D0857418

HOLY CROSS

HOLY CROSS

A Century of Anglican Monasticism

Adam Dunbar McCoy, OHC

Morehouse-Barlow
Wilton, CT.

Morehouse-Barlow Co., Inc.
78 Danbury Road
Wilton, Connecticut 06897

Library of Congress Cataloging-in-Publication Data

McCoy, Adam Dunbar, 1946-
Holy Cross; a century of Anglican monasticism.

Bibliography: p. 246
Includes index.
1. Order of the Holy Cross—History.   I. Title.
BX5971.073M33   1987   271′.8   87-5513

ISBN 0-8192-1403-5

Printed in the United States of America

Contents

Illustrations follow page 116.

Foreword

The idea of producing a history of the Order of the Holy Cross as part of our Centennial celebration was first discussed in the late 1970s. In 1981, Fr. Adam McCoy, OHC, was commissioned to write the history, and he began sorting through the Order's archives at West Park and in Austin, TX. He interviewed many members of the Order and some friends of the Order who would have personal knowledge of its history. None of us realized what an enormous job this would be. Instead of being ready for publication in the year of our Centennial, 1984, it is just now ready to go to the printers.

This massive work was not undertaken just as an added "extra" for the Centennial celebration. It has a more important purpose than that. Any group of people which wishes to know who it is and where it is going must know where it has been. Someone has defined a "self" as "a past and a future," and this is equally valid whether the self is an individual or an institution. If the Order of the Holy Cross is to be able to make plans and project its life into the future, it needs to understand clearly how it is rooted in the past.

It is also true that the history of a group is affected by its present self-understanding. This history would have been quite different if it had been written twenty years ago, and it would be different had it been delayed twenty years into the future. The discerning reader will be able to tell much about how Holy Cross understands itself in 1986, for it is from that understanding that the history is interpreted.

The one instruction given to Fr. McCoy was that this history was to present Holy Cross "warts and all." It does not focus on the unhappy and painful episodes of the past, but neither does it gloss over them. These events, too, have made the Order what it is today and will influence what it will be in the future.

I speak on behalf of all the members, associates, and friends of Holy Cross in thanking Fr. McCoy for the magnificent job he has done. I commend the book to the Church, and I ask for the prayers of those who read it. May God bless the life and prayer and ministry of the Order in its second hundred years as he has in its first.

Clark Gregory W. Trafton, OHC
Superior
Solemnity of James Otis Sargent
Huntington, OHC
November 25, 1986

Preface & Acknowledgments

The Order of the Holy Cross is the largest and in some ways the pioneer American monastic community. Its story is of interest to students of Anglican institutions, of course, but also to those interested in the development of the history of monasticism on a larger stage, for in Holy Cross we see a new type of monasticism, growing out of American and Episcopalian soil. Its genesis is in the ferment of the mid-Victorian intelligentsia of the Northeast, the same milieu which brought forth the Transcendentalists and Brook Farm in an earlier generation.

Its development is not along simple lines, but encompasses the radical social movements of the turn of the century, the Anglo-Catholic tide of the Episcopal Church through World War II, and the vast reform of Christendom initiated in Vatican II. Its personalities are vivid, and its accomplishments are many, surely more than could have been expected from a relatively small group of men working within an essentially hostile or indifferent ecclesiastical environment. In its way the history of Holy Cross is both brilliant and significant for American and late Christian culture alike.

Holy Cross's almost inexorable movement toward the Benedictine ideal of monasticism is perhaps the most significant case of the convergence of monasticism of independent origins toward that most pervasive of Western monastic models. In this the story of Holy Cross is important for the whole monastic world, Roman and Orthodox (and Reformed) as well as Anglican.

This study is primarily an institutional history, because that is the first need of the community. Not every concern could be fully addressed in it. In particular, it does not supply a theology of monastic life and practice, or a deep and searching look into the inner lives of the members of the Order. That must wait for subsequent work. But in this book a framework of fact and history has been laid which may enable other, more specialized accounts.

Those interested in the particular institutions begun by Holy Cross, especially St. Andrew's and Kent schools and the Bolahun Mission will need to look elsewhere for detailed accounts of those works. To have told their stories in detail would have swamped what is a history of Holy Cross itself as an institution. Their stories are told from the perspective of the Order that created them.

Finally, a word about politics. There is in some quarters of the religiously minded world a feeling that religious people, and *a fortiori* monks, should be above the sweaty struggles of human politics. Much of this history details the political life of a monastic order. It is the author's conviction that politics, as part of life, is an arena for the Holy Spirit, and that God is not ashamed to use as instruments the ordinary passions of ambition and desire as well as the loftier virtues to accomplish his ends. The monks detailed here are men like others, graced perhaps by their consecration, but playing their part with the gifts and limitations of their creation.

This project has lasted more than four and a-half years, and the author is indebted to more people than he can remember. Fr. Clark Trafton, OHC, the Superior, assigned the task and supported it consistently. Fr. Bonnell Spencer, OHC, began a similar project and relinquished his notes in assistance. The Brethren stationed at Mount Calvary Retreat House during these years have borne the joys and sorrows of this project patiently and helpfully.

Prof. V. Nelle Bellamy, the Archivist of the Episcopal Church and Professor of Church History at the Episcopal Theological School of the Southwest in Austin, TX, was of inestimable help in delving through the OHC Archives deposited to her care. Fr. James B. Simpson, an Associate of Holy Cross and editor and author gave consistent support. Hilary Ross edited the work, and along the way taught the author to simplify. Dr. Gretchen Burnett was a creative listener to the traumas associated with creation.

Several persons have read and commented helpfully on the completed manuscript. They are of course in no way responsible for its inevitable errors, but have contributed many helpful suggestions. The Rt. Rev'd. Richard Grein, Bishop of Kansas; Prof. Samuel M. Garrett, retired from the Church Divinity School of the Pacific; Prof. V. Nelle Bellamy, of the Episcopal Theological School of the Southwest; Prof. J. Robert Wright of the General Theological Seminary; Mrs. Avery Brooke of Noroton, CT; the Rev'd. William P. Clancey, Jr., of Berkeley, CA; the Rev'd. Clark Trafton, OHC; and the Rev'd. H. Bonnell Spencer, OHC, all read and commented helpfully on it, and much of its accuracy is due to their insightful reading.

It is no small thing to move from a mass of unfiled paper and unsubstantiated myth and legend to a more or less adequately documented history. To all who helped, the author gives his grateful thanks.

Mount Calvary Monastery
Santa Barbara
Sts. Ignatius of Antioch &
Philip Quaque
October 17, 1986.

1

Backgrounds

On November 25, 1884, James Otis Sargent Huntington, then 30 and an Episcopal priest, knelt in a small convent chapel in New York City and vowed: "I desire for love of Jesus, to devote myself body, soul and spirit to the service of Almighty God in the religious life as a member of the Order of the Holy Cross, and to that end to take upon me of my own free will the vows of Religious Poverty, Chastity and Obedience."

The community he formed by this act was four years in preparation, and has endured a century. From its earliest work on the Lower East Side of New York City, Holy Cross has spread across the North American continent and to West Africa. In slum and suburb, rain forest and city, illiterate pagans and sophisticated westerners alike have drawn strength from the life of Holy Cross.

The love of God that inspired Fr. Huntington and gave him strength to continue for more than fifty years continues to draw men from widely different backgrounds. The story of the Order of the Holy Cross is the story of weakness and strength, success and failure, because it is a very human story about a very human community, a very American community in its formation, a very universal community today.

The secret of God, according to St. Paul, is not in power but in weakness. "The human mind and heart are a mystery," adds the psalmist. The monastic life is an attempt to embrace the source of God's power through weakness, the cross, and monastic history—the history of the Order of the Holy Cross—exhibits God's power through transfigured human weakness.

The three founders of the Order of the Holy Cross were Robert Stockton Dod, James Gibbon Cameron and James Otis Sargent Huntington. Cameron and Huntington were trained for ordination together and shared a common missionary emphasis. Huntington and Dod exhibit a close

1

similarity in their patrician family backgrounds, their training and their interests at the time of their call to the monastic life in November, 1880.

Robert Stockton Dod was 25 years old that autumn. He was born Jan. 13, 1855, the son of William Armstrong Dod, a Presbyterian minister with charges in Philadelphia and Princeton, NJ. Dod's father, a lecturer on fine arts at Princeton from 1855 to 1866, was ordained an Episcopal priest in 1859, and soon became Rector of Trinity Church, Princeton. His mother, Catherine Elizabeth Stockton, was the daughter of Admiral Robert Field Stockton.

Admiral Stockton's history gives a sense of the Dod family tradition. Grandson of Richard Stockton, a signer of the Declaration of Independence, native of Princeton, he joined the Navy and saw action against the Barbary Pirates. As captain of the schooner *Alligator* he secured the land which became Liberia for the American Colonization Society to Africa. He refused a seat in Tyler's Cabinet, delivered the annexation resolution to Texas in 1845, and commanded the U.S. forces in California, ultimately winning Alta California from Mexico for the Union. He set up the first American government there and was its first governor. He was a U.S. Senator from 1851 to 1853, retiring to build the Delaware and Raritan Canal.

Such was the family background of the man who provided the inspiration and original design for the Order of the Holy Cross. Ancestors who achieved academic, military and civic distinction provided Fr. Dod with a legacy of vision, courage and confidence that equipped him for the course he chose.

Dod attended Princeton and graduated in 1873. He taught for eighteen months, went to Europe for half a year, and in 1875 entered General Theological Seminary in New York, graduating in 1878. "While at General, Dod witnessed the attempted murder of a young girl in broad daylight within sight of the Seminary's Chapel on West 29th Street. This sordid episode brought the conditions of life among the poor in New York vividly before the young student. He looked back to his experience in regard to that tragedy as the first indication to him of his vocation."[1]

As a result, Dod was fired with zeal to work among the poor, and he found his place at the newly founded Mission of the Holy Cross for German immigrants run by the Sisters of St. John the Baptist on the Lower East Side of New York. He was ordained a deacon shortly after graduation, on June 9, 1878, but his ordination to the priesthood was somewhat delayed because of frail health. Nevertheless, on Aug. 24, 1880, he was ordained a priest and added further responsibilities at the Mission. Less than three months later he met James Huntington at St. Clement's, Philadelphia.

James Cameron was older than Dod and Huntington by about seven years, making him 32 in November, 1880. The son of James Cameron and Diana P. Merchant, he attended St. Andrew's Seminary in Syracuse, founded by Bishop Huntington, and graduated a year behind Fr. Huntington in 1879. He was ordained a deacon on June 8, 1871, and a priest in the same service with Fr. Huntington on May 28, 1880, both times by Bishop Huntington. His first ministry was to Onondaga Indians near Syracuse in 1879-80. He joined Dod in the work of the Holy Cross Mission in 1880.

James Otis Sargent Huntington was, like Dod, from a patrician American family. Born July 23, 1854, six months older than Dod, his family was bound up with the religious history of New England. His grandfather on his father's side, Dan Huntington, was a Yale graduate and a tutor at Williams College, having studied at Yale under Timothy Dwight. Dan's wife, Elizabeth Phelps, brought to the marriage her family farm, Forty Acres, at Hadley, MA. Dan was called to the Congregational ministry but could not support his family on the income, and the family retired to Forty Acres. Dan and Elizabeth were interested in the growing Unitarian movement toward liberal Christianity. They doubted the doctrine of the damnation of unbaptized infants, and Dan was denied membership in the First Congregational Church of Hadley, while Elizabeth, already a member, was tried for heresy. Their son, Frederick Dan Huntington, Fr. Huntington's father, remembered the incident vividly, and abhorrence of intolerance became a key element in his religious character. Elizabeth Phelps Huntington was, he says,[2]

> . . . a noble-hearted, devout woman . . . on account of a deliberate and well-weighed change of opinions, followed after, persecuted, threatened . . . at last roughly excommunicated from a Church of which she had been for years an untiring benefactor, and which her blameless spirit had so long adorned. The tears and anxiety we used to see with our child's eyes, after those impudent deacons and sly ambassadors . . . had withdrawn from one of those cruel interviews, left an impression that will not lose its horribleness while we remember anything. This was in the heart of our old Massachusetts, in the midst of its valleys and free air, some of the loveliest scenery in the world, indeed, but not beautiful enough to move and soften the gloomy features of that stern, forbidding, unrelenting Calvinism.

Frederick Dan Huntington went to Amherst, then Harvard Divinity School, graduating in 1842, and was called as the Unitarian minister of the South Congregational Church in Boston. His successor there, Edward

Everett Hale, wrote:[3]

> Never was a ministry more successful. The church was full; the charities were admirably administered; the Sunday School was in perfect order. More than this, oh so much more than this, hearts had found living food here that had hungered and thirsted elsewhere. . . . Here were exiles who had been lost and were found. . . .

But true to his family tradition, it was religious truth that Fr. Huntington's father thirsted for, not just successful ministry. Despite growing doubts about Unitarianism, he was appointed Preacher to Harvard University and Plummer Professor of Christian Morals in 1855. His tenure there was successful, but filled with questions of faith. When his mother died in 1847, he came into possession of her private journal, filled with meditations on a God passionately involved, feeling and suffering with his created world, a far cry from the intellectual detachment of mid-nineteenth century Unitarianism. Moreover, this God was in Christ, incarnate, offering salvation that transcended moral exertion, convicting and absolving humanity of sin.

In 1859 he resigned his Harvard positions, Unitarian faith being one of their requirements. He was confirmed an Episcopalian with his wife and two older children, George and Arria, by Manton Eastburn, Bishop of Massachusetts, on March 25, 1860, ordained a priest the following year, and soon became Rector of Emmanuel Church, Boston, and then first Bishop of the Diocese of Central New York in Syracuse. He was a tireless social activist, working openly for social causes long before the causes were fashionable. He promoted ministries to the Indians of his diocese (he ordained David Oakerhater, the great Oklahoma missionary), he enlisted the support of the Church for the labor movement, and established relief ministries to the poor as well as a preparatory school and seminary. Never an Anglo-Catholic, he encouraged his son and respected the integrity of his vocation. Elizabeth Phelps's persecution bore a double fruit: the episcopal ministry of her son and the monastic life of her grandson.

James Huntington attended a private grammar school on Boylston Street, Boston, until 1860, then for two years the Brimmer School, followed by private tutoring at home, a year (1868-9) at the Roxbury Latin School in Boston, and finished his secondary education at St. John's School, Manlius, NY, founded by his father near Syracuse. He entered Harvard in 1871, graduating in 1875. He was one of the founding company of the Harvard *Magenta,* later the *Crimson*. Upon graduation he returned home to enter the first class of the seminary his father had begun in

Syracuse, St. Andrew's, which he attended from October, 1876, until June,

10⁰⁶ Jeff

10¹⁹ mn Lisa

from

603 653-9500

3 mn

register for blood pressure test

Then give blood/urine

other decent and undesecrated places of assemblage, or of spots in the open air—all these have their legitimate place in the manifold distributions of the Heavenly Grace, under one comprehensive, Catholic law.

He hoped for clergy who would be available for the mission of the Church at the discretion of their Bishop.

James showed his interest in the ministry early at Harvard, and was elected president of St. Paul's Society for Episcopal students. In his junior year he wrote to his father: "I hope I am making this choice for the right reasons—the desire to fulfill my baptismal vows. It is very hard to tell whether notions do not form part of the motive, but I hope that the ideas of self-sacrifice I have now, however obtained at first, may be sanctified as I realize them in my life."[5]

He was also attracted to social service while at Harvard. He visited Pine Farm, a Methodist farm near Newton, Mass., for underprivileged boys. The aim there was to teach the boys practical work skills in a Christian atmosphere. James was moved:[6]

Oh, how much good such an institution can do. Why is our Church the last to do this work? For myself, though I know that can never be, I could hardly wish for myself a position I should more enjoy despite all the trouble and disappointments, than teaching and training just such boys. And what Christian body is better fitted for it than our own part of the Catholic Church where superstition does not endanger and cold stiffness, bare walls, and unattractive services do not hinder or alienate. But others do the work imperfectly or wrongly and we wait.

His personal spirituality was also undergoing development. Late in his time in seminary he wrote to his brother George: "If one is to reach the dull and ignorant one must have a mind sharpened by study and cleared by thought and quickened by exercise as well as purified and warmed by love."[7] The cadences recall the Rule he would later write, but the sentiments are as yet unfocused. During Lent of the same year, 1878, he asked his father for time to concentrate on uninterrupted study of theology, philosophy, Hebrew and German, which he felt he could not "possibly do while I am in charge of a parish and systematically neglecting it in things which ought to be done."[8] James used his father's refusal as an exercise in willed obedience:[9]

I had grace enough to be able to say, and that truthfully, that I should yield a ready obedience, that what I wanted most of all was to be under direction and (as he had spoken of crossing my wishes) to have my wishes crossed by a superior whom I know I ought to follow.

He responded obediently to his father by undertaking more, not less, active work. After his ordination as a deacon, St. Mark's Mission, Syracuse was added to his responsibilities, and he took to visiting inmates in the penitentiary and poorhouse, working with the county shelter, the Bureau of Labor and Charities, and the Society for the Prevention of Cruelty to Children.

If Bishop Huntington had expected unremitting labor in the active ministry to diminish James's growing Anglo-Catholic tendencies, he was mistaken. If anything they grew. James wrote:[10]

Whatever may be said of me as an extreme man it cannot, I think, be said that I am either morbid, effeminate or dreamy. I have too good an appetite and am too busy for the first, I walk too much for the second, and the atmosphere of police courts and county houses is not favorable to the state of mind described by the third. In the rightness and advantage of two things I strongly believe—religious orders of men and women, and confession. But I do not view either of these with a sickly sentimentalism or an enthusiasm that cannot see the evils to which they may so easily be led. On the contrary I could paint the bad consequences of both in as dark colors as would satisfy even the Am. Prot. Union.

In the same letter to his father he reveals that he had heard the first confessions of two elderly men who, though baptized, had never received communion, thinking they were unworthy. The confessions had released the load of sin and guilt they were carrying, and they were able for the first time to receive the sacrament, to their inexpressible joy.

There is one further indication of the state of his mind at this time. Commenting on the story of the rich young man (Mt. 19:16-22), a standard text for the monastic life, James told his brother:[11]

The condition of one who *refuses* to receive a call to adopt the counsel of perfection must be essentially different from the state of him who simply chooses one of two courses of action, either of which would be equally conformed to the will of God.

The rich young man's question to the Lord is "What must I do to inherit eternal life?" And the Lord's response: "Keep the commandments." But the rich young man wants to do more, so the Lord advises him, " 'If you wish to be perfect, go and sell what you own and give the money to the poor, and you will have treasure in heaven; then come, follow me.' But when the young man heard these words, he went away sad, for he was a man of great wealth.'' In the third century this same parable launched St. Anthony, the father of Christian monasticism, on his ascetical career. James's statement indicates that he feels such a call might come, and if it did, he would not refuse it.

Bishop Huntington wrote in 1881, as James was preparing to enter the new Order: "But how could I hold him back—knowing his heart, seeing what he has done for me, and fully believing with him that the Church sorely needs both a standard of holy living in the Ministry and a leaven of Evangelization supplementing our miserable, halting, half-secular Parochial system.''[12] Bp. Huntington had done his work well. His son was launched on the double path of holy living and evangelization, the path down which Fr. Huntington would lead the Order of the Holy Cross.

The idea of the Order of the Holy Cross was born in 1880. What was the world like for Dod, Cameron and Huntington then? Fifteen years after the end of the Civil War the United States was engaged in vast economic expansion. The depression of 1877-78 was over. Railroads had just spanned the continent. The movement from farm to factory had begun. Cities overflowed with jobseekers. The riches of the few contrasted sharply with destitution among the working classes. Utopian theories and new ideas of progress challenged theories of class struggle and revolution. New states were added to the Union. It was a time of founding new institutions: labor unions, universities and schools, the Metropolitan Opera. New inventions crowded one after another: the incandescent light bulb, the typewriter, the phonograph and the telephone. The 1880s were a time of confidence that progress was possible, and even the ideologies of protest witnessed to the prevailing spirit of optimism.

The Episcopal Church in the 1880s grew along with the nation. In the hundred years since the Revolution it had successfully separated from the Church of England, and in the 1820s had broken out of the comfortable cities and tidewater plantations to become a truly national church. It had divided and then reunited peacefully at the time of the Civil War. And it had begun an expansion which would more than triple its membership between 1870 and 1900, from 207,762 communicants to 712,997, with corresponding increases in churches and clergy.[13]

Of the twelve million immigrants who entered American ports between 1870 and 1900, some prospered and soon moved west, but many crowded into cities in living conditions of almost indescribable misery. Because the government provided little in the way of social service, helping the hungry, the homeless and the sick was left to private charity, largely through the churches.

Reacting to this ferment, radical and Marxist denunciations rose from many platforms. The Knights of Labor, founded in 1869, spearheaded a labor movement spurred on by the Great Railway Strike of 1877. Henry George published his Single Tax Theory in *Progress and Poverty* in 1879. Threatened American political institutions became entrenched. The Republicans firmly controlled national politics, while the Democrats controlled the South and many city halls. Both parties seemed more responsive to money and power than to human need.

The Anglo-Catholic movement was part of this ferment and experimentalism. Anglo-Catholics in the later years of the nineteenth century were inspired by the possibility of change, and by the belief that what the Church does in her worship and prayer life matters directly for the world as well as for herself. The battles over ritual and theology were not merely theoretical. They were practical and social as well, and involved the change of a whole order of assumptions about the place of the Church in society. Unless this social fact is understood, the vitriolic reactions which greeted almost every attempt at change initiated by the Anglo-Catholics in the nineteenth century cannot be understood. The battle was not over altar tabernacles and priestly vestments; the battle was over class privilege, an established order of society which the Church had been expected to uphold, or at least to confirm by muting its criticisms and adopting a non-threatening institutional stance.

The doctrine of the Incarnation can be a political statement as well as a theological one, because its conclusion is the equality of all persons before God. The value of Christ's humanity makes the value of the least man or woman infinite. The presence of Christ in the eucharist is the presence of God in the world, making the world itself, and not just heaven, the focus of God's attention and love. Anglo-Catholicism, spurred by these doctrines, not only fostered personal and private devotion leading to individual holiness, but also hoped to lead the Church to become the agent of real and fundamental change in society. Anglo-Catholics could contemplate the rearrangement of wealth and power as part of the bringing in of the Kingdom of God. And as they saw in the Church the objective sign of God's presence and work in the world, so they expected the Kingdom to have a real and objective manifestation in the world, not simply in the hearts of believers.

Accordingly, many Anglo-Catholic parishes faced opposition because they held that Catholic belief and practice were necessary to save the world around them. The parish where Frs. Dod and Huntington met and first conceived the idea of the Order of the Holy Cross was such a parish. At that very moment in 1880 it was in the midst of a controversy over ritual and belief. This conflict illustrates Church polity in the 1880s.[14]

The Rev. Herman Griswold Batterson, since 1869 the Rector of St. Clement's, Philadelphia, had taught fasting and abstinence in preparation for communion, which he hoped would be frequent. At that time a monthly celebration of the eucharist was considered frequent. He introduced the choral service, cross and candlesticks on the altar, lighted candles in the chancel, and other high ritualist innovations. Armed with a new canon against ritual practices passed by the General Convention of 1874, the Bishop of Pennsylvania, William Stevens, accused Batterson of teaching private confession, prayers for the dead, bowing to the eucharistic elements at the time of consecration, and other "deviations" from Episcopal practice. The matter went to civil court and Batterson won, but resigned, exhausted. Dr. Theodore M. Riley was called as rector, and the Bishop demanded he sign a statement foreswearing colored vestments, the mixed chalice (water with wine), bowing to the altar, elevation of the elements at the consecration in the eucharist, unnecessary candles, prayers from outside the *Book of Common Prayer*, and private confession. Dr. Riley would not sign.

The vestry then invited the Society of St. John the Evangelist, recently come to Boston, to take the parish. Fr. Oliver Sherman Prescott was to be rector. He was an American, and had been part of the early experiment in monasticism at Valle Crucis. He arrived in 1876 with Frs. Maturin and Convers of the Society. Prescott went even further than Batterson, introducing daily eucharist. The Bishop again threatened prosecution, and Fr. Prescott agreed to modest changes. But Bishop Stevens pressed on, and in the spring of 1880 brought suit. Fr. Prescott was found guilty of bowing to the altar, the use of candles, wearing vestments, elevating the consecrated elements, and celebrating the eucharist alone. The Cowley Fathers resigned the parish, but continued to minister there, conforming to the Bishop's usage until Fr. Maturin was elected rector in 1881. This was the state of affairs which greeted Huntington and Dod in 1880.

A century later it is difficult to understand the furor. Most of these dangerous innovations are standard in all but the lowest-church Episcopal parishes. Indeed, not just stoles but eucharistic vestments are now virtually standard, as is weekly (and often daily) eucharist, and the *Book of Common Prayer* has not one but two forms for private confession. But in 1880, there were the symbols of a profound change in the Episcopal Church. The Anglo-Catholics were calling the Church to be itself, to proclaim the faith visibly as well as loudly, and to claim its place as the herald of the Kingdom, not a subordinate agency whose function was to bless society.

The Religious Life was far from unknown in the American Church in 1880. The Cowley Fathers had arrived in Boston in 1870, four years after their foundation in England, and were precariously established in Philadelphia as well. Three English sisterhoods had also begun work in America. The Society of St. Margaret sent their first Sister to Boston in 1871. The All Saints Sisters came to Baltimore at the invitation of Fr. Richey of Mount Calvary Church in 1872. And the Community of St. John the Baptist began work in New York City in 1874.

Americans had also tried to establish the Religious Life, and the women had succeeded. The Order of the Holy Cross was not the first attempt in America, and its antecedents in the American Church are important. For women, the first stirrings of the Religious Life were at the Church of the Holy Communion in New York City, under William Augustus Muhlenberg:[15]

> Six months after the foundation of the first English Sisterhood in 1845, a young American woman, Miss Anne Ayres, was greatly moved by a sermon on Jephtha's daughter, preached by Dr. Muhlenberg. She related in after years that this sermon had "an application glancing at the blessedness of giving oneself undividedly to God's service." The immediate result was that Miss Ayres resolved to dedicate herself to her Saviour.

Nurses were needed for Dr. Muhlenberg's new St. Luke's Hospital in New York, and so the Sisterhood of the Holy Communion was born in 1852. But Dr. Muhlenberg envisioned a protestant deaconess society and did not allow the sisters to take vows. In 1863 Miss Ayres resigned as "First Sister" in dissatisfaction, and the community was dissolved. Revived under more conventional rules by Muhlenberg's successor in 1871, it continued until 1934.

Harriett Starr Cannon and three other members of the former Sisterhood of the Holy Communion came together in 1863 to staff a House of Mercy in New York City for the rehabilitation of prostitutes. By 1864 they had decided to form a religious community. On Feb. 2, 1865, at St. Michael's Church in New York City, Bishop Horatio Potter presided at the profession of five sisters of the new Community of St. Mary. They did not take vows, but intended to dedicate themselves irrevocably to the Religious Life. Dr. Morgan Dix, Rector of Trinity Church, became their spiritual director, and Miss Cannon, now Mother Harriett, remained

Mother Superior until her death in 1896. The community's work grew rapidly, and from their headquarters in Peekskill, NY, it soon spread to Memphis and Sewanee, TN. It was in Memphis that four Sisters of St. Mary gave their lives nursing in a yellow fever epidemic, and became known as the Memphis Martyrs.

The first attempts at the Religious Life for men in the Anglican Communion were made in America, not England. But by 1880 there still was no American men's community, even though three attempts had been made. The first was the initial community of the Nashotah Mission in Wisconsin. In 1840 an appeal was made to the students of the General Theological Seminary in New York for young men who would remain unmarried, be obedient to the bishop in community, and hold property in common. Bishop Jackson Kemper of the vast Northwest Territory welcomed three young deacons: James Lloyd Breck, William Adams and John Henry Hobart, Jr., son of the Bishop of New York. The Religious Life of the small community gradually evolved into the semi-monastic system of Nashotah House Seminary. It is difficult to pinpoint when this first Anglican attempt at a men's community ceased to be monastic. But it was the first in the Anglican Communion, earlier than John Henry Newman's attempts at Littlemore, near Oxford.

A second, little-known attempt was made in New York State shortly after the Nashotah experiment, in 1845:[16]

> After being ordained deacon, the Reverend Edgar P. Wadhams was placed in charge of a rural district in Essex County, New York. There he was joined by a Mr. Clarence E. Walworth and another deacon, named McVicker. They tried to imitate a sort of monastic establishment, but it did not succeed. Within a year all its members had been received into the Roman Church.

The third attempt is most colorful. Levi Silliman Ives, Bishop of North Carolina from 1831-53, and the son-in-law of Bishop Hobart of New York, bought a piece of property in a lovely North Carolina valley near the Tennessee border. He wished to found an agricultural school for Appalachian boys and a clergy training school for his diocese. He called it Valle Crucis, after a Welsh Cistercian monastery. A young man named William Skiles was placed in charge of the school, and soon Bishop Ives conceived a plan to found a religious community modeled on the Jesuits, obedient to himself. Among the first members were William Glenny French, who was made Superior, William Skiles, and Oliver Prescott, later a member of the Cowley Fathers and Rector of St. Clement's, Philadelphia. Bishop Ives professed the members of the new Society of the Holy Cross (whose name is its only direct link with the Order of the Holy Cross) in St. Luke's Chapel, Hudson Street, New York City, during the General Convention of 1847. The Bishop encouraged extreme asceticism and an openness to reunion with Rome, and he and the Society came under fierce attack. By 1851 Bishop Ives stated that the Society had ceased to exist in 1849, and in 1852 he became a Roman Catholic, confirming the worst suspicions of those who opposed the Religious Life as a sure path to Rome.

But Br. William Skiles continued a life of quiet holiness at Valle Crucis, ministering as a deacon to the people there and true to his monastic vows. Ives's successor, Thomas Atkinson, arrived in the winter of 1862 to dedicate a little church that Br. Skiles had built with his own hands.[17]

> That service was the crown of the good brother's life. He never entered the church again, but died of cancer soon afterwards. . . . The troubled times (of the war between the Northern and Southern states) made it necessary to bury him in the garden of the house, but later on his body was removed to a place beside his little church. So died in faith the first man in the Anglican Communion since Reformation times to persevere in the dedicated life of poverty, chastity and obedience, under vows. . . . He fell asleep in the Lord on the Feast of the Conception, December 8, 1862.

Fr. Prescott in time joined the Society of St. John the Evangelist, and so this curious experiment had two results for the future: Fr. Prescott's membership in the Cowley Fathers, and Br. William Skiles's holy and dedicated life.

By 1880 the American Church was well acquainted with the Religious Life. New York, Boston, Philadelphia, Baltimore, Memphis and other smaller places had functioning Anglican religious communities. William Skiles and the Memphis Martyrs, Sisters Constance, Thecla, Ruth and Frances, had been faithful to the end. Still, no lasting community for men had been formed in the Episcopal Church. Into this situation stepped Robert Dod, James Cameron and James Huntington, young, all ordained priests within the year. They were fired with a vision, and were determined to establish the Religious Life for American men in the American Church, along American lines. That they succeeded is due to the founding vision of Robert Dod, and to the persevering strength and generous heart of James Huntington.

The Order's Earliest Days (1880-1884)

In the autumn of 1880, the Rev. William John Knox-Little, Canon Residentiary of Worcester Cathedral in England, and a leading Ritualist, gave a retreat for priests at St. Clement's Church, the Cowley Fathers' parish in Philadelphia. Knox-Little's retreat, from November 8-13, attracted Robert Dod and James Huntington. Both had thought of joining a religious community before the retreat. But here they met, were inspired to act, and made their first plans to found an American Order for men.

The retreat made a strong impact on James Huntington. To his brother George he wrote on November 23:[1]

> I wish you could have been with me at the Retreat. It was wonderfully helpful. I do not care to think what might have become of me without it. It seems to me not too much to say that it was God's provision for saving my soul.

He took full notes, he said, but all that has survived is an outline of the retreat in another letter.[2] From this it is clear that Knox-Little aimed at focusing the retreatant's will on God's purpose in creating him, leading him through participation in the life and passion of Christ, and sustaining him in the Holy Spirit's working in society, sacrament and the hope of eternal life. So moving was it that when Knox-Little recounted the Passion, "the silence was broken only by the sobs of strong men," and at the end of the retreat Fr. Huntington went back into the Church and as he knelt in the stillness, he burst into tears.

For Fr. Huntington, the retreat drew the connection between his nature and his purpose, what God had created him to be, and what God intended him to do with himself. Nothing less than the direct imitation of Christ would do, and for Fr. Huntington, that meant the Religious Life. As he himself put it, "To act out the answer (to the question Who am I?

Why am I?) was really to have lived. To discover God's call is to discover the path to fullest life.'' Fr. Huntington believed that as a result of the retreat he had found the path of his life. From that time on he never looked back.

Dod also felt the same call, and as they took the train back to New York together, they talked of their experience, and formed their first plans for a new Order. Dod was already working at the Holy Cross Mission on the Lower East Side, where he was in daily contact with the St. John Baptist Sisters, and where the Cowley Fathers occasionally visited and worked. Huntington returned to Syracuse and his work at Calvary Church and St. Mark's. Dod's action in response to their call was immediate. He made his way to England in December or January and was received as a postulant at Cowley on Feb. 4, 1881. When he arrived there he found that James Cameron had already been received as a postulant on Dec. 23, 1880. Dod stayed less than three months, Cameron apparently into the summer of 1881. But it did not take long before the two Americans decided that their future lay in founding a specifically American Order.

Fr. Huntington's interest in the monastic life led his father, who as Bishop was also his ecclesiastical superior, to propose the foundation of a mission-preaching ministry, not quite but almost monastic in character. James wrote to his brother:[3]

> Oddly enough, I came back [from the retreat] to find Father possessed of the idea of *Missions,* that name being used in a wide sense for services continued through a number of days and not simply of a stirring but also of an instructive character. He wants me to live here but go off frequently for a week or ten days at a time to localities where the Church has never been presented. . . . It would be strange but not impossible if Father should send me eventually to Oxford [i.e., Cowley] to be trained for the particular kind of work which he thinks may be useful when men are ready to devote themselves entirely to it.

This is a prescient description of the kind of mission work Fr. Huntington and his brethren would in fact do so much of in the years to come. But the plan was not carried out, and he continued in Syracuse through the winter and spring of 1880-81, corresponding with Dod in England.

On March 6, 1881, Fr. Dod wrote to Huntington concerning his motives for seeking the Religious Life, in a letter which constitutes a foundation document of the Order:[4]

> I was led by the Spirit, I trust, to desire the *religious life,* by which

I mean giving up of one's whole self to God and making Him the object and end of every, even the most trifling, action. The active work I look upon as secondary, but also as a means of bringing me nearer to a perfect walking with God as an imitation of my Master. The primary end of work would be the glory of God and therefore would consist largely in mental prayer and Meditation, works of mercy springing from them. To accomplish this one should be associated with others under obedience and for this we have the example of all the ages of the Church and can see their mistakes and follow their virtues. Above all I felt that entire giving up of my own will was necessary, first to God's guidance and secondly to some human will as Superior. Where was I to find this? Once found, there must be no going back, no disputing, but a thorough and complete obedience.

On April 27, 1881, Dod left Cowley and went to the Mother House of the Community of St. John the Baptist at Clewer, Windsor. There he acted as hospital chaplain at the Sisters' St. Andrew's Hospital. The community had been founded in 1851 by Canon Thomas Thelusson Carter (1808-1901) and guided by the remarkable Mother Harriett Monsell until her strength failed in 1876. Dod may or may not have had her counsel from her place of retirement at Folkestone, but Canon Carter was at Clewer, and Dod had many conversations with him about the foundation of the new Order.

Canon Carter was a remarkable figure. Prominent in the Oxford Movement since its earliest days, and especially in controversies in its later Ritualist phase, he had been Rector of Clewer since 1844. He had been active in the ministry to prostitutes, and founded the Sisters of St. John the Baptist to staff the House of Mercy, a recovery and rehabilitation center for prostitutes, which he opened in 1847. He had directed the Sisters together with Mother Harriett since their founding, and as it grew the community had gradually taken on many other socially useful works, among which was the work started in New York with immigrants in 1874. Carter was a leading authority on the Religious Life, and unlike Pusey and Neale, based his writings on experience rather than primarily on theory. His books on the Religious Life were standard for Anglicans by the end of the nineteenth century. When Dod met him he was at his height, and Dod reaped the benefit of thirty years' experience with the St. John the Baptist Sisters. While he was at Clewer, Dod wrote preliminary notes for a Rule and Constitution, which formed the basis for the documents he wrote later in the year.

On May 18 Dod wrote to Huntington about his plans:[5]

Can we but gather together a few willing thus to give up everything

I feel that, under God, we are assured of success in the highest sense. It is a very serious step to which I feel compelled—the breaking away from an established order of things and undertaking to start alone as we do with but little experience.

He gave Huntington a general survey of monastic ideals and life, and then proposed the work of the new community:

Above all we should be men of prayer and learned in the sacred scriptures. The outgrowth of such a life must be works of love—and I should propose missionary work among the neglected poor of our large cities—and holding missions & retreats whenever we are able—and in time to make the mother house a place of spiritual retreat and rest for our secular brethren hoping thereby to deepen the spiritual life among the clergy generally.

He did not place much confidence in his own foundation, but saw it rather as a first step in the development of monastic life for men in America: "I do not look forward to any great outward success. I shall be perfectly satisfied to be the first of the failures which some predict must precede the establishment of an order."

Huntington answered Dod on June 7, in a letter now lost. He asked Dod if he should resign his work and was ready with characteristic directness to begin immediately. Dod advised that they wait until support for the new venture was forthcoming, and their own intentions were clear. Dod thought he should remain in England for the time being to learn all he could:[6]

I am trying to use the time that remains here as a time of preparation. I have had some training, thanks to Fr. Benson, and I daily receive help & encouragement from Canon Carter and others here—I have adopted as a means of preparation a rule of life such as I hope to see introduced in America and am endeavoring to carry it out as far as the distraction of the work in the hospital will allow.

James Cameron was uncertain whether to follow Dod, but made up his mind to leave Cowley in midsummer. Dod was continually modest about the prospect of success for his venture, but his real uncertainty was his own health: "There is another reason why you should not take any steps toward immediate resignation of your work, viz.—that my own health may prevent my starting as soon as I hope to do."[7]

Huntington regarded the plans to form the community as virtually complete by July 7. On that date he wrote:[8]

I expect to leave here in a few weeks and next autumn three of us, all Priests of the American Church, hope to begin a community life together, looking forward to the founding of an American Order for Priests. The other two have been at Cowley for some months and one is now with Canon Carter at Clewer. We all feel very deeply how unworthy we are to be called to such a work, yet we firmly believe that we *are* called and dangerous as the task is we feel that we must undertake it, whatever the end may be. My father sympathizes very heartily with us and will give us his assistance. He gives me up willingly though I know that it costs him much. I shall find it hard to leave my poor people here and some of them will miss me for a time.

Dod sailed from England on August 18 and landed in New York on the 27th. Soon after, Huntington went to New York to talk with him. Dod made a short visit to the Huntington family farm at Hadley, MA. Fr. Huntington wrote on September 11:[9]

Matters have been gradually taking shape since I saw you. I went to New York to see Dod and he has been up here for a few hours. It is settled now, so far as we can see, that we are to begin in New York in a few weeks, having a three-story house with Chapel in it near the Wilson Industrial School and taking up work in connection with the Mission of the Holy Cross. This is a Mission, largely among the Germans, founded and carried on by the Sisters of St. John the Baptist. There is a German Priest. We shall take up the English side of the work, working three or four hours only each day, spending the rest of the time in study, meditation, celebrating or alternating celebrations and reciting the offices. I expect to go to New York week after next. Cameron will stay in Syracuse till someone can be found to take up the work at Calvary Church.

I had not realized how important it is that we should be quiet for two or three years and have that inner discipline which alone can fit one for the separated life. Bye-and-bye I will send you a time-table so that you may see how our day is spent.

I think you would like Dod very much. He is only 26 but seems older than I do. He is a tall, handsome fellow, thoroughly bright and manly, has spent a great deal of time in outdoor exercise. He seems to be rapidly gaining in strength and there is no present likelihood of his being troubled with asthma etc.

Four days later Huntington wrote of his uncertainty about the new community, and his determination to begin:[10]

We know little about the future. It must be years before an Order can really be begun. We must be postulants and novices ourselves first. We only feel, that whatever failures, disappointments, distresses may await us, we have all received the summons and we *must* go on. We do not anticipate much of what the world calls success. If we are working in the supernatural order, the best results of what we do must, in the nature of things, be invisible.

One additional arrangement had been made. The Rector of the Church of the Transfiguration, Dr. George Hendric Houghton, was to be the director of the new Order. He acted in a similar capacity to the Sisters, and was well known as a spiritual guide and friend of the Religious Life. Fr. Huntington wrote of him: "Probably there is no one in New York that has proved more helpful to people than Dr. Houghton, of the Church of the Transfiguration. I suppose he confesses half the penitents of our Church in and about New York. I can say to you, in strict confidence, that he will be our guide and director in this new work."[11]

James Huntington joined Robert Dod in New York on Oct. 1, 1881, and they moved into the first house of the Order of the Holy Cross at 276 East 7th Street. Before the end of October, James Cameron, who had left Cowley and briefly succeeded Fr. Huntington at Calvary Church, Syracuse, joined them. Dod was to lead the community as a novice, and to undertake the active work at the Holy Cross Mission which would materially support the new community. Huntington and Cameron, as postulants, would for the first six months lead a quiet and contemplative life. The three wrote their friends to keep a novena for the new Order in the first week of October,[12] asking for perseverance of those called; faithfulness and wisdom; that what they do might be for the glory of God; for their advancement in the spiritual life; that the Order might be for the good of the Church; for the increase of the Order; for other religious orders, the bishops and clergy, and for the Church at large.

The day before the formal beginning of community life Huntington addressed some of the real concerns expressed by his family:[13]

This will reach you tomorrow morning, I hope. It cannot be a real answer to your most suggestive letters because there is very little time and I have not thought over them enough. They raise in my mind the distressing question whether you really believe that in leaving Syracuse, breaking away from attachments there, giving up home life, grieving kind hearts, perplexing friends, whether in all this I have been acting contrary to the will of GOD. You do not really think it? Surely I have not acted hastily in this matter and I did not leave Syracuse because I thought I should be more successful, or more widely known, or even *do more good,* as the saying is, elsewhere. Work on the "east side" of New York is not likely to be exactly encouraging and we are far from having a *model Mission,* anything like St. Augustine's, for example.

Nor have I reasoned and studied the life as you suppose, I have only tried to live it and in doing so I have begun to discover what a real, separate, distinct thing it is, with experiences, temptations, sorrows, and joys not altogether peculiar to this life of course, yet characteristic of it in the sense of being *always* found where the life is earnestly followed and *not* always found in good lives, even in the lives of Priests, living in the world. I do not mean that I realize all this in myself yet, only I see that it must come and know something of it through the lives of others about me.

But you must not think that I mean that the life in a religious Order is a complicated and elaborate form of religious experience. On the contrary I seem to be growing much simpler in my faith and devotion, One's own sins and shortcomings and GOD's overflowing and unfathomable mercy and a continual giving up of oneself to our Blessed Lord to be made like Him through study of His Life and receiving Him in the Sacrament of his Love, these are the thoughts that form the subject of meditations, prayers, hopes, fears.

The Mission of the Holy Cross, which had offered employment to the new community, was six years old in 1881. It had been founded by Sr. Helen Margaret, CSJB. Known in the world as Helen Stuyvesant Folsom, an American, she had entered the Community of St. John the Baptist in December, 1871, and was professed on July 6, 1874. She had decided to dedicate her life and her real-estate holdings on the Lower East Side of New York, which she had inherited from her father (George Folsom, U.S. Minister to Holland, 1850-53), to God and to the ministry among the poor. The autumn after her profession some of the Sisters of CSJB began ministry among the immigrants on the Lower East Side, using the Folsom family house as the mother house. Sr. Helen Margaret arrived in the Spring of 1875 and continued the work until she died April 26, 1883.

Working at first from rented rooms in a tenement on Fifth Street near Avenue C, in the winter of 1875 the Sisters began visiting families, giving classes in religion and domestic skills to children, and gathering a congregation. Arrangements were made to use the church building of the Church of the Nativity, with the support of the Rector, The Rev'd. Caleb Clapp; the first service was held there on Whitsunday, 1875. Known as the Mission of the Holy Cross, the work grew rapidly. By 1879 the Sunday school had grown to 400 children. In 1880 the Sisters made 2,931 visits, and there were 205 families on the register and 300 communicants. But Clapp died in 1879 and the vestry, hostile to the Sisters and their Mission, evicted them in May, 1879. The Mission met temporarily in the Sisters' convent chapel on 17th Street, many blocks from where most of the people lived. Still, they filled the tiny chapel to overflowing. In the autumn of 1879 a bank building on the corner of Avenue C and 7th Street was rented, the ground floor fitted for a chapel and two upper floors for Sunday school and guild use. At the time of the Knox-Little retreat Fr. Dod was already working in the Mission, under the direction of the Rev'd. C.P.A. Burnett, who had charge of the English work of the Mission.

The Sisters of St. John the Baptist had a great effect on the early days of the Order of the Holy Cross. The Order took its name from their mission, and they provided nearly everything of substance for the new community: its work, its place in the ministry of the Church, its income, introduction to Canon Carter and Dr. Houghton, and a large share of the encouragement and advice which made the enterprise possible in its beginnings. It is not too much to say that without the Community of St. John the Baptist the Order of the Holy Cross probably would not have begun at all.

But it was Fr. Dod who was really responsible for founding the Order. Fr. Huntington credited Dod for establishing its first Rule and distinctive observances, and also for forming the first idea of community and carrying it through to reality:[14]

> You must remember that we did *not* meet together and say "Come, let us make a Religious Order" and then go on piecing this and that together. I doubt if any Religious Order that lasted long has had its origin in that way. The outline, the conception of the Life and the Community as a whole must exist in some single mind to begin with, not of course in all its details, but in the main purpose and *ethos* of the society. The conception of a Religious Order in our Church did present itself to the mind of Fr. Dod. He embodied it in a Rule drawn from sources ancient and modern and with advice from Canon Carter and Mother Harriett of the C.S.J.B., but directed and shaped by the model before his own mind. I believe that in this he was guided by GOD.

When Dod, Huntington and Cameron formally began to live the Religious Life on November 1, 1881, they already possessed a fully formed structure. Dod had drawn up a preliminary constitution and rule while at

Clewer. By November 1, he had completed three founding documents for the Order: a Rule of Life, a Constitution and a House Rule.[15] These documents governed the Order until 1894, and in modified form until 1901.

Dod's principal ideas of the Religious Life are seen in three mottoes at the beginning of the Rule. The first, in Greek, is Ecclesiasticus 2:1: "My son, if you aspire to be a servant of the Lord, prepare yourself for testing." The second is 2 Corinthians 12:9: "My power is made perfect in weakness." The third is a statement about the nature of the Religious Life:

> The way of perfection lies in the faithful observance of Rule, through the power of Divine Love, and ardent aspiration after God, with the pure intention of seeking Him, and winning others to glorify Him, so that shining forth in heavenly virtues and active duties we may reveal Him who is the pure and perfect Light.

The dominant ideas of these mottoes are testing as a path to the service of God, weakness as a path to the power of God, and the seeking after perfection. Purity, faithfulness and light are dominant images of that perfection. Dod's Rule is a development of these ideas. The life he sets forth is one of unremitting prayer and work, with the strictest limitation of self under obedience, all for the sake of the search for perfection.

The Rule is divided into two parts. The first describes specific duties: Prayer, which comprises Holy Communion, offices, meditation, reading scripture and spiritual works, and retreats; Penance, including self-examination, confession, the discipline, fasts, days of abstinence, sleep, silences, recreation and the habit; and Good Works, among which he describes study and active work. The second part of the Rule consists of Counsels: Of the Life, the Holy Eucharist (written especially for the Order by Canon Carter), Work, the Superior, Employments, Duty to Our Companions, Recreation, Intercourse with the Outer World, Temptations, Faults and Monthly Observances. These seem to be the fruit of Dod's discussions with Canon Carter, and are sentences of advice, not unlike proverbs. The tenor of these sayings may be felt from some from one section, Of Duty to Our Companions:

Bear all from them without giving them anything to bear from you.

Do not speak of them unless you speak well of them.

Do not speak to them except in love.

Bear their faults as you would wish them to bear yours.

Of the words and deeds of others judge nothing rashly.

Never make mortifying remarks, avoid partisanships, never find fault with anyone, unless it is your place to do so, and then always in meekness and love.

Practice mutual edification, courtesy, forbearance, gentleness, unselfishness, patience and universal charity.

Be ready on every opportunity to oblige and help each other, yet taking care not to interfere, against rule, in another's charge.

No detail of life was so small that it might not be brought under rule to serve the search for perfection. No hour was left unscheduled in the "ardent aspiration after God." Within two months the Order had evolved a schedule, derived from the prayer and work required by Dod's Rule, adapted to the needs of the ministry at the Holy Cross Mission. It is rigorous:[16]

5:30 a.m.	Rise
6:00	Breviary Office of Lauds from St. Margaret's Book. Prime and Preparation for Holy Communion
6:30	Holy Communion (7:00 if at St. John Baptist House) followed by a Thanksgiving and a Eucharistic Meditation
8:30	Breakfast
9:00-10:00	Principal Meditation
10:00	Terce and Matins
10:30-11:00	Reading of Scriptural Theology
11:00-11:30	Reading of New Testament (on knees)
11:30-12:30	Study of Theology
12:30 p.m.	Sext and Self-Examination
1:00	Dinner (reading by community member)
1:30-2:30	Recreation in the library
2:00	None
2:30-5:30	Reading and Study, except on Wed. and Fri. James leaves after dinner to do some teaching. German kept up.
5:30	Evensong
6:00-6:30	Vespers and Eucharistic Meditation.
7:00	Presentation of abstract of a sermon on Tues. Written sermon due on Thurs. Guild of boys at house on Tuesday.
9:30	Compline and Matins (Nocturns)
11:00	Lights out

The practical details of life were spelled out in the House Rule. Not only was time strictly regulated, but the physical details of life were correspondingly ascetic. The House Rule prescribes minutely times for rising and retiring, for services, ringing the bell, silences, recreation, the use of the library, visitors, leaving the house, meals, furnishings, clothing, possessions and the work of the community. It was very austere, but also wholesome:

No food can be had at any other times (save regular meals) except by permission of Fr. in Charge.

The food shall be such as the Superior shall direct, from time to time, plain & simple but cleanly & of sufficient quantity to preserve health in the community.

Great care should be taken that there be no waste.

There shall be no meat served on days of Abstinence, and no food except to sick and visitors, on fast days until after 6 p.m., when there shall be a light refection.

No alcoholic drinks shall be drunk in the House except as medicine.

No smoking is allowed except by visitors in their parlor.

The cells of the community may be furnished with an iron bedstead & straw bed, a table, a chair, a wash stand & necessaries, a small looking glass and a suitable receptacle for clothing. There may be a Prie-Dieu & crucifix but not pictures, curtains or carpets. The cell must be kept thoroughly clean & swept by the occupant once a week, and scrubbed by him when necessary. There shall be no easy chairs or lounges in the House except in the visitors' room.

The third document Dod prepared for the new Order was the Constitution. Here he defines the Order and its purpose and vows, as well as the duties of its officers. It specifies the methods of election of officers and details of admission and profession, with a service of profession which would be the basis for Fr. Huntington's profession three years later. The Order of the Holy Cross intends as its purpose "For the love of Jesus to serve God in the Religious Life by prayer, fasting & good works, especially mission work among the city poor and holding missions and retreats."

Dod places the voting membership, called Chapter, first in the political arrangement of the Order: "The Chapter shall deliberate and decide all that concerns the Order. The Rule cannot be altered or added to without consent of Chapter. . . . The Superior cannot impose a command contrary to the decision of Chapter." This is a democratic, American institution, with all the life-professed members enfranchised in Chapter, and the obedience due to the Superior tempered by recourse to popular will. But the Superior is also a strong figure to whom, within the limits of conscience and Chapter's decisions, absolute obedience is due. He is not unlike a Benedictine abbot, with complete discretion within the limits set by Chapter and Rule, and a paternal character as well: "The first duty of the Superior is to promote the inner life of the Community. He governs the Order with loving care as a father his sons."

The heart of the Religious Life is in the vows kept by its members. In giving the self to God through poverty, chastity and obedience, the vows taken signify a complete turn toward God, and ultimate dedication of self to the coming Kingdom. This is made possible through redirection of the fundamental impulses of human life. To one not called, the vows are burdensome, absurd, death-giving. But to one called they are the path of life itself: "In his will is our peace," as Augustine of Hippo says. The mark of true vocation is the joy and fruitfulness of the life under vows. This does not happen without pain and struggle, nor does it manifest at every moment a superficial happiness, but the truth of the vocation is in a determined and productive adult decision to live one's life for God. Dod's formulation of the vows is a clear statement of the intention of the early life of the Order. He speaks as much of behavior and action as of interior intention, making a unity of the two. These quotations give a sense of Dod's theology of the three vows:

> Religious poverty is understood to mean the entire surrender of all that may be possessed, even to the least article of personal use or enjoyment, so as to have no longer any property whatever at one's own disposal. . . . Religious poverty does not relate merely to outward possession or use. It is an interior law of self-renunciation which unites the soul to its Lord, and most perfectly exhibits His mind, who "for our sakes became poor that he might make many rich." It implies a surrender of all desires or intentions as to outward things, according to the apostolic precept, "having food and raiment let us be content."

Of chastity he says:

> The holy example of our virgin Lord and the spotlessness of His Virgin Mother furnish to the Religious a perpetual incentive to interior purity of mind and heart and to the strictest guarding of the senses against whatever may distract the soul or tend to withdraw it from heavenly things.

And concerning obedience:

It must be ever borne in mind, that a constant humility is the only safeguard of the habitual self-surrender which this great principle of the Religious Life requires, and which the example of our Blessed Lord had endeared to us as the ground work of his own perfect obedience by which "many are made righteous."

In his Rule, Constitution and House Rule Dod held the banner of the Religious Life as high as he possibly could. His Order would be both democratic and obedient, and as fully active and as fully contemplative as it could possibly be at one and the same time. Its energy would derive from the strictest austerity and the most willing self-giving possible under vows. The Order he dreamed of would be an instrument of perfection, nothing less.

And so the life of the new community began. The first months saw Dod taking most of the outside work so that Huntington and Cameron might immerse themselves in the contemplative life necessary for the first steps as religious. Dod described the new community in a letter of December 15: "We three form a little community and are beginning to be aware of the effect on our life. We exclude the world and almost all work from our lives and our minds—leaving just enough to keep us from growing morbid. The necessary work in the H. C. Mission—I do. A number of men have expressed a desire to join with us—to all I have said *wait*."[17] And in a charming letter written December 12, a young cousin of Fr. Huntington describes his visit to Holy Cross House:[18]

They see about the wretchedest and wickedest side of life in New York. Several times they have had paving stones thrown at them, "not very hard," James said, by roughs, but have had no serious trouble.

They rise at half past five, work and have services till half past eight, when they take breakfast. They have a great many services, nine a day, I think. He seems thoroughly happy in his work, and looks, and says he is, very well.

Silence is always kept in the entries, stairways and chapel. On going down in the morning, no one speaks until Father D. says something; then at breakfast all stand while one of the Fathers reads a chapter from the Bible, then bow while grace is said.

The house is very old and quaint, with wooden dadoes and small squares of glass in the windows. The inner wall of my room . . . had settled a foot or more, making quite a hill from one side to another. The first thing I noticed in the room was a kind of shrine or altar at one side. It was made of wood, shaped something like a small bookcase, and had a large crucifix painted on the back.

Indeed, all that evening, as I sat by the fire in the library, filled with musty leather-bound books, old engravings of saints, and a cross over the mantle, the two priests in their long black gowns and the dim light which made the room look large and hid all modern incongruities. . . . I could hardly realize that I was not in some old monastery.

I think on some days, Fridays for one, they do not speak all day except when necessary. . . . Cousin James wears his long black gown all the time, indoors and out. I noticed that when he spoke of a clergyman he said "priest." . . . I forgot to say that they had almost sixty boys there the night before, playing checkers and other simple games.

The question of the work of the Order has been a constant feature in Holy Cross conversation from that day to this: which has precedence, prayer or active work? Huntington tried to explain the Order's position in a letter:[19]

I am so glad that you realize the value of the life apart from *work*. Not that we mean to go "out of the world" or found a purely contemplative order, only that we want to realize a *separated* life in ourselves *first*, to learn a real detachment from the world and from self, to bring every thought, every impulse, every emotion into the obedience of Christ, *then* we shall be ready for any work, no matter how intense or active, in which God shall see fit to employ us.

At the beginning of Lent in 1882, after the community's first four months, Dod gave the Order a retreat. His notes have survived, and give a clear picture of Dod's understanding of the Religious Life and what he hoped his new community would become. The Order must not confuse its vocation with the ordinary parish ministry: "If our all is to serve God as parish priests this is *not* the way. We are losing time and *not* fulfilling our vocation. . . . The social visits, the business meetings and other pleasant and profitable necessary duties of a good and holy parish priest are not for us any more than the sweet and holy pleasures of a happy christian home. The time that they would consume would leave us no time for prayer."[20] He went on:

[The religious house] must be a monastery from which all the world is excluded. Its spirit is seclusion, the aim of the inmates is not to show a life or a teaching that may effect a reformation in the Church. (All this may be effected, but it is not the aim.) The aim is our own perfection—the intensity of holiness—the offering to God of our whole selves—not offering ourselves as examples or helps to men—but offering to God and image, *eikon* of his Son which by the Spirit is made perfect in holiness, going on from glory to glory, from grace to grace.

In his second instruction Dod enlarges on the theme of perfection: "Perfection is not only the absence of sin, but fulness of virtue." The purpose of perfection is not merely personal development, but union with God. Nine obstacles stand in the way of perfection leading to union: self love, love of the creature, desire to satisfy the senses more than is proper, pride, anger, self will, mere curiosity of wit, fickleness and carelessness. Dod's purpose is to change the inclination of the natural man from building the false self to building the true one, from self-preoccupation to union with the Creator. The third instruction is on prayer: "The constant intercourse of the soul with God is unceasing prayer. . . . It is the very life of the soul, not only the sign of that life. It is the power of communion or fellowship with God." Union with God through ascesis is the aim of the Religious Life. The fourth and fifth instructions give the means, after prayer, by which the ascetic union is reached: penance and study.

Dod is a thorough rigorist. For him, the full person must be engaged in a struggle for perfection, purity, union with God, not simply the moral self, but the intellectual and emotional and physical self as well. His ascetical doctrine brings to mind the practices of the Desert Fathers. Like many founders, he held an extreme vision, one which in fact eventually consumed him. But that extreme vision staked out the territory for his new American community. In a Church with relatively few examples of ascetical community life, such as Little Gidding, and in a Church and a society which distrusted such a life, Dod's firm and uncompromising theology of the struggle to perfection broke definitely with the present age. In clearing a wide space for the new community, he gave it the gift of room for development. Here was no half-hearted, apologetic attempt, only barely discernible from its surroundings. Dod uttered the full-blooded cry of ancient monasticism: separate from the world, discipline the self, mistrust anything which serves the senses, devote the self entirely to God, care for nothing else: "Love God above all things and your neighbor in God and for his sake." For Dod, God is all and the self exists as the means for relating to God. This places Dod's concern squarely in modern religious thought: What is the nature of the self, and what is that self in relation to ultimate reality, to God? Dod spoke this concern clearly to the new Order, and it took up his cry.

Huntington and Cameron made a retreat of six days at St. Gabriel's

School, of the Community of St. Mary, at Peekskill, NY, before they were clothed as novices. That retreat gave Huntington an opportunity to crystallize his thoughts about the Religious Life, and his notes are preserved. They provide a compelling contrast with Dod, not so much in conflict as in a different emphasis. For Dod the basis of the monastic life was in the relation of self, in all its various faculties, to God. The monastic, indeed, the Christian life was for Dod a struggle for perfection. For Huntington the basis of Christian life and monasticism was the self-giving love of God in the Incarnation and in the Passion of Christ on the Cross. The emphases of the two men were so different it is difficult to believe, reading the notes of their two retreats, made less than two months apart, that they were from the same milieu. And yet they are strangely complementary. If anything, Dod's emphasis is closer to that of our day, preoccupied with self as the place where salvation is wrought. But it is also repellant in its extreme conclusions, while Huntington's seems to breathe sweet reason and a more liberal spirit. But Huntington's emphasis was no less radical than Dod's, and as it was built on the more abstract base of deductive theology, rather than the immediate base of the active self, it was also somehow distant. Dod was deeply engaged, constantly, earnestly struggling in his addresses, a personality which could not easily be ignored, which would demand response and elicit devotion. With Huntington there was a reserve, a commitment to theoretical conclusions, an intellect which pervades and invites, but more by example than by direct personal claim.

Huntington's first thoughts set the scene for his theology of monasticism:[21]

The Religious Life is a great fact, whence does it come? GOD has created it as a life of special union with Him through prayer and suffering. It exists only in the Christian Church raised to a high place of glory and power thro' the Incarnation, by which alone indeed and by its results working backward as well as forward is any abiding union of man with GOD possible. To us Christians the Religious Life is the creation of GOD's Love through the Life and Death of JESUS. Union with GOD through the Perfect Humanity loved and initiated. "Sell all that thou hast—take up thy cross—follow me." Yes—the Cross, before us and in us the Fountain of the Religious Life—the Love of GOD, the sufferings of JESUS. Prayer through the One Mediator; suffering in the strength of the Crucified. That I might realize my vocation He must die. Oh can I trifle with my calling when I reflect what it has cost.

He passes on to the purpose of the Religious Life:

> The Religious Life, so unlike the life of most, involving such real sacrifices—what is it for? The Glory of GOD. GOD may be glorified by *my life*. *Ego se edoxasa epi tes ges.* To present to GOD a faint image of his dear Son,—in humility, obedience, suffering. To witness for GOD. To the awfulness of sin, to the joy of redemption, to the abiding care of GOD for his children, to the poverty of earth, to the riches of Heaven, to the Cross of Christ. *Umeis de este martures touton.* To intercede for the world. "More things are wrought by prayer than this world dreams of." The Religious, on his knees before the crucifix in his cell, or pleading the Holy Sacrifice at that Altar is labouring for the salvation of the world. JESUS CHRIST loved the world enough to die for it. Cannot we, in union with Him, live and suffer for it?
>
> To preach and teach, to warn and comfort, to arouse and edify, to hear confessions, to minister to the sick and dying,—all in union with JESUS, freed from self. " 'Tis angel's work below" "Angels he calls you, be your strife to lead on earth an Angel's life."

For Huntington the Religious Life begins in relation with God, and moves ever outward, embracing the world in a Christ-like love which is born of the willingness to share the Cross.

He then details the realities of vocation: sufferings in body, mind and affections, and spirit. The duties of the Religious Life include prayer in all its forms, fasting and good works. But the Religious Life has supports as well: a deepening sense of vocation, the Blessed Sacrament both received and celebrated, and community life. And it has virtues proper to it: humility, obedience, charity and suffering gained from the love of the Cross. The fruits of such a life are inner, toward God and towards others: "The Religious Life, if faithfully followed, gives us what we most need in finding our way to the hearts of others—a deepening knowledge of our sinfulness and weakness and of GOD's infinite Love and Patience,—self-forgetfulness, gentleness, courage and some faint far-off likeness to JESUS."

On the Feast of the Finding of the Cross, May 3, 1882, Frs. Huntington and Cameron were admitted as novices in the Order of the Holy Cross. Dr. Houghton, the Order's spiritual director, was the officiant, and Bp. Huntington gave the benediction at the end of the service, which was held in the Sisters' chapel on 17th Street. The Order now consisted of three novices, with Fr. Dod acting as Superior, under the direction of Dr. Houghton. They settled in to live the life they had desired to establish.

In May or June of 1882 the three young monks moved from their first house at 276 East 7th Street to a house at 95 Avenue D, in the midst of the worst tenement area. Fr. Dod continued to take most of the work at the Mission, but Fr. Huntington and Fr. Cameron began to work outside the confines of the monastery as well. Dod, however, showed the strain of leadership and work. A somewhat later letter, its recipient unnamed, reveals Dod's nervous hysteria at the violation of a very small point in the Rule:[22]

> I heard this evening from Mr. Stockton that he had seen you smoking and I write at once to ask you to forgive me, for I fear *my example* may have led you to break your rule, but by God's help I will never let it be so again, for I shall not hereafter use tobacco in any form even as medicine, lest my "meat cause my brother to offend." But O Brother remember the first fervor with which you came to us, to offer yourself to God, resolved to take every opportunity of denying self & all appetites for his dear sake, how gladly you then promised, not me but *God,* to give up all for Him, how glad to be received here.

Full of nervous energy, holding an ideal before the new community almost impossible to fulfill, working full time at the Mission, and keeping the community exercises in all their strictness as well, it is no wonder that Dod, exposed to the unsanitary conditions of the Lower East Side tenement district, and never strong to begin with, began to decline. On Oct. 8, 1882, Fr. Huntington wrote that, although he was well himself, "certainly better in health since coming to N.Y. than I have been for some years," Dod's health was a concern: "Fr. Dod is not strong, but Fr. Cameron and I are almost always well."[23]

Fr. Huntington's relatives were becoming alarmed at his new life. His mother regarded it as morbid, and asked, "Does such a life fit him to do battle with the sin of a city like New York and work with a man's strength and vigor in the battlefield of the Lord? Perhaps he is girding himself for the future in some way that I do not understand."[24] To his brother George Fr. Huntington wrote on Jan. 17, 1883:[25]

> Thank you for your kind letters and excellent hygienic advice. Was this prompted by Aunt F's declaration which Uncle James heard her make in a horse-car lately that "a High Church Episcopalian 'had told her that we live entirely on bread and water' "?

To one of his aunts he wrote reassuringly at the end of 1883:[26]

> As to food, we breakfast on cereal, molasses, milk, bread, butter

and sugar, and the same for supper with hominy in the place of oatmeal. For dinner we have at this season soup, meat, two kinds of vegetables, and apples, beside bread and crackers. We can have coffee when we wish for it, but do not think it best to drink it as a regular thing. We have good meat, and our food is always well-cooked. I cannot remember when I made a meal on anything [nothing?] but bread and water—it might be a good thing occasionally, and of course we are grateful to Aunt F for suggesting it, only do not tell her so. No, really, we do not aim to do queer things, but just to make our lives as simple and real as we can. Thank you for the money you sent. We live pretty close to the wind (is that the correct nautical expression?). You need not fear but that your gift was very acceptable.

By January, 1883, Fr. Dod's health had deteriorated even further, enough to worry Fr. Huntington: "Fr. Dod is *very* unwell and the future of our active work is very uncertain. Please remember us specially next Sunday. Thank GOD the Order is established—I think we feel that no one of us is *necessary* to its continuance."[27] At this time Dod's health problems were connected with his lifelong bout with asthma. But by Holy Week of 1883 (Palm Sunday was on March 18 that year) Dod was seriously ill:[28]

The health of the Fr. Superior had become more and more "difficult" and the asthma, from which he had suffered for many years, came back more and more frequently. At length, in Holy Week 1883, the Father was attacked by typhoid fever and for many weeks lay dangerously ill at St. Luke's Hospital. The Order had been obliged to move into a smaller house, 95 Avenue D, and it was felt that, if the Father recovered, he ought not to return to the unsanitary conditions of that locality.

So, the community moved in the spring of 1883 to its third house in less than eighteen months, at 330 East 13th Street. Fr. Dod returned from the hospital in the early summer, and retained his health until the following winter.

Fr. Allen recalled the house on 13th Street:[29]

[It] was a high stooped brick house, three or four stories and basement with cellar underneath. On the first floor was a good sized room intended as a parlor but used as a reception room for callers. Back of this a room with windows on the rear yard used for a chapel. . . . Going from the chapel downstairs, the refectory occupied the front room and at the back was the kitchen with pantry and store room between the rooms. . . . On the second floor the rear room served as a library. . . In the front were cells and between the front and rear, closets and a bath room. On the top floor or floors were cells.

The conditions of life on the Lower East Side were very difficult. Masses of immigrants poured into New York daily, some of course pushing west as soon as they could, but many settling in New York City. The physical structure of the city could not easily accommodate them, and their own poverty, the poor living and sanitary conditions, the chronic under- and unemployment, the lack of linguistic and cultural skills to assimilate easily into American culture, and above all, the alienation many immigrants experienced—cut off from their homelands and not yet accepted in the new—all these conspired to make their lot in New York City a harsh and difficult one. Dod described the scene:[30]

That part of the City of New York from 7th Street as far down as Division and up to 16th Street that lies along the East River extending back to Avenue A or 1st Avenue, is a district to many utterly unknown though near at hand. There are numerous factories in the quarter and the old houses, once private residences, have been converted into tenement houses, filled and often overcrowded with the factory hands and others too poor to find homes. Other houses have been built 4 and 5 stories high. On each floor there are 2 families at least if not four, and in the yards of many of these houses is a rear house shutting out light and air. Poverty, disease and dirt are everywhere. The overcrowding of this densely populated quarter makes it a centre of vice and crimes. The police say it is almost impossible to make an arrest there. The blind courts and alleys afford hiding places for criminals and for the accumulation of great piles of filth and rotting garbage.

In order to minister to the people of the Lower East Side the Holy Cross Mission provided several kinds of activity. Guilds were formed for men and women, boys and girls, to give them the simplest of comforts: a safe, clean place to be away from home:[31]

A guild [for men] has been formed of about 40 members. They meet in their guild room, a cold, bare, cheerless place enough, and read and smoke and rest, instead of spending their time in beer saloons, in drunken brawls, or gambling away the wages needed so sorely by their wives and children. One man said there is no place where a man can go and spend the evening in pleasure and not feel ashamed of himself when he goes home.

The guild of women numbers about 200. It would do your heart good to see these poor women as they gather in their room to knit or sew and talk and listen to the reading or words of comfort and sound kind advice about their troubles and worries.

The Order particularly worked with boys. Throughout the years of the Order's work at the Mission many groups were formed to meet one need or another. All had the same ultimate object: to bring the children of these almost destitute immigrants into contact with something which could give them hope. One of those boys, Fr. Edward Henry Schlueter, who in later years became Fr. Huntington's close friend, recalled some of the attempts the boys' groups made to change the tenor of the neighborhood:[32]

New Year's Day on the East Side was a very wild day with much drunkenness and debauchery. Things seemed right on that day that seemed right at no other time: and very young boys in crowds went off calling and came home at night drunk. On one occasion on New Year's Day he [Fr. Huntington] got together the choirs of the various churches. He began with his own choir and went down to the Epiphany and joined with their choir and went down to St. Augustine's and on down to All Saints and around to St. Mark's and then back to Holy Cross. The boys sang hymns as they went; they were vested; and there were processional crosses. I think it did a lot for the boys; I do not know what it did for the neighborhood. The hope was that it would arouse opposition; but the more or less phlegmatic East Side just looked on and smiled and let it go by. On the other hand, who knows—some mother may have seen this sight and drawn her boy closer to herself.

In the summer of 1883 a fresh-air work for boys was begun on a farm of about sixty acres near Farmingdale, Long Island. The Sisters had already established a similar work for women and girls there, and to it was added St. Andrew's Cottage, providing a wholesome vacation spot for boys who were, at very early ages, compelled to work long hours in the factories, and had very little decent place of recreation. Fr. Allen described it thus:[33]

The plan included eventually a sort of agricultural and industrial house for relief of the congested life in the tenements on the East Side. Meantime a start was to be made in a cottage to take in boys for a week or two for a summer outing. . . . A large barn was erected and arranged to accommodate the boys. The barn floor was partitioned on one side for cells for the Fathers and caretakers and also a chapel and wash room. One corner of the other side was set off for a kitchen.

The remaining part of that side was used for a refectory. Tables and benches were placed transversely to the length of the room. The whole middle of the floor was left free for the boys' use. There were broad sliding doors at each end as is usual in a barn. On either side were lofts used as dormitories for the boys. Subsequently a floor was placed over the central part of the barn above the lofts to which the chapel was transferred. . . . The outside was painted but the interior left in the natural state. . . . The boys would gather at the 34th Street Ferry to Hunters Point, Long Island City with their bundles. The depot at Long Island City was a crude affair and trains poor. The line ran through a dreary array of slipshod houses and back yards. . . . Arrived at Farmingdale we walked out to St. Andrew's. Monday morning the boys returned to New York, sometimes in [the] charge of an older boy.

Fr. Schlueter remembered the work from a somewhat later time:[34]

It was really hardly what one would call a fresh-air work; it was a kind of religious house with 50 or 60 fellows around. [Fr. Huntington] was not often there himself. . . . The background of all this was the chapel with its bells tolling out seven times a day, calling to office. . . . Each night there was an instruction in the chapel for the boys. One thing which I learned there, which I have never seen in any other fresh air work except at West Cornwall, was that those in charge ate with the children and ate what they ate: there was no separate table for the priests or the gentlemen! The first few years they tried farm work; I remember my helping to harvest several acres of oats. One year there was a kitchen garden—but East Side boys don't make good farmers, and it cost more than could be raised.

In the summer of 1883, as many as sixty-seven boys at once spent time at St. Andrew's, and the numbers grew every year.

It soon became clear that the Dry Dock Bank building on Avenue C and 7th Street was inadequate, and a plan for building a new church was made. By 1883 there were more than 400 communicants and about 700 children, and they needed more room. Mr. Folsom had pledged the land, and some amount of money, but the building would cost $50,000. A smaller plant could be built for as little as $15,000. The advantage of the larger building would afford a more permanent home for the Order: "When we still thought of a larger church we hoped it might be handed over to us and become our conventual chapel with a Community House attached to it."[35] Fr. Huntington envisioned another house in the country as well, seeing a dual-monastery establishment of city and country, a combination which the Order would not realize until some ninety years later:[36]

> When the Church is built, as I have said to you before, the money will be forthcoming for the monastery. In the course of years, if our members should increase, we should hope to have a house in the country, probably connected with some permanent institution such as an orphanage, where novices could be trained, and where those who work in the city could go for rest and change of air. If the Mission and the Church should be also in our hand we should then be fully equipped. Those who are preparing to enter the Order could then have their time of seclusion out of town and could also be sent in to the city-house for a definite time to be trained in active work in the Mission.

But it did not happen as Fr. Huntington dreamed. Fundraising began but fell short of the larger goal, and work on the smaller church building began in 1885.

Sometime after early October, 1883, Cameron left the novitiate, "feeling after long deliberation that his vocation lay along different lines."[37] Dod and Huntington carried on the monastic life at home and the work of the Mission. But Dod grew gradually weaker, and his asthma returned. In November, Mrs. Huntington noted that Dod was "somewhat of an invalid but they hope he is gaining on the whole."[38] By January Dod had collapsed almost entirely. The illness seems not entirely physical in nature. Fr. Huntington wrote:[39]

> He rarely sleeps now before three or four o'clock in the morning and often he is unable even to say an Office on his bed or do anything but read a child's story book. The thought of such weakness makes me feel how great is the responsibility of my strength and how much I have got to learn. . . . I trust I am able to do it in a more detached and submissive spirit. I do not feel the same alternations of hopes and discouragements or the same natural eagerness I once did. Yet I think I care for the souls to whom I minister more than ever.

Worn out by physical work and a religious regimen stricter in practice than it may have seemed in theory, and perhaps worn out as well because of his intense idealism, Dod left on March 18, 1884: "Fr. Dod has, quite suddenly at last, realized that he cannot go on, his own conviction is that he will never go on with the work and life. He took off his habit this morning and went to Princeton."[40] Dod traveled to Sewanee, TN, where his cousin was Vice Chancellor of the University of the South. He returned briefly to New York in the summer, and then sailed to Galveston in late October, making his way to Brady, TX, about 125 miles northwest of San Antonio. He wrote to Huntington frequently, and his letters portray a perfectionist aristocrat, educated in all the classical disciplines, confronting the realities of frontier life:[41]

> I think you would be amused could you see my dress and accoutrements. I find time to sing an office on horseback occasionally but not much else. We keep moving while it is light, and when not driving, which engages one's attention, we are hunting for dinner.

Dod's leaving was a difficult blow to Huntington. He wrote to his father:[42]

> The wrench was a very hard one to make but he has made it and feels sure that he is doing God's will. It seems as if he could not be happy under such a disappointment to the hopes of years yet his inner life is so deep and true that I think he will be happy and at peace. Of course he lays aside the life entirely. He has taken no vows and is free to marry. He wished you to know this, but please do not say outside anything further than he has gone away for his health. I must succeed him. It is a crushing weight. God help me to bear it.

It was clear to Huntington that Dod would never return, but not so clear to Dod. When he left in March he passed on his duties as Novice Master to Fr. Huntington, but did not resign control of the Order as Superior until early summer. He continued to hope to return, but gradually realized that he never would.

Fr. Huntington was not left alone, however. There were constant guests in the small monastery, and a layman who had been admitted as a postulant some time before, whose memory survives only in Fr. Allen's memoirs. Fr. Sturges Allen had arrived in March, 1884. Thirty-four years old, from Hyde Park, NY, Fr. Allen was a graduate of the City University of New York and General Seminary, and had assisted in parishes in Kansas City, MO, and Newburgh, NY. He described the household he found, apart from Dod and Huntington:[43]

> There was in the house a priest, Fr. Warren, as a guest, and a layman, Valentine by name, who after much persuasion on his part succeeded in being admitted as a Postulant taking the name of Br. Louis. He had lived a dissipated life, but had repented and made his confession and was very eager to serve God in Religion. He besought the Order to allow him to make a trial. He was attached to Fr. Dod and admired

him greatly though he received sharp correction from him. Under these conditions we were thrown together a good deal and he was an endless talker. He talked of his past life and of his present life and was free in his criticism of the one in authority in the place of Fr. Dod. Fr. Warren was staying for a time helping out with Masses and in search of a permanent work. Brother Louis was 50 years old and Fr. Warren probably older.

After a short stay as a guest it was thought well to admit me as a Postulant, although my intention was to make a visit to England and the Continent for a couple of months. This was considered as consistent with the actions of a Postulant as his obligations were very slight. This also made an escape from an awkward situation as otherwise Br. Louis being a Postulant would be in charge, which was extremely undesirable.

The house was full, but in reality the continuance of the Order depended entirely on James Huntington's faithfulness. Guests came and went, the incorrigible Br. Louis departed soon after March, 1884, and Allen did persevere. But in the summer and autumn of 1884, the whole weight of the Order fell on Fr. Huntington's shoulders. It is in this sense that Fr. Huntington became Fr. Founder: not that he had the founding vision, but that he had the founding strength to remain faithful, and his faithfulness raised up a mighty work. Fr. Allen went abroad and returned, the monastic life continued, and the day for Fr. Huntington's Life Profession drew near.

3

Profession, Social Questions and Slum Work (1884-1892)

Fr. Huntington's Life Profession was scheduled for November 25, 1884. Fr. Allen returned from England in the fall, and Brother Louis had left the community. Guests at the small monastery were set to issue and answer invitations. Two weeks before the date of the profession Fr. Huntington went into a long retreat. "He confined himself to the small room at the top of the house [330 East 13th Street] and had no intercourse with the outside world beyond what was absolutely necessary to him"[1] He copied Dod's Rule by hand, a custom later observed by Frs. Allen and Sargent as well.

At 10:00 a.m. on Tuesday, November 25, 1884, in the Chapel of the Sisters of St. John the Baptist, 233 East 17th Street at Stuyvesant Square, the service of profession took place. Present were forty-one priests, including such leading figures as Morgan Dix, Rector of Trinity Church, Arthur Ritchie of St. Ignatius Church and John Shackleford of the Church of the Redeemer. The Sisters of St. John the Baptist were all there, and seminarians from General Seminary, and many others. Charles T. Quintard, Bishop of Tennessee, was in the sanctuary; Bp. Huntington, Fr. Huntington's father, presided at the eucharist; Dr. Houghton, Rector of the Church of the Transfiguration and spiritual director of the Order, preached the sermon. And Henry Codman Potter, Assistant Bishop of New York, received Fr. Huntington's vows.

The promise he made was the same every monk of Holy Cross has made ever since:

I desire for the love of Jesus, to devote myself body, soul and spirit to the service of Almighty God in the religious life as a member of the Order of the Holy Cross, and to that end to take upon me of my own free will the vows of Religious Poverty, Chastity and Obedience.

39

Bishop Potter then questioned him closely as to the meaning of the vows he was taking upon himself, giving him an ebony cross as a reminder of his poverty and his only possession, a cincture to remind him of chastity, and the Rule for obedience. The hymn *Veni Creator* was sung, Bishop Potter took Fr. Huntington by the right hand and declared him admitted to the Order of the Holy Cross.[2]

The cross he received was the plain black ebony cross of the novices of the Community of St. John the Baptist, and still signifies the Order's enduring filial relationship to the St. John Baptist Sisters.

And so, Fr. Huntington became the first Episcopal priest to take the threefold monastic vow in an American religious community. Three bishops of the Church witnessed and consented to his vow in a service well advertised and attended by a large number of clergy. It was not an official act of the Church because it was not included in the *Book of Common Prayer* or in canon law. But it was also not forbidden by them. It was authorized, witnessed and consented to by the Church in every way short of official sanction.

The tiny community returned to 13th Street, Fr. Huntington now officially its Superior and only permanent member, and quietly took up its work again at the Holy Cross Mission. But it was not long before a storm of criticism broke upon the Order and Bishop Potter.

William Reed Huntington, Rector of Grace Church in New York and a distant relative, wrote to Fr. Huntington on Jan. 9, in a typical reaction:[3]

> I am filled with sorrowful dismay at the transaction in which you have lately taken part. It is a difficult, but by no means impossible thing to keep one's personal friendships unhurt by differences of opinion and belief, and if you find me in the future opposing with all my might the introduction into our Church of the ascetic theology and the practices and terminology associated with it, I hope that you will remember that I have written this and will believe that I am as truly actuated by principle in my hostility to as you are in your advocacy of the revival of monasticism.

The church press was soon full of letters both opposing and defending the introduction of the monastic life for men in the Episcopal Church. The most prominent question was whether vows should be taken for life.[4] "Nothing for years has so startled me. . . . Is it wise, is it right, to encourage young people in the ardor of their early enthusiasm to add life-long 'vows'? . . . May they not become a curse to them?" wrote Samuel Benedict of St. Paul's, Cincinnati. Robert Wilson of St. Luke's, Charleston, SC, asked a second typical question: Is this not reversion to a discredited past?

"The outlook today is inevitable and inexorably *backward*—backward through the long vista of monastery and abbey, of cowl and tonsure, of bitter controversy between bishop and abbot, between parochial clergy and religious orders, closed in by the dark cloud of oppression, license and robbery, which the necessity of suppression produced." Many other comments simply expressed a hysterical anti-Roman Catholic bias.

But the most important correspondent in the controversy was the Presiding Bishop of the Episcopal Church, the Rt. Rev'd. Alfred Lee, Bishop of Delaware.[5] He wrote to Bishop Potter of his "astonishment and distress occasioned by your recent unexampled act, the admission of Mr. Huntington to a so-called religious order, after requiring of him the well-known Romish vows." He objected that by his action, Bishop Potter had sanctioned the whole monastic system, even attributing it to divine inspiration, as the language of the Ordinal of the *Book of Common Prayer* had been used. He then continued with a scathing denunciation of monasticism not untypical of the anti-Catholic propaganda of the time:

> This system is no untried experiment. It has been on trial for hundreds of years, and with whatever of sincerity and zeal started under different forms, the fruits have been evil and pernicious. It was utterly repudiated by the Church of England at the Reformation, and has since been rejected with loathing by several Roman Catholic countries. Sacerdotal celibacy has a history of shame, suffering and sin, traced in indelible characters. The corrupt morals of the priesthood wherever Romanism is in the ascendant is a notorious fact and frightful comment on the attempt to override God's laws and to set up a purer standard than the Holy Scriptures. No attempt, however specious, to introduce the system in our Church can fail to awake earnest and indignant condemnation.

Bishop Potter replied with a passionate defense of the new community and his own action, pointing out that the Church had not ceased to develop different institutions, and that such development was essential if the needs of modern society were to be met.[6]

> The Church was reformed, while religious orders, in England, on the other hand, were destroyed. On the theory that the Reformation was a finality (which is, I know, the theory, or rather the profound belief of many excellent men) there is no appeal from this action, and there can be, it is assumed, no question as to its wisdom. But I cannot say that, in my judgment, the Reformation was a finality.

Turning to the specific case of Fr. Huntington and his companions, he continues:

> Here are, first one young man and then another, who feel profoundly moved by the condition of the godless thousands and ten thousands who crowd our tenement houses in New York. Do you know, my dear and honored Presiding Bishop, what a tenement house in New York is? Do you know the profound and widespread apathy of the Christian community concerning these schools of poverty, misery and almost inevitable vice? Do you know that our own Church's mission work has, thus far, but touched the fringe of this awful mass of sorrow and sin? All this these young men came to see and know by personal observation and actual contact. And then they said, and said as I believe rightly, "If we are to reach these people we must, first of all, *live among them.* It will not answer to have a home and interests elsewhere, and then to walk over to the Mission Chapel and go about among the tenement population three or four times a week. If we are to get close to their hearts we must get close to their lives.

Presiding Bishop Lee shot back on Jan. 19 in an immense 3000-word reply.[7] He failed to see the connection between doing tenement work and taking monastic vows: "there are many effective laborers . . . working unostentatiously without calling upon the world to behold and applaud their self-devotion and heroism. Is there no danger of less pure and exalted motives insinuating themselves when the consecration to a self-sacrificing service is published abroad and enacted as a spectacle before an admiring congregation?" Religious orders have "shown an inveterate tendency to degeneracy and corruption." As to the vows being revocable, as Bishop Potter had stated, Lee thought their language clear: "The vow is really made to God, not to man. I cannot see what human authority can release the devotee. . . . And herein lies a most forcible and weighty objection against encouraging an enthusiastic person to assume obligations . . . which may be a snare and a burden in after years." His final comment, however, is to link the excesses of both license and discipline: "Asceticism and licentiousness are the outgrowths of the same unsound social condition, and both flourish in the degree that sober, consistent, practical godliness declines." Ironically, Fr. Huntington agreed with this. In his Rule of 1901 he included a strikingly similar sentiment: "It is to be remembered that a persistent and long-continued self-denial is often harder and of more spiritual benefit than an excessive austerity alternating with abandonment to appetite."

After reaching fever pitch in January, the controversy gradually died away. Bishop Potter, aware of the anxiety Fr. Huntington was feeling, wrote to him at its height:[8]

> As to the journalistic and other criticism of my part in your profession, you must not give yourself a moment's concern. I am glad to have the whole matter thoroughly "talked out," and, incidentally, to feel that I am, presumably no longer in danger of the anathema pronounced against those of whom all the world speaks well.

Bishop Potter's approval of the new Order was strongly linked to the work it did among the poor, and he likely would not have sanctioned Fr. Huntington's profession without that work. In this Potter was one with Lee, but more generous in recognizing vocation and encouraging new growth in the Church. But the right of a monastic community to exist in itself, apart from any work it might do, was still far from accepted. Nineteenth-century Anglicanism looked to the practical benefits of celibacy, poverty and obedience in community, and saw laborers to work where others could or would not. It would seem that Fr. Huntington did not discourage Bishop Potter in this view. To do so would raise an issue which, in the Church climate of the day, might have made the establishment of the Order an impossibility. But Huntington was also becoming more and more passionately devoted to the social ministry which Potter valued so highly. Probably Huntington saw no contradiction in his position: God's purpose would be served doubly, in mission and in monastery. The social work of the Order would give it legitimacy in the eyes of those for whom no more direct appeal would be possible. But there was no dialectic or separation of motives with Huntington. How could there be when God was clearly calling him to both works?

Controversy or no controversy, Fr. Huntington and Fr. Allen (admitted as a novice on Feb. 7, 1885) returned after the profession to their work at the Holy Cross Mission. It had grown to 300 families and counted some 1500 people in affiliation. The Rev'd. Augustus Hoehing had been hired by the Sisters to work among the German immigrants, as the Order had been hired for the English-speaking ministry. Fr. Huntington and Fr. Allen concentrated on work with men and boys and provided the sacramental ministrations for the Sisters at their convent on 17th Street as well as the services in English at the mission.

The work load for the two priests was immense. Constant meetings of various guilds competed with what would today be called social work, and all had to be fitted into the rigorous monastic program laid out in the Rule by Fr. Dod. St. Andrew's Guild for older boys and young men undertook to walk shop girls home when they worked late at night, and organized huge outings for neighborhood folk, as many as six hundred at a time, to summer picnics on the islands in the East River. There was no gymnasium for the young men and boys, so Fr. Huntington organized one in the by-now abandoned Church of the Nativity on Avenue C and 5th Street. Out of this grew regular boxing matches, which were an occasional feature of the weekly socials at the monastery designed to give a glimpse of settled, civilized life to these cramped tenement dwellers. One boy present at those events remembered:[9]

> There were always readings of stories. I remember especially reading Ruskin's "The King of the Golden River." There were always efforts to draw us out, sometimes pitifully responded to. [Fr. Huntington] wanted to know what we thought, even as small boys. There were usually "eats" after these meetings. I remember suppers, etc.; I cannot recall anything that we ate, but I can never forget the beauty of the table. I recall one supper especially. As we entered the dining room, there was an outburst of "Ah!" from the boys. This is a lesson, too, I never forgot. In all his dealings with us there was never a sense of "Oh these people, what do they know? Anything is good enough!" Rather it was, "Nothing is too good."

In the summer St. Andrew's Cottage reopened in Farmingdale, demanding even more time and attention. And out of it there grew in 1885 a scheme, never realized, for a trade school in Farmingdale for tenement boys, and a "colony" out West to resettle boys once they had learned a trade. The scheme was publicized, funds were solicited, but nothing came of it.

About $35,000 did come in for the church building, however. The mission had been meeting in the Dry Dock Bank building since its eviction from the Church of the Nativity in 1879. In an appeal for funds, the bank-chapel was described:[10]

> The inconveniences of the present chapel are very great. The vestibule is so small it is very difficult for a funeral to enter or leave the chapel. The rooms above are used as Sunday School rooms & the noise of the children going up & down the stairs is & the singing hymns &c is very disturbing to the congregation in the Chapel. The ventilation is very imperfect & in winter the overheated air in the crowded room is almost unbearable. And in the summer people frequently leave the chapel almost fainting & we have carried strong men out of the chapel in a dead faint from the great heat.

The new church was designed by Henry Vaughn. It was a brick and stone Gothic structure placed in the middle of the block, with the northeast corner of the block left vacant for the clergy house and parish hall. On April 19, 1885, the cornerstone was laid by Fr. Huntington. The construction lasted all summer, and, in addition to his other duties, he kept a close eye on the work. The building rose swiftly, and by September it was ready for consecration.

On Holy Cross Day, Sept. 14, Bishop Potter consecrated the church. Even though he was a consistent supporter of the Mission, the Sisters and the new Order, he was careful not to allow himself to be seen as endorsing their Anglo-Catholic positions entirely, and so he wrote to Fr. Huntington of his concern about the reservation of the Blessed Sacrament:[11]

> I trust there will be no erections or constructions, in connection with the structure of the sanctuary, for the reservation of the Sacrament. I do not know, and I do not care to know, your opinions on that subject; but the most strenuous claimant for what the Church may *allow,* in that direction, will not pretend that the question has been *settled affirmatively,* so far as the right, or propriety, of reservation is concerned. And until it is, I can not undertake to consecrate a Church which, as a permanent part of the fabric, implies that the question *is* so settled.

The service was both solemn and beautiful. Bishops Potter and Huntington were there, with every Sister of St. John the Baptist, twenty-five in all, in procession. There was no tabernacle.

That evening the Bishop came for the confirmation of seventy people. A Sister remembered that service:[12]

> Fr. Huntington had expected a crowd, so instead of having the chairs set in rows, he had left them piled up, thinking people would stand and so have more room. There was a policeman at the door to admit people and keep order; but he seemed to let everyone in. Not merely our own people, but all kinds, Hebrews and foreigners, all whose curiosity had been roused by the building of the Church, poured in. They had no notion of Church behavior, pulled down the chairs, and arranged them in circles and groups all over the Church, and talked steadily. Some, of course, had to stand. The service went on, but could not be heard for the hubbub; with difficulty were the Confirmation candidates squeezed through the crowd to the Bishop. They were confirmed and the Bishop tried to preach, but was not listened to. At last it was over, and we went home.

Earlier in the summer, Fr. Hoehing had contracted typhus and died, leaving the direction of the Mission entirely in the hands of Fr. Huntington and Fr. Allen. A German seminarian at General Seminary, Henry Meissner, came to work temporarily and after ordination undertook the German work entirely.

Huntington and Allen had told the Bishop that they intended to live among the poor, and so in March, 1885, they had left their relatively comfortable dwelling on 13th Street for a tenement lodging at 711 East 12th Street. It was "a double tenement house five stories high with a central hall on each floor and two sets of apartments on each side of the hall. Huntington and Allen took two of the four first floor apartments and for additional space the front apartment on the floor above."[13] This was "an effort on our part," wrote Fr. Huntington, "to get into closer fellowship with the people by sharing in some measure their discomforts and dreary surroundings."[14]

And dreary they were. Packed in, 2000 people to a typical tenement block, 290,000 people to each square mile in the immigrant districts in New York City, a family of five typically had three rooms, a single sink on each floor, outdoor privies in the back yard, and virtually no ventilation, often little or no heat in winter, and stifling heat in summertime. Above all, there was no privacy. Families were bombarded constantly with the smells, sights and sounds of every sort of human life, both decent and desperate. Drunkenness and debauchery were open to the view of impressionable children. For nine months the young monks lived in such a tenement, using their home for social gatherings for parishioners, directing an occasional retreat for a visiting priest (the fame of the little monastery had spread) and above all, trying to keep the strict schedule of prayer and study laid down by Fr. Dod. But the strain caused by overwork, crowding and noise was too much. And their original purpose had not been achieved:[15]

> We found that such physical propinquity brought no more intimate social contact. There is really very little neighborliness in a tenement house. Each family, to secure any privacy at all, keeps to its own limited quarters. Perhaps if we could have taken up work in a factory and supported ourselves on the wages we received, we might have gained a place in the ranks of the proletariat, but that seemed impracticable.

On New Year's Day, 1886, they moved to a small house at 60 Avenue D.[16]

> It was an old-fashioned house, low stoop, with a basement. . . . front room, refectory, rear kitchen. The coal was stored in the wood house in the back yard which also contained the outside toilet.

One of the principal reasons why the Order had to move from its tenement on 13th Street at the end of 1885 was the increasing number of laymen who were indicating their desire to enter the Religious Life. There had been one layman already who had tried his vocation with the Order, and it had not worked. Among those who presented themselves, some were too exotic, unrealistically believing that in the Order of the Holy Cross they would find both an answer to their personal problems and a perfection of religious observance which could really only be had in fantasy. But in the course of time several practical and realistic men applied. It was decided to form a community for laymen, parallel to but independent of the Order of the Holy Cross, which still thought of itself as a community for priests. And so the idea for the Order of the Brothers of Nazareth was conceived.

First to arrive was Eugene Wood, from Ascension Church in Chicago, who came just after the Order had moved to 60 Avenue D. Wood was a musician and began training the small monastic choir in plainsong. He came to know one of the friends of the Order, Ann Livingston, and persuaded her to donate a purple cope. Fr. Huntington, thinking how little a purple cope might be needed in the tiny chapel in the house, made Wood return it, and induced her to give a gong instead to announce the entrance of the priest from the sacristy at Mass. Wood was joined by a man named Connery from Stevens Point, WI. He was a fine cook, but soon tired and left.

With the arrival of Gilbert Tompkins, the Brothers found their leader. From Poughkeepsie, he had worked as a layman in Episcopal churches in Milton and Highland, NY, and had entered the novitiate of the Cowley Fathers, but had not been professed. He had for some time been in charge of church work with boys in Providence, RI. He arrived in January, 1886, and immediately took charge of the housework and cleaning of the small monastery on Avenue D, and began work with the guilds of men and boys in the Mission.

On St. Benedict's Day, March 21, 1886, Gilbert Tompkins was admitted as a novice of the Order of the Brothers of Nazareth. A year later he was professed for three years, in a great service at Holy Cross Mission. Fr. Huntington received his vow, Dr. Morgan Dix of Trinity Church preached, and many attended. Louis Lorey had already joined the Brotherhood as a novice, while Connery and Wood had left the preceding summer.

Beginning with the summer of 1886, much of the work at St. Andrew's Cottage was put into Br. Gilbert's hands; Br. Louis Lorey also proved gifted in dealing with the boys there. Fr. Allen wrote of him later:[17]

Br. Louis, now our Fr. Lorey, was a wonder. Slight and active and indefatigable, he worked day and night like a Trojan, taking the duty of the cook and the general housekeeper, baking all the bread for that big family of hungry boys, and scrubbing floors as though he had nothing else to do. And above all taking all the discipline and instruction of the boys and carrying on the musical services, playing the organ and leading the singing, throwing his whole heart into the work. His figure rises up before me with his hands in the dough, which after thoroughly kneading, he signed with the holy symbol of our Religion and commended it to the processes of nature, as we say.

At the end of the summer the virtue of Brs. Gilbert and Louis had so established itself that there was no further question that they would remain mere helpers of Holy Cross, but should begin some work of their own. It was decided to open a convalescent hospital for men and boys discharged from hospital but not yet strong enough to work. With the help of friends, Br. Gilbert engaged Bishop Potter's interest, raised funds, and leased a large family mansion in Harlem (then a fashionable neighborhood) on 120th Street near Pleasant Avenue, close to the fresh air from the East River. It was named All Saints Convalescent Home and was opened with a formal service on Dec. 8, 1886.

The Brothers of Nazareth remained a small community. They continued to work closely with the Holy Cross Fathers at St. Andrew's Cottage. The work in Harlem continued with quiet success for some years, and work with teenaged boys was added to it. Every summer the Brothers would remove their patients to Cragsmoor, near Ellenville, NY. Out of this grew the eventual removal of the community from New York City. In the spring of 1890 they were given a tract of land at Verbank, near Milbrook, Dutchess Co., NY, where they built a facility large enough to accommodate their works. The community seems to have lost its drive in the later 1890s, and eventually disbanded, Br. Gilbert returning to secular life. Br. Louis Lorey was ordained in 1905, joined Holy Cross in 1906 and was life professed in 1907.

Eighteen eighty-five was a tumultuous, busy year, and Fr. Huntington and Fr. Allen must have had little time to reflect on the course of their community and individual lives. That year brought the new church building, Fr. Hoehing's death, the constant and growing demands of the Mission, the strains of life in the tenement, and not least, their own rigorously ascetical Rule. But as they moved to Avenue D and Brs. Gilbert and Louis added their help, the excitement and strain must have lessened, letting out pent-up frustration. Certainly a fundamental change came over Fr. Huntington in the course of 1886, and no doubt Fr. Allen experienced some of the same feelings.

With Fr. Huntington it took the form of depression. In his own words he recalled:[18]

> The tragedy of the situation gradually pressed itself upon me. Contact, day and night, with a seething mass of humanity; the constant sense of poverty and squalor and wretchedness; the sight of young lives marred and mutilated and ruined; the apparent hopelessness, for them, of any escape from the treadmill of toil and disease and degradation; all this bred in me a fierce resentment. I could feel my teeth grind as I went up and down stairways to dreary attics, or foul basements and listened to piteous tales of hardship and heartbreak. I had begun my work in New York with an acceptance—largely the result of inheritance—of the Christian Faith. But I could feel that conviction weakening and threatening to give way under the weight of the conditions that bewildered my mind and crushed my spirit.

Typically for a New England Brahmin, the salvation for this depression lay in a book:[19]

> Just at that time, notice appeared in the papers that Henry George was coming to the city. I knew very little of him, nothing of his teaching. But I took down from the shelves of the library of our Mission House a copy of *Progress and Poverty.*

In Henry George's book Fr. Huntington found both a resolution of his social questionings and, more significantly, something akin to a mystical experience:[20]

> The truth dawned upon me. There had been no mistake in the ordering of the world. The shameful contrast that had tortured me, was not due to God but to man. It was not of the Lord that the people labored in the fire and were weary. On the contrary, there was provision in the very growth of population that the needs which that increase created should be met without impoverishing any section of society, without the piling up of fortunes that ruined those who claimed them, or doomed to ignorance and crime those who created them. I was like a man who wakes from a torturing dream to the light of a summer morning; yet who rises, renewed in vigor, to answer a call to a bracing adventure.

Henry George's theory of economy held that land was the original base of economic value, and that by adjusting the tax system to reflect properly the value of land, the resources which might otherwise be selfishly hoarded would be properly distributed and used, assuring a fair return for capital and labor alike, and producing a general prosperity. This theory, and the political program which followed from it, came to be called the Single Tax. Fr. Huntington (and Fr. Allen) advocated it passionately all their lives, long after the meteoric rise and fall of Henry George was but a memory.

Henry George declared himself a candidate for mayor of New York City in the autumn of 1886. Fr. Huntington was drawn to a meeting at Chickering Hall on Oct. 2, at which Henry George was nominated for mayor by a labor coalition which included many business and professional men. Fr. Huntington recalled the exultant mood: "The audience rose as one man with a shout which might have raised the roof. It was the birth cry of a new movement."[21] After the meeting Huntington lingered until he was the last person to leave the hall. The man who had been accepting donations asked if he would like to meet Mr. George:[22]

> We walked down Fifth Avenue together in the autumn air. As we reached the entrance of the hotel, a short man with a red beard came down the steps and greeted us with, "Well, boys, how did the meeting go?" That was my introduction to Henry George. We went in with him and found a small company of people, a sort of family party. And one remark of Mr. George's that night seemed to give me a side-light on his character—its self-forgetfulness and simplicity and absolute sincerity. Two of the men present opened the tin box and counted the contents. After a little while, one of them turned to Mr. George, who was on the other side of the room engaged in conversation, and said, "Just seventy-five dollars, Mr. George." "That's good," said Mr. George, "that'll about pay for the hall, will it not?" There was no thought, apparently, of the hundreds of thousands of dollars that would be poured out by the old parties to prevent his election, but only that his friends and supporters would not be put to too large an expense in his interest.

Fr. Huntington was drawn to George by his upright character and his exemplary personal life. The two became lifelong friends, Fr. Huntington acting as a sort of family chaplain for many years, officiating at weddings and baptisms for the George clan.

Fr. Huntington immediately plunged into the mayoral campaign. He made speeches for Henry George, and even used his pulpit for the advancement of the cause. The account of the campaign issued by George's supporters describes Fr. Huntington, the "Protestant monk," joining the many speakers in a unique outdoor campaign:[23]

The usual method was to call a meeting at a street corner, and just before the appointed hour to draw up a truck, from the tail of which one speaker after another addressed the crowd that came. It was the great number of meetings of this kind that gave the campaign the name of the "tail-board" campaign. Speakers went from one truck to another, often many blocks apart, making two and three, and sometimes five and six, speeches in a night. Around these trucks, to the number of hundreds and often of thousands, the common people of the city gathered, women as well as men. Standing in the open air, and packed closely together, at times straining to catch the words of the speaker above the din and rattle of surface car or elevated train, they listened with intelligent eagerness, not to eloquent perorations or funny stories, but to plain expositions of the labor problem.

News of Fr. Huntington's participation in the campaign was reported in the press, and Bishop Potter, attending a meeting of the House of Bishops in Chicago, wrote on Oct. 10, eight days after Fr. Huntington began to campaign:[24]

I see by the papers that you are speaking for Mr. Henry George. I do not challenge your entire right to do so, but all the same, if I were you, I wouldn't do it,—simply because, in the long run, I think such a course tends to secularize a clergyman and to weaken his influence with his people.

The Bishop then suggested that Huntington prepare for him a "digest of the spiritual statistics of your neighborhood," no doubt wishing to channel the young monk's energy rather than stifle it.

The reaction from the principal patron of the Mission was more direct. George Folsom, brother of Sr. Helen Margaret and chairman of the Mission's Board of Trustees, wrote to Fr. Huntington on Oct. 15:[25]

The course you are taking in regard to the campaign for the election of mayor is likely to affect the usefulness of the Church of the Holy Cross, and antagonize many who might help it. . . . The worst of the matter to my mind is that all this wild talk of his [George's] is likely to disturb the minds of the working man, to increase the number of strikes, and throw many men out of employment, thus depriving their families of the means of living.

Fr. Huntington wrote back with spirit that if his course was hindering the Mission, he should resign. He tried to explain the economic reasons for supporting Henry George. Folsom replied that he fully appreciated "the great values of your services there [at the Mission] and your thorough self-devotion—the arduous and difficult duties of the Mission, and that it would be a grave mistake to make any change."[26] Huntington withdrew on Oct. 20 from active participation in the campaign, and wrote to Bishop Potter:[27]

> I have spoken briefly five times at meetings of workingmen with regard to the principles of the movement which has led to the nomination of Henry George for mayor. I do not think you would disapprove of what I *said*. I regarded the occasion as an exceptional one and therefore not governed by the wise rule for ordinary occasions that "parsons should not go into politics." I had already decided before receiving your letter, that having sufficiently indicated my positions, I would not go to any more public meetings in this campaign. . . . I have of course been severely censured in some quarters for what I have done, but I do not think I have in any way harmed the people under my charge—who are to a man in favor of Henry George—and I venture to think that, could I talk the matter over with you, you would not disapprove of my actions so strongly as some do who have been kind to me heretofore have felt it right to do.

The election resulted in the defeat of Henry George by the Tammany Democrat Abram S. Hewitt. But George outpolled the Republican, Theodore Roosevelt, and there remained the suspicion that the Democratic machine at Tammany Hall had stolen the election.

Only eighteen days elapsed between the Chickering Hall meeting and Huntington's withdrawal, but two results issued from this exciting campaign for him. The first was an abiding commitment to speak out publicly for the laboring man, for the poor and for the mobilization of Church and society on their behalf. The second was the article suggested by the Bishop published early in July, 1887, called "Tenement House Morality." A review of the article in the New York *Tribune* editorialized:[28]

> Father J.O.S. Huntington's article in the July "Forum" on "Tenement House Morality" ought to make the people of this city hang down their heads with shame. For two facts are brought out with startling clearness in that article: First, that vast numbers of people in this city are so crowded together in vile and unhealthy tenements that, as two eminent clergymen have recently said, morality is practically impossible; and secondly, that the responsibility for this state of affairs rests upon the shoulders of the so-called better

classes. Many of the tenements of this city which are a shame and a scandal to our common humanity are owned by men who call themselves respectable, who move in good society, and who are members in good standing of the Christian church. They are nevertheless content to live off the blood-money of the poor wretches who are compelled to exist in their death-traps, and apparently neither the law of the land nor public opinion has anything to say to them.

And then the editorial eulogizes the new Order, bringing it to the attention of the New York secular public for perhaps the first time:

It is proper to say that Father Huntington is setting an example to the ministers of the Christian churches which is as noble as it is needed. He has not only consecrated his life to the service of the poor and the afflicted in the tenements of the East Side, but he has gone to live in one of these tenements himself. Without ostentation, without any sense of doing these people a great and unwonted favor, he goes among them sharing their joys and sorrows and ministering to them the consolations of religion. He and his associates in this work are there to stay; they are not there to make a reputation which will help them to get a good parish or to reach after the honors and emoluments of their church. Would it not be well for all Christian denominations in this city to call such men for this work? Call them what you will, priests, monks, missioners, exhorters, revivalists, or simply Christian workers, the name is of little consequence so long as they are filled with the spirit of the founder of Christianity.

Almost immediately after his withdrawal from the mayoral campaign, Fr. Huntington and Fr. Allen both joined the Knights of Labor and the Anti-Poverty Society. The former, founded in 1869, was the oldest and largest union in America, led by the fiery Terence V. Powderly. The latter was founded on March 26, 1887, and headed by Fr. Edward McGlynn, a Roman Catholic priest who had supported George, and who later would be excommunicated for his radical views. Throughout 1887 Huntington spoke on behalf of the workingman at rallies and Anti-Poverty Society meetings. At one such meeting, on July 17, 1887, at the New York Academy of Music, the press reported:[29]

Mr. Huntington made a long speech, which he began by telling of a slave he knew in his boyhood who had paid for himself three times over, and was forced back into slavery each time. Then he said: "There are workingmen in this country who have paid for themselves not three times but thirty times, and they do not belong to themselves yet. . . . Make them free," he said, "and make the land free, and you will have what God meant to be."

He made many such speeches that year, and afterward, always drawing the theme of justice for the workingman from the Gospel and from ordinary human experience.

Fr. Allen recalled a Knights of Labor meeting: "Our local assembly was on 53rd St. and Third Ave. Weekly meetings were held. There was some sort of initiation and a pass word. There was some oratory of an inflammatory character, but the Master or whatever the head of the circle was called was a rather mild-spoken man."[30]

Huntington and Allen were not content to allow the Episcopal Church to engage the labor movement through individual effort alone. They decided to form a Church organization to work for the laboring man in both his individual and collective needs. They called a meeting at Holy Cross House at 60 Avenue D on May 18, 1887. Bishop Huntington attended and presided, and the general lines of the organization, to be called the Church Association for the Advancement of Labor (CAIL), were drawn up. The principles of the organization were drawn up, nine in number:[31]

1. God is the Father of all men, and hence all are brothers.
2. God alone possesses the earth, with man as steward.
3. All must work for the common good.
4. No class is to be favored over another in legislation.
5. Employers should be legally responsible for worker safety.
6. Child labor should be prohibited, and children required to attend school.
7. Freedom of conscience and expression should be maintained.
8. Women and men should receive equal pay for equal work.
9. Workers should not be overworked, and should be compensated adequately for a reasonable amount of work.

The members of CAIL pledged themselves to disseminate these principles by prayer, sermons using the Gospel as guides to labor questions, tracts and secular addresses; by using personal influence to advance the just cause of labor, encouraging conscientious use of the ballot, attending meetings of other labor organizations, and joining them. Each member was to take or read at least one labor journal, to join one other labor organization, and to devote time to the study of the social problems of the day in the light of the Incarnation.

In its initial stages CAIL attracted the membership of several prominent clergymen, including Bishop Huntington; its first president, Dr. B. F.

DaCosta; the chairman of the Oct. 26 meeting, Bishop Potter; the Rev'd. James H. Darlington of Christ Church, Brooklyn; Dr. Rainsford; Dr. Rylance; Dr. Sill, Vicar of St. Athanasius Chapel (and father of the future Fr. Sill, O.H.C.); the Rev'd. W. D. P. Bliss; and the Rev'd. Edward Kenney. While the goals of the organization might have been radical for a church as well connected as the Episcopal Church, CAIL began with strong backing from leading members of the clergy, and was almost immediately recognized as an important force for labor.

The passion with which Fr. Huntington undertook the founding of CAIL is evident in the address he made to its first general meeting, placing its mission squarely in the evangelical duty of the Church:[32]

> An idea has prevailed that the highest object of the Church is to prepare mankind for another world; to save a few individuals out of the world, rather than save the world itself. This association [CAIL] springs from a desire to deserve a granting of the universal prayer "Thy kingdom come"; the bringing into harmony all nations and races of mankind. . . . it points to a time when the declared adherents of Christianity will not persist in teaching that the spiritual is entirely distinct from the material, but will insist upon the great fundamental truth that the Spirit of God is indwelling, pervading the universe: that the proper work of the Church is the hallowing of all social conditions.

To this philosophical statement he added:[33]

> I am a Knight of Labor and a member of the United Labor Party. My association with the workingmen and the men of the lowest classes has proven to me that they look upon clergymen with profound distrust. They think we prefer the rich man to the poor man, and to a certain extent, I think they are right.

He went on:[34]

> [Workingmen] look at the Church as an assembly of respectable people, who are willing to uphold the present commercial spirit of moneygetting. They read the New Testament, and find its teachings different from the Church practices. They have asked for bread and been given a stone. Too many of us think that a good man with money is better than one without money. I am a Knight of Labor and the principles of that order aim to make industrial and moral worth—not wealth—the true standard of individual and national greatness. How many of us are willing to preach that to our congregations—that the millionaire is not in the highest but in the lowest grade, if he

does not render an equivalent for his support. This movement has a deeper purpose than mere politics. It teaches that every man must work in order to live. It is a gospel of work, not a gospel of idleness.

It did not take long for CAIL to enter into controversy. The Haymarket riot in Chicago of May, 1886, had issued in the sentencing to death of seven anarchists. Their appeals had been rejected by the Supreme Court on Nov. 2, 1886. A nationwide appeal for clemency to the Governor of Illinois arose, and CAIL added its voice. Fr. Huntington wrote a letter for CAIL demanding clemency "not because I consider the prisoners guiltless, but for the reason that in the minds of hundreds of thousands of men the question of their execution is regarded as an issue between the present holders of wealth and power and the vast multitude of the underprivileged and defenseless."[35] He joined Bob Ingersoll, the agnostic Republican, in a similar appeal. Gov. Oglesby commuted two of the sentences to life, but on Nov. 11, 1887, four of the condemned men were executed. Six years later the government admitted that all had been innocent of murder, and those remaining were pardoned.

In the winter of 1887 the first associate group founded by the Order came into existence. There was a need (as Fr. Allen put it) "to draw together the earnest members of the congregation (of the Mission) and to strengthen them in their spiritual life."[36] The Rule of the Confraternity of the Christian Life comprised daily prayer, weekly communion, fellowship with the Order, and serious attention to the spiritual life. It was a rule for laypeople, and was meant to be easy to keep. Almost from the beginning there was a CCL newsletter, which in 1892 became the *Holy Cross Magazine.* Fr. Allen remembered the trials of getting out the little paper:[37]

> I recall the pains and trouble it cost—the difficulty of making a good
> stencil and then the trouble it involved in getting a good print. Often
> it was late at night before the job was finished in much agony.

The CCL proved so popular that it soon spread to other parishes, and formed at that early time a nucleus of devoted laypeople supporting the work of the Order. It was also the model for the several Associate groups which soon developed: Priests Associate, the Society of the Oblates of Mount Calvary (for celibate priests), and the Confraternity of the Love of God, centered around eucharistic meditation.

One of the great events of the winter of 1887-88 was the blizzard which struck the eastern seaboard on March 12, 1888. The entire city of New York was cut off from the outside world. Fr. Allen remembered how quickly supplies ran out:[38]

> The most serious lack was milk. The little grocery stores soon sold out their supply of condensed milk. Indeed, the shelves were well emptied of every kind of provision. . . . Impassable streets made coal unobtainable. For the fire at the Mission Church coal was carried in sacks on the backs of men. We had an ample supply at 60 Avenue D, so that when in the afternoon a number of men from the General Theological Seminary came over to see what they could do in the way of relieving the distress we could send by them buckets of coal to our needy people.

During that same winter the second stage of the Mission Church building plant was under construction. The Mission, or Clergy, House was built on the corner of Avenue C and 4th Street next to the church. The five-story brick building still stands, now derelict. The 4th Street side had a wide hall and staircase entering into the church. The ground floor was a store rented to a druggist, the second and third stories were for Sunday school and guild rooms, the fourth floor was for the Order of the Holy Cross and the top floor was used by the Sisters. There was a suite for Fr. Meissner and a large library with two open fireplaces, a very pleasant room. The Order moved there in May, 1888, from 60 Avenue D.

It was during this period that the man who would become the third member of the Order began to associate himself with the Mission. The Rev'd. Henry Rufus Sargent had spent much of the summer of 1887 with the Order when it lived on Avenue D. Later, after a time as a parish priest at Mount Calvary Church, Baltimore, he had tried his vocation with the Cowley Fathers in England, leaving them in 1888. He had been interested in the monastic life for some time, and upon his return to America, he helped at the Holy Cross Mission in the autumn and winter of 1888. The Englishness of the Cowley Fathers dismayed him, and he wrote to Fr. Huntington asking for advice:[39]

> There is something lacking at Cowley, something that I fancy that some of the Englishmen feel—a restraint, a hardness of life that is immaterial. . . . Certainly I have to thank GOD that thro' Fr. Benson's instructions, he has given me in some measure to feel a spirit of detachment, but detachment ought not to destroy charity—and this I felt greatly to be wanting.

Sargent felt called to work in a black parish, and Fr. Huntington encouraged him, perhaps thinking that his sensitive nature was not yet ready for the Order of the Holy Cross, less rigid perhaps than Cowley, but certainly rougher, more strenuous, more improvisational, more American. As a result of Fr. Huntington's counsel, he became Vicar of Emmanuel Church, a black mission in Memphis, early in 1889, where he remained until he joined the Order in 1891.

The work of the Mission continued as usual throughout 1888. Fr. Huntington and to a lesser extent Fr. Allen continued their interests in CAIL, in the Anti-Poverty Society and in Henry George's crusade for the Single Tax. In addition they were busy with the many activities of social work on the Lower East Side, all the time maintaining the monastic life. Some flavor of their life in those years, 1884-89, between Fr. Huntington's profession and the time of leaving the Mission, is evoked by Fr. Allen in his memoirs. There was a continual succession of cooks, some more competent than others. From a very early date bishops and others took to referring problem persons to Holy Cross, in the hope that an atmosphere of prayer could help them. A typical case was described by Fr. Allen, humorous but also deeply sad:[40]

About this time [summer 1885] a guest was sent to us, as to a sort of asylum. A deposed priest by the name of Clarke. A remarkable character. His first appearance will give some notion of his case. He arrived shabby and dirty, one might say out of the gutter, probably from some lodging house in the Bowery. Father Huntington gave him an outfit of clothes and sent him to the bathroom to get cleaned up. After he was thus rehabilitated he turned to Fr. Huntington and said, "How often have I had this done to me," quite as a matter of course and with the insinuation of the hopelessness of the situation.

Many such men came and went, some helped, some not, all given what little the Order could manage and the blessing of love, attention and prayer.

Fr. Huntington began, as the fall of 1888 drew near, to widen his circle of contact and to take mission preaching engagements outside New York City. The week of Oct. 13 he preached a mission at Calvary Church, Syracuse, his old parish. The following month, Nov. 11-19, he conducted a similar mission at Christ Church, Milford, DE. The congregation's reaction to his message was almost violent. On the last night of the mission he spoke on "Christ the Social Leader":[41]

The Sunday evening lecture in Dorsey Hall by Rev. J.O.S. Huntington of the Episcopal Mission in New York was attended by eight hundred and twenty-two persons. The very best society of Milford formed a large part of the audience, and there is division of opinion as to the usefulness of the lecture in Milford; but none deny it to be one of much ability. The audience was displeased with the socialistic remarks and the espousal of Henry George's principles in regard to land. In a bitter vein of sarcasm the speaker denounced landlords, and claimed that, as a class, they are more oppressive to the poor than the landlords of Ireland; "and yet," said he, "this is your free America; the land of the brave and the home of the free." Landlords he termed "little gods, yea little gods almighty." He claimed that the land should be held in common, and every tiller or occupier of the soil be compelled to pay its rental value as a tax into one common fund, and that all other taxes be abolished. . . . Had the speaker been more familiar with the condition of the Negro race in this and other southern states, he would not have given utterance to the sentiments he did on the subject. In plain language, he accused the white race of keeping colored women in a species of subjugation for immoral purposes. . . . The speaker then made an appeal for the elevation of the colored race, and claimed that they can never be elevated to an equality with the white race until the churches and schools were thrown open to them for use in common with the whites. At this point marked dissatisfaction was shown . . . and more than fifty left the hall.

Never one to mince words, and having become a fiery platform speaker in the two years since the mayoral race in 1886, Fr. Huntington was becoming a national figure and a well-known, and not always welcome, voice, adding racial discrimination to the condition of labor and ownership of land as his social themes.

In the fall of 1888 William Dean Howells, formerly the editor of *The Atlantic Monthly* and probably the most influential literary man in America, visited the Holy Cross community at the Mission House.[42] Howells was deeply interested in the social ferment of the period, which he expressed in novels of realistic detail. In *A Hazard of New Fortunes*, published in 1890, he unmistakably refers to the Order and to Fr. Huntington. Two characters, a young upper-class woman and a saintly, sensitive son of a nouveau-riche German family, attach themselves to a mission very like Holy Cross, and its spellbinding monk-priest, Fr. Benedict. The hero's father heaps scorn on his son, and the mother defends his new-found piety:[43]

They ain't the kind of Catholics we been used to; some sort of 'Piscopalians; and they do a heap o' good amongst the poor folks over there. He says we ain't got any idea how folks lives in them tenement houses, hundreds of 'em in one house, and whole families in a room; and it burns in his heart to help 'em like them fathers, as he calls 'em, that gives their lives to it. He can't be a father, he says, because he can't git the eddication; but he can be a brother.

The young man spends a summer helping at what is unmistakably St. Andrew's Cottage in Farmingdale. At the climax of the novel he is shot to death in a strike, an unmerited death precipitated by his generous action, a Christ-like act which somehow redeems his family.

Howells' view of the young Order is significant. His is an important secular voice taking notice of this new movement. He sees strange, almost outlandish behavior issuing in kindly, compassionate action for the poor, and contrasts the ideal of redemptive self-giving with both the coldhearted charity of the rich and the cynical, fanatical politics of the striking anarchists.

With the denunciations of the Delaware press in his ears, Fr. Huntington returned to New York City for the Life Profession of Fr. Allen on Dec. 1, 1888. Allen, who had been a novice for almost four years, had withdrawn for a week to the Brothers of Nazareth on 120th Street, where he made his retreat, including a general confession to Dr. Houghton (still the spiritual director of the Order), and returned the night before the service to the Mission House. Silence was kept:[44]

> A certain signal was agreed upon for me to come down to the Church. For some reason the signal was not heard and while I waited in perplexity the congregation wondered whether there would be any profession. However, venturing to investigate and finding that the time had arrived and the ceremony was halted by my non-appearance, on my arrival the service proceeded. Fr. Sargent sang the Mass and Bishop Potter received the vows, according to our custom of the day.

The preacher was Dr. Morgan Dix, Rector of Trinity Church, Wall Street. The service was followed by a festive breakfast.

Sturges Allen probably had more formative influence on the Order of the Holy Cross than any man save Fr. Dod and Fr. Huntington. Born June 25, 1850, at Hyde Park, NY, he was 38 at his Life Profession, four years older than Fr. Huntington. He attended schools in New York City, graduating with a B.S. in bookkeeping from the College of the City of New York (CCNY) in 1869. His elegant copperplate hand comes as a welcome relief after Fr. Huntington's angular illegibility. After working for some years he entered General Seminary in New York, graduated in 1880, was ordained deacon on May 18, 1880, and ministered at Trinity

Church, St. Louis. He was ordained priest Jan. 15, 1882, at St. George's Church, Newburgh, NY, where he was then a curate.

Two significant delays can be seen in Fr. Allen's early career: a longer than usual time spent both as a deacon and as a novice. Why this was is not clear. Allen did not immediately impress those who first met him; he was short, he stuttered so badly that he rarely preached, and he seems to have been a man whose intelligence, while considerable, was as practical as Fr. Huntington's was theoretical. Nevertheless, he was Superior for two important periods, 1888-94 and 1906-15. Indeed, at the end of his last term in 1915, Allen had been Superior as long as Huntington had been. But, "He was not happy either as an executive or a preacher. He liked to stay at home, say his prayers, and do the housework. . . . In a community, most of whose members were busy preaching missions all over the Church or founding schools . . . Fr. Allen must have been a much needed stabilizing force in the home monastery."[45] A slow starter, but impressive in the finish, he ended his life as a mystic and a missionary.

Fr. Huntington immediately made Allen Superior. This act was the formative political act of the Order of the Holy Cross. By doing so, Huntington relinquished that control over his community that so many founders exercise, and stamps their communities immutably with their personal character. Jesuits, Franciscans, Dominicans, and even the Cowley Fathers bear the stamp of their powerful founders. Perhaps because it was not Huntington but Dod who conceived and first nurtured the Order of the Holy Cross; perhaps because of some lingering sense of being the son of a strong father and not wanting to repeat that pattern himself; perhaps because of an awareness of some interior passivity; perhaps because he understood and respected institutions as institutions and not simply as personal vehicles; for whatever reason, Huntington relinquished control and became subject to the obedience of a man whose formation he had just concluded. It was an act of great trust. No doubt he would find some aspects of Allen trying; no doubt they would disagree. But by his willing obedience in community he set the Order of the Holy Cross on the path of stable leadership from which it has rarely deviated. Never since has there been the fear on the part of the Chapter that "Father might not approve," which can so hamper the mature development of communities, although Fr. Hughson came close to dominating the Order in this way in the 1930s. And as a consequence the vivid, strong, even strange, but never weak, personalities of those who have persevered in Holy Cross have never been cast in a founder's mold. A Holy Cross man is a monk, is himself, but is not recognizably a Huntingtonian.

The selection of Allen as Superior freed Fr. Huntington to roam even wider in his preaching and proselytizing for labor, the Single Tax, and the Lord. He spoke several times in the spring of 1889 for CAIL and for the Single Tax. But his energies seem to have worn down, and in the summer he embarked on a project at once bold and puzzling. In May he hired himself out as a day laborer on a farm near Meridian, NY, near Syracuse. In part he wished to experience the grinding tiredness of a farm hand. But his interests were all urban. If it was his intention to experience hard labor, why not a job in a factory? It would seem that this episode is the first in a series of near-breakdowns in Fr. Huntington's health, presaged by a need for more physical exercise and a time away from the rigorous demands of community life. Whatever the reasons, by June 4 his activity had been discovered by the papers. This short notice is typical:[46]

The Rev. J.O.S. Huntington of New York, son of Bishop Huntington of this city, has been revealing to the farmer folk of western Onondaga what a man will do under the influence of religious ardor. The life of asceticism he has lived with other members of the holy order to which he belongs has shattered his health and made it necessary for him for the time being to leave his work in Five Points in order to try the benefits of country air. Unknown as a clergyman or priest of the Episcopal Church, Father Huntington applied for work near the village of Meridian, in this county, and was hired as a farmer. Father Huntington worked in the fields with the others, and acquired strength by the exercise.

After nightfall he usually walked to the village, and wherever he could find a knot of men spoke to them of religion. His earnestness and bearing prevented him from being made the butt of ridicule. For two Sundays he has preached in the open air at Meridian to the villagers. Not until a day or two ago was his identity made known by a friend of his school days who chanced to be in the village. Since it has come out that he is something besides a common farm hand the Wednesday evening prayer meeting in the village has been deserted. He gets the audiences.

Fr. Allen commented:[47]

Fr. Huntington was taken to task by the farmer for his lack of skill and he had a good taste of the disagreeable features of farm jobs. He realized the contrast between the remuneration received for a hard day's labor and that which he was paid for a couple of hours writing for a periodical after his day's work was done.

Later in the summer Fr. Huntington returned refreshed. But there was a pressing call which drew him into his most active labor role.

Back in New York he found his friends at Henry George's paper *The Standard* fighting among themselves. George himself had been abroad in the spring of 1889 and during his absence a dispute had broken out between some of his ablest lieutenants and his son Henry George, Jr., who was managing the paper. The younger George felt the paper should narrow its focus to the issue of the Single Tax, while the others felt that the many issues—labor, wages, racism among them —which went hand in hand with the Single Tax ideal, should have their place as well. Huntington tried to mediate between the Georges and their followers, but to no avail. When the division came, he remained loyal to George, no doubt because of the warmth of their mutual friendship.

For some time there had been a dispute in progress between the miners and the coal company of W.L. Scott in and around Streator, IL, halfway between Chicago and Peoria. Scott had tried to reduce the effective wages of the miners by half, and to put an end to collective bargaining. Fr. Huntington was called in as a mediator, as he was a Knight of Labor and a man who might gain a hearing with the management of the company. But Huntington's sympathy was clearly on the side of the strikers. He left Syracuse, where he was visiting his family, on August 18 and spent about ten days in the strike area. He sent dispatches to the New York and Chicago papers, enlisting public sympathy for the strikers. In the end he was able to obtain a more just wage, and his efforts ended the strike. One press account described his impact:[48]

> The appearance of Father James O. S. Huntington of this city on the streets of that town, clad in his black cassock, caused a sensation, which was heightened by his admission to the secret meetings of the striking miners. . . . He prevailed upon the strikers to rescind the violent resolutions adopted at a previous meeting and to consent to more moderate measures.

Upon his return he wrote an essay, published in *The Churchman,* called "Miners and Ministers" in which he set forth the essential goodness of the miners and the justice of their cause. He urged the Church to take up their cause and make it her own. He ended with a challenge:[49]

> Two persons, one an ecclesiastic, the other an unbeliever, have lately said to me, "The Protestant Episcopal Church will never take up the cause of labor, she is too deeply compromised with wealth." I do

not believe it, for I believe that, as men said in yet darker times, *Christus vincit, Christus regnat, Christus imperat.*

All this time that Fr. Huntington was away, or working on behalf of the Single Tax, Fr. Allen had the Mission to take care of. He and Fr. Meissner had the aid of seminarians and visiting clergy, but it must have been a strain to maintain the active life of the Mission alone and essentially unaided by Fr. Huntington. It must have weighed on Fr. Allen, practical as he was, that Fr. Huntington's withdrawal from the work of the Mission (for that is what, to all intents and purposes, he had done) might be symptomatic of something deeper. Fr. Dod had had a breakdown which resulted from overwork and the taxing demands of the ascetical program he had laid out for the Order. Might Fr. Huntington be suffering the first stages of the same course? If so, something must be done.

In September, 1889, Fr. Allen wrote to the trustees of the Holy Cross Mission, explaining to them that it would be impossible for the Order to remain sole minister for the English work of the Mission. His intent was to request that someone else assume direction of the work, while the Order remained to help. But he was taken to mean that the Order wished to resign the work entirely, and upon reflection, both Allen and Huntington decided to follow that course. The advantage, as Fr. Allen put it, was that the Order would be free "to give its services to the whole Church as they were needed."[50] But their departure from the Mission meant the loss of their home in the Mission House and the salary paid them for their work in the Mission. They withdrew formally on Sept. 21, 1889, at the end of the Octave of the Feast of the Holy Cross.

At this juncture Fr. Allen turned for advice to the founder of the Order, Fr. Robert Dod. Still in Brady, Texas, working with his rancher relatives, Dod wrote to Allen that leaving the Mission "was always contemplated when the time came."[51] Allen had suggested to him that in the future the Order proposed to be disconnected from any parish in particular in order to be "engaged in preaching and ministering to the poor in the great cities and to be content simply with a cell in which to pray." To this seeming simplicity Dod reacted violently. The monastic life must have priority over any work, and it needs, above all, space:

Dear Father, for yourself and other professed in the Religious Life this would do [having simply a cell]—but what gives the Religious his strength if not the training of his novitiate in the *community.* Where does the Religious turn when human weakness weighs down the extended arms but to the community? Look back on your own experience and tell me, has what you have gained in self-renunciation grown more from your own life or from the community life? Ask Father Huntington what period of his life he looks back on as most helpful and I think he will tell you when he was sweeping the floor or filling the lamps in the old house on Avenue D. You can have a high *spiritual* life in the individual anywhere in any occupation or any rank of life. You can *not* have the *religious* life without the community—the retirement not of the cell (that you can get anywhere) but of the cloister. Now this community life can be had only where there is a house or a portion of a house entirely set apart to the religious.

Allen's suggestion would, to Dod, break up the Order as a community. For the sake of a small economy and the accommodation of the present interests of himself and Fr. Huntington he would make it impossible for the Order to grow and become what it was intended to be:

> The object of joining the Order is not primarily to war against the evils social or spiritual yourselves but to build up in the Order a mighty power in the Church which will hereafter, when grown to its full stature, nourished by the grace of God, become a weapon ready to the hands of the Bishops of the Church with which to beat down the giants of spiritual and social evils in their very stronghold as God gives them opportunity.

He urged Allen not to lose heart in this temporary situation, but trust that the seed planted in the new Order would indeed grow.

Still, the problem of support and housing was acute. A benefactress appeared, offering for a short time $250 each month to help the Order carry on its work, and to distribute to the poor. And in late September the two monks began a four-month time in which they had no fixed dwelling. They went first, in late September, to the Huntington family home at Hadley, MA. In October they spent the month taking care of the Episcopal Church in Gloversville, NY, Fr. Allen taking the first half of the month and Fr. Huntington the second. Early in October Fr. Huntington spoke at the national convention of the Brotherhood of St. Andrew in Cleveland.

An offer arrived to join together with an incipient Benedictine community, actually only one priest, the Rev'd. T. C. Foote, and a layman. They were located in Tennessee on a remote farm. Fr. Allen decided to investigate the offer, so early in November he set out. He took the train to Robbins, TN, and then walked the rest of the way:[52]

It was wild country indeed, only two or three cabins on the way, if that many. The road led through a forest and trying to follow the directions and asking my way at one cabin, a real backwoods cabin, and taking what seemed to me the right road where the road parted, only to see the road disappear in a river and then returning to the fork on the road and following the other trail, a small cavalcade of four or five horsemen dressed in what looked like burlap blouses and long shaggy hair and beard met me. This looked like a holdup. However on accosting them [Allen was wearing the black cassock and cord of the Order, and must have looked equally strange to them!] they showed no signs of being highwaymen and answered peaceably my questions. They assured me that the path leading to the river was the right one and that Fr. Foote lived across the "branch" and would respond to a call. So retracing my steps and again coming to the river, an effort was made to attract Fr. Foote, but in vain. However at that moment a native appeared and told me he was going to cross the stream in a skiff which was lying near the bank a little distance from the ford. He offered to take me across with him, which was agreeable to me. He was uncouth and wild in appearance like the horsemen, and carried a gun, and when he landed me on the shore I was much relieved.

Fr. Foote and his companion were finally found. Fr. Allen spent the night and the next day talking and looking over the situation, and then returned to St. Louis to see his family. Nothing came of the venture.

While Fr. Allen was gone, Br. Gilbert of the Brothers of Nazareth had come up with a solution to the problem of housing. There was a frame house at 417 Pleasant Avenue in Harlem, adjacent to the house of the O.B.N. for young working men, and near the All Saints Convalescent Home. It could be rented for $50 a month, renovated for a monastery, and joined to the working boys' home. It was decided to accept the offer, and most of November and December was taken up with the renovation. Allen and Huntington spent a month at Holy Comforter Church, Poughkeepsie, on a mission late in November, and in December Huntington went on a speaking tour to the Midwest while Allen lived at the Convalescent Home waiting for the house to be readied. In January the move was made, transporting books and furniture by horse-drawn wagon from the Mission House on 4th Street.

The house on Pleasant Avenue was a four-story frame building with a mansard roof. The basement held the kitchen and a cellar for wood and coal. On the first floor were the chapel in front and refectory in the rear. The entire second floor was library, two cells and a bathroom were on the third floor and three cells on the top floor. This house, home to the Order for two and a half years, was large enough to accommodate more members as well as guests, and Allen and Huntington began to pray earnestly for more vocations.

The small Order settled down into the pattern of life that carried it into 1892. Fr. Huntington was frequently gone on speaking tours and missions, sometimes for weeks at a time. Fr. Allen stayed home, taking services at the Convalescent Home and other Episcopal institutions, kept the prayer life alive, and saw to the continuity of community life. The Order continued active in CAIL, which held monthly meetings that Allen and Huntington attended faithfully.

Fr. Huntington's social crusading reached its peak during these years. In late December, 1889, he was in Chicago preaching and giving his message of social justice, support for the laboring man and the Single Tax. His speech on "The Church and its Attitude to Social Problems" in Recital Hall in Chicago on Dec. 29 was reported as far away as Detroit. In February he was in East St. Louis and St. Louis, in March in Omaha, Baltimore and Minneapolis, and in May in Camden, NJ and Syracuse. Everywhere he attracted publicity by his black cassock, cross and girdle; using the curiosity thus aroused, he led audiences to consider his message seriously by his engaging character. One correspondent described him as "a man of fine physique and of marvelously winning manner; and those who heard him carried away a deep impression of his wonderfully strong and intense personality."[53]

But Fr. Huntington's health gave way again, as it had the year before, and under doctors' orders he sailed in July for Europe aboard a ship carrying petroleum. "Fr. Huntington, a miserable sailor, had a miserable voyage, not ameliorated by the savory cargo,"[54] reported Fr. Allen. While in Europe he attended the Passion Play at Oberammergau. He also rendezvoused in London with Henry George with whom he was invited to meet Cardinal Manning. The Cardinal was vitally interested in the labor cause, and had mediated a dock strike a year before. Fr. Huntington's memory of the meeting is amusing:[55]

We went to the Cardinal's palace in Westminster, and were ushered into a room of state. After a few minutes, the sliding doors slipped back and his chaplains came into the room. The Cardinal was then an old man—he died a year later—but there was a flash in his eye and a ring to his high-pitched voice, and an air of mingled grace and dignity in his movements. He asked us to be seated, and entered into an animated conversation with Henry George. At a pause in their confab, the Cardinal, with a certain archness in his tone, said, "Mr. George, I think you had better leave that young man with me. I see he's got a cassock on already." As we left the Cardinal said, "Well, Mr. George, if you come to London again, and I'm alive, you'll come to see me, won't you?" I am sure that Cardinal Manning understood and appreciated Henry George, and valued his friendship, and Henry George on his part recognized the noble qualities, the large-heartedness and courage of the Cardinal.

Fr. Huntington returned in September, 1890, and immediately plunged back into his hectic and controversial work. On Sept. 21 there was a meeting of more than 125 clergymen in New York to support the People's Municipal League in its effort to dethrone Tammany Hall from its corrupt control of New York City politics. All was going smoothly until Fr. Huntington spoke, moving that the meeting agree to support no candidate for mayor who was not acceptable to the majority of labor organizations in New York City. He said,[56]

> Brethren, this is the Municipal League of the people of New York City. Who are the people? We believe that they are the folk gathered together by the Holy Ghost, for good and sufficient reasons. The great bulk of the people are wageworkers, and the only way that they have a voice is by coming together and organizing. There are thousands of self-respecting workingmen in this city who do not go to church because they see the criminal classes welcomed by our large and fashionable churches.

At this the meeting broke into an uproar, almost causing the League to dissolve on the spot. Fr. Huntington was not allowed to continue after speaking for five minutes, under the rules, and went to his seat "in a dudgeon." The meeting ended by inviting the cooperation of labor organizations, a compromise which saved the day.

In November, 1890, Fr. Huntington was in Lexington, then in Memphis. In January, 1891, he was in Toronto and Kingston, Ont., where his social speeches stirred up angry criticism. More than one correspondent to the press accused him of "high church socialism." But he won as much support as criticism: "Fr. Huntington will no doubt be much gratified to know of these attacks," ran one editorial, "as they will evidence to him that the object of his mission, to make the consciences of those yet unsubmerged uneasy about the hard fate of their submerged brethren."[57]

Late in October he addressed a meeting of clergy in Baltimore about

CAIL, and aroused the wrath of the Bishop of Maryland, William Paret, who wrote:[58]

> Had my advice been asked, as I think it should have been, before a movement to organize the clergy of Baltimore in a matter touching the relations of different classes, I should have said that it would not be wise or helpful to undertake it now, if at any time. There are special reasons which to my mind make it important that there should be no such organization in Baltimore at this time; and since some have somewhat tardily sought my advice, I have given it to that effect. It seems to me that any organized movement of the clergy should have the Bishop's advice and cooperation, and I venture to ask you, in obedience to certain principles of ancient Church principles and maxims, to let this matter rest for the present.

Bishop Paret, as the Order would discover upon moving to Maryland in 1892, was a man obsessed with his own position and determined to control every aspect of the life of the Church and the clergy in his diocese. Fr. Allen, as Superior, wrote back that Fr. Huntington was acting privately and as a member of CAIL, a recognized Church organization, and that he was unfamiliar with any tradition of the ancient Church which might have been infringed. Bishop Paret shot back, refusing to recognize Allen or the Order: "If the Rev. Mr. Huntington does not choose to accept my Counsel, I have nothing further to say. But I must decline to discuss the matter with other persons and a different organization. I thought he might make kindly answer to a kindly letter."[59]

And with this flourish began a long and acrimonious controversy between Bp. Paret and the Order which poisoned the ecclesiastical relation of the Order to him, and to other diocesan bishops, for years. Bp. Paret's hostility taught the young Order that not every bishop was as solicitous for the Religious Life as Bp. Potter had been.

The year 1891 saw the first answer to the Order's prayers for vocations. Fr. Henry Rufus Sargent joined the Order as a postulant on June 17, 1891, and was clothed as a novice in the little chapel at 417 Pleasant Avenue on Dec. 17. A newspaper report of the service noted, "Although he was born in Boston and educated in Harvard University, he has no taint of the false liberalism which prevails there."[60] This is an apt description of Fr. Sargent, whose previous experience with Cowley and many visits to other religious communities while in England, and whose adherence to the most rigid sort of Anglo-Catholicism, made him a strong figure in the Order almost immediately. He had a great concern for the right appearance of things, which shows itself in a curious memory of Fr. Allen: "Fr.

Sargent used to tell me that when he and I were alone in the choir [on Pleasant Avenue] he would simulate other voices to make passersby on the street think that we had a larger choir."[61]

That winter Fr. Sargent fell ill, and spent most of the rest of the cold season temporarily in charge of Calvary Church, Americus, Ga. Fr. Huntington continued his extensive travels. A typical itinerary from February and March of 1892 has survived: Feb. 2 in West Haven, CT; Feb. 6-11 in Baltimore; Feb. 11-15 back in New York with at least three speaking engagements; Feb. 19-20 in Washington, DC; Feb. 25-28 in St. Louis; March 4 in Kenosha, WI; March 5-6 in Detroit; March 9 in Philadelphia; and March 13-19 in Princeton, NJ.[62] Again, Fr. Allen was alone.

In the spring of 1892, Fr. Huntington made one final dramatic public statement about the plight of the workers. But this time it was not a fiery speech. He called reporters to 417 Pleasant Avenue on April 30, 1892, and told them, "What I intend to do is to introduce some of the dwellers in tenement houses to some of our wealthy people. We will meet tonight and have a friendly chat. There will be questions and answers, and I expect the result will be very entertaining."[63] He hoped that from this encounter would grow a Board of Conciliation from all classes which would meet regularly and establish useful communications between different segments of society. The meeting took place at a mansion on 34th Street, with about twenty working people and twenty of the capitalist class. A factory girl, a mechanic and other laborers described their work and lives, and lively conversation ensued. The press was interested in this meeting, indeed, it was a media event, conceived and staged with publicity in view. But it did not issue in the organization he hoped for.

As the spring and summer wore on, the financial situation grew more and more serious. Despite the fact that they were living frugally (Fr. Allen estimated that yearly household expenses at that time came to $330), it was difficult. And it was clear that the Order was not growing in its current situation. Fr. Huntington was almost always away, had suffered two serious breaks in his health already, and Fr. Sargent, after only six months, was also ill.

A fortuitous proposal arrived in the spring of 1892. The house at 417 Pleasant Avenue had been sold, and the new owner was unwilling to sign a lease, the tenancy thus being from month to month with no assurance of permanence. Miss Lucretia Van Bibber, a pious, wealthy lady had built a large house next to the parish church in Westminster, MD, for a niece. The niece had died, and Miss Van Bibber offered the house to the All Saints Sisters in Baltimore. The Mother Superior declined the offer, but knowing of the Order's predicament, suggested that it be offered to Holy Cross. After visiting Westminster, it was decided to move. And so, after eleven tumultuous years in New York City, the tiny community set out in August for rural Maryland, trusting God to provide new growth and a different life.

4

Westminster (1892-1904)

Before the crates from New York were unpacked on the day of arrival in Westminster, Fr. Allen celebrated Mass in the new monastery. With this act the Order took up residence in Maryland. It was the feast of St. Dominic, August 4, and ever since Dominic has been a patron saint of the Order. Fr. Huntington and Fr. Sargent soon followed, and the twelve-year residence of the Order in Maryland began.

The life in the Westminster monastery seemed at first to differ from Pleasant Avenue mainly in its setting. The rigorous daily timetable was unchanged, with its round of Divine Office, daily eucharist, times for private meditation, silence and community activities. Fr. Huntington was on the road as much as before, and so, increasingly, was Fr. Sargent, both preaching missions, and Fr. Huntington continuing to speak on behalf of social causes.

For several reasons the Westminster stay was a period of remarkable development and expansion. But which of the new factors brought about the change in the Order's fortunes is not easy to discern. Perhaps it was because of the less stressful character of a charming village on the border between North and South, where memories of the Civil War, or War of Northern Aggression, were still recent; perhaps it was because of the implied commitment the move made to strengthening the inner life of the Order; or perhaps it was because of the friendliness with which the local people welcomed the three monks. Whatever the cause, twelve years after the move the Order numbered six men, and had formed its distinctive character, at once ascetic and homely, deeply rooted in local surroundings and yet able to adapt with remarkable speed to new situations.

The natural setting of Westminster was important in this process. Where before there had been the prospect of a filthy tenement street, or the dusty highways of New York residential neighborhoods, now there was the glorious surrounding of Maryland's rolling hill country. For exercise the community began taking long walks together, in the approved Victorian fashion:[1]

> One favorite expedition was to what we styled Monastery Hill, which we thought would make an attractive site for our house. It commanded a wide view to the east towards Baltimore, a range of hills gave a delightful bit of mountainous landscape with several villages dotted on the hills. To the west were cultivated farms with Westminster in the foreground. Another prospect was found on Sunset Hill. . . . From Sunset Hill you had not only a fine panorama of Westminster at your feet and climbing the hill to the eastward, but also in the opposite direction you got a beautiful view of the Blue Mountains. The favorable situation for a sunset gave it its name. We made frequent excursions to Monastery Hill to spend the day and picnic. Many happy days we enjoyed in this fashion and many friends visiting shared the pleasure. We also went to the old Van Bibber homestead, about two miles east of Westminster, a brick house with suggestions of former greatness. Near this house, at the railway station, Spring Mills, I think, was a picnic grove, very pleasant and in the vicinity of an ice cream factory, which afforded an agreeable adjunct to our lunch.

Furthermore, the house itself stood on a scenic half-acre and was spacious.

The neighbors immediately welcomed the Order, invited the monks to dinner, and sent vegetables, sausage, spare ribs, and at Christmas, a can of lard. One family, the Reifsniders, introduced the community to gardening. For years the garden was a source of joy, frustrated attempts at commerce and humor. By turns experiments were made to raise pigs, tomatoes, peas, dairy cows, Belgian hares, chickens, fantailed pigeons, strawberries, raspberries, grapes. None of these succeeded as economic ventures, though the pigs provided some meat, the cows some butter and skim milk, and there was one year of glorious berries and a few meals of rabbit. Fr. Allen recalled:[2]

> One year we put up over a hundred quarts of tomatoes in tin cans. We had a surplus of peas, which we put up in like manner. The tomatoes kept very well, but the peas—oh! The first explosion made one think of firearms and murder, but subsequent ones merely betokened another can gone.

The first autumn brought Fr. Richard Meux Benson to Westminster for the first of a series of annual long retreats which he gave the Order in that period. He had resigned as Superior of Cowley in 1890, and spent the next decade in America. Fr. Huntington recalled those visits in a memoir after Benson's death in 1915:[3]

> He always took the kindliest interest in our surroundings and life in Westminster. He would go across the road to call on Miss Lucretia Van Bibber, to whose generosity we owed the house in which we lived, and then go down to the kitchen to say a word to "Parker," the old colored man who, in an extraordinary headgear, a sort of combination of a linen mitre and a fireman's helmet, cooked our meals.
>
> Who will lose the mental image of that face and form, as he [Fr. Benson] sat among us in our little oratory, his hands thrust into his wide sleeves, his body erect, his head thrown back and his countenance turned upward, as if (and how could we doubt it?) though his eyes were closed, yet by some inner faculty of vision he were gazing into celestial regions? Or who of us has quite let go the impression that was ours when, the meditation over, as we knelt in silence, we listened to Fr. Benson's footfalls as he went up the creaky stairs to his room at the top of the house? (A strange fancy used sometimes to seize me, that he would keep on and on, up some invisible stairway, and return to us no more. And now he has done so.)

Frs. Dod and Cameron had begun their religious life with Fr. Benson at Cowley, and so had Fr. Sargent. Fr. Benson's visits to Westminster year after year, usually in the spring, gave the American Order a sense of continuity, and the great man's presence and teaching provided much-needed confirmation of their monastic direction.

The Episcopal parish in Westminster, Ascension Church, was hospitable to the Order, and soon invited Fr. Huntington to preach. The relationship grew even warmer after the installation of the Rev'd. Jesse Higgins as rector. Higgins had been a classmate of Fr. Allen's in seminary, and became a staunch supporter of the Order. The parish lent its cooperation to two summer schools the Order put on for priests. In 1893 Fr. William McGarvey lectured on liturgics, Fr. Webb on moral theology, Silas McBee on church architecture, Dr. Mortimer on preaching, and Fr. Cowl on the Dupanloup Catechism. The following year, in conjunction with the jubilee celebration of the parish, Bishop Grafton, who had a childhood connection with Ascension Church, also lectured.

By contrast, the relation with the Bishop of Maryland was not cordial. His constant demand was to control the Order, even though he clearly disapproved of it and everything it stood for. Time and again he demanded that the members of the Order come under his jurisdiction. Letters dimissory would be provided, and he would reject them, since none of the three priests had a formal pastoral or parochial connection to the Diocese of Maryland. At one time it was thought appropriate to invite him to be the Visitor of the Order, but it became apparent that he was so out of sympathy with the Order's ideals that he would probably have changed it beyond recognition. Many attempts were made to establish good relations with him in the twelve years that the Order stayed in Maryland, but to no avail.

Bishop William Paret, the sixth Bishop of Maryland (1885-1911) was a High Churchman of the old school. He held an uncompromising view of the beliefs, practices and worship of the Church, derived from a severely restrictive interpretation of the *Book of Common Prayer,* and an equally strong opinion of the bishop's place in the administration of the Church. He always conducted himself with courtly politeness, but his manner was that of the lawyer so sure of his case that he need reveal his strategy only as necessity might demand a new tack. His 1892 letter to Allen about Fr. Huntington's activities on behalf of CAIL had revealed many of these traits.

For some time things went along satisfactorily. Then in April, 1893, Fr. Sargent, with characteristically tactless vigor, took the Bishop to task about his churchmanship:[4]

> You say, my Lord, that you have been "startled and pained" by some of the things reported in the Holy Cross Magazine, but when we speak of things painful and startling, there is another side to be considered which I am sure you will permit me to suggest in all respect. I have myself been startled and pained in seeing things tabooed and forbidden by those in authority, things that in our Communion are matters of difference even among the Bishops themselves, and that in other portions of Catholic Christendom are of ordinary use—as in earlier centuries of Church life they were of general use.

The Bishop replied: "When a Presbyter of the Diocese of Tennessee [where Sargent was then canonically resident] assumes to rebuke and censure the Bishop of Maryland for the Bishop's official decisions and counsels to the Clergy, it shows conclusively that there is a necessity for strict canonical action."[5] He asked for Sargent's Letter Dimissory from Tennessee, and inhibited him from priestly function until it came. When it arrived, he rejected it. In addition, he forbade any member of the Order to minister in Ascension Parish during the interim between rectors before Fr. Higgins arrived:[6]

I do not want, and would not approve, the taking charge of the

Parish by yourself or any Clergyman of your special Order. I do not approve even your taking temporary duty there. It will be far better, in my judgment, to leave the Parish practically vacant and let its services be suspended, in the hope that this may induce them to take more earnest measures to secure a permanent Rector.

Upon the arrival of Fr. Higgins in the summer of 1893 a fresh dispute broke out over the reservation of the Blessed Sacrament, which Bishop Paret would under no circumstances permit. The controversy between Paret and the Order ran on and on.

By the spring of 1894 Fr. Sargent was ready to make his Life Profession. The service took place on May 26 in Sewanee, TN, with Bishop Quintard presiding. Bp. Quintard asked that Fr. Sargent be placed in charge of the mission to black people for the whole Diocese of Tennessee, but that was not possible.

The Life Profession of Fr. Sargent meant that the Order now had three members, and could constitute a valid Chapter for the first time. Since its founding in 1881 the Order had lived by the Rule and Constitution written by Fr. Dod, lacking the legal capacity to modify its formularies. Further, the leadership of the community had in a sense been informal: Fr. Huntington had become the Superior in 1884 because he was the only original member left when Fr. Dod departed, and then was the only member in profession after November, 1884. Fr. Allen had become Superior by agreement between himself and Fr. Huntington at the time of his profession in 1888. But now there were enough members to begin the formal, legally constituted decision making of the Order. On June 13, 1894, the first meeting of Chapter was held, and Fr. Allen resigned as Superior, directing a three-day period of prayer before the election of a Superior.

The Chapter then proceeded to the question of the Rule. Fr. Huntington had been appointed a committee of one to revise the Rule, and he presented to Chapter a slimmed-down version of Dod's original, whose chief feature was its brevity. The Rule Huntington drafted was for priests alone, the question of a rule for laymen being left aside temporarily. It was, as was Dod's original, divided into three parts: Prayer, Penitence and Good Works. However, the section of "Counsels" was omitted entirely, Huntington explaining that:[7]

> The Rule of Life should stand by itself, containing the actual duties of a professed member of the Order and that then a body of counsels and explanations of the Rule should be gradually arranged but kept distinct from the Rule.

He consulted the rules of the Cowley Fathers and the Sisterhood of the Holy Nativity, which had been founded in 1882 by Bishop Grafton of Fond du Lac. He did not consult the Rule of St. Benedict, but noted apologetically that "it had been before those who drew up the Rules just referred to and probably essential features had been retained." This statement seems to imply that to Fr. Huntington the Rule of St. Benedict has a claim in framing any modern monastic rule. Essentially the Rule of 1894 is a digest of actions required of members of the Order, the only scriptural allusions being those of the headings from the original. It remains Dod's in all essential features. Modified by subsequent Chapters, it remained the Rule of the Order until the adoption of Fr. Huntington's Rule in 1901. But its inadequacy was clear. Not only was it revised in 1894, but in 1897 the Chapter asked Fr. Huntington to prepare a "permanent" rule, a request repeated in 1898. It took Fr. Huntington more than four years to draw up materials and write his final Rule, evidence of the care he gave it, and of the reluctance with which he entered into the process of writing the present Rule of the Order.

On Saturday June 16, 1894, the Chapter elected Fr. Sargent Superior, thus continuing the tradition of making the newest life professed member of the Order Superior. Fr. Sargent was temperamentally different from both Fr. Allen and Fr. Huntington. Where Huntington was inclined to lenience, Sargent was strict. Where Allen preferred indirection and patience in working out problems, Sargent was direct. His previous connection with Bp. Paret, who had ordained him, might have been an advantage, but turned into a disaster. His already wide experience of religious communities and his strong ritualistic bent energized the Order in some interesting directions, and, coming to fruition after his term as Superior, issued in the adoption of a new habit, a new rule, and the determination to build a new monastery and open a school for boys. His rigor in governing the community became legendary, and he himself recalled years later:[8]

> When I ceased to hold the office of Superior [in 1897], I said to Fr. Huntington that perhaps I had failed in my direction of affairs, and in perhaps not ordering the life sufficiently. He said, "System! Why, you systematized us to the highest degree. We had enough, to be sure." He was quite right. I was too young, and too certain that I knew all that my office required.

And he added an interesting comment on the nature of the life in the little monastery in Westminster:

> There in the quietness and aloofness of a small town the atmosphere

of the house was that of a religious community. Probably we were over-strict, and probably believed that we must bend Aristotle's stitch "the other way" in order to emphasize a feature of uncommonness in Anglicanism, the (technical) Religious Life.

A certain awareness of the artificiality of their life must have been constantly present to the Order, must have colored their views of the Church, and must have attracted to them some whose purposes were even more arcane than their own.

Through all of this the ministry of the Order went on. Fr. Allen continued his quiet life of prayer and work at home, and Fr. Huntington continued his extensive preaching and speaking tours. The simplicity of Fr. Huntington's preaching and the direct appeal he made is well illustrated in a sermon he gave on March 14, 1894, to the Brotherhood of St. Andrew in Syracuse:[9]

> To know God we must know him by a personal relation. It takes time to know God, just as it takes time to know a friend. Meet a man to-day for the first time and for the next six months give him just as much time as you spend with God. How much will you know about him at the end of that time? If we have not cultivated the acquaintance of God and do not know Him, how can we love Him?

He also continued active in his social ministry. The same newspaper report quoted above states that his "life at present is devoted to the advocacy of social reform, industrial reform and tax reform. On these subjects he delivers lectures in all parts of the country, and he goes from Maine to Nebraska holding these meetings." The divorce from the Holy Cross Mission in New York and the subsequent removal to Maryland had in no way diminished Fr. Huntington's social convictions or his work on their behalf.

In the spring of 1895 matters heated up again with Bp. Paret. In March he withdrew his permission for the Order to officiate in the Diocese of Maryland altogether:[10]

> If at any time I may have seemed by silence or by conditional or temporary assent, to have allowed you to officiate, such silence or conditional assent does not constitute the License required. Any such silent, conditional, or temporary assent is now withdrawn. I ask that in obedience to the law of the Church, you do not minister in any way within the Diocese of Maryland until you shall have the Bishop's Conditional License.

Such a license he refused to issue. The Rector of Ascension Church, Fr. Jesse Higgins, was shocked, and wrote to the Bishop:[11]

> The community will have the impression that they have done something wrong here; and the question will be "what" and my inability to answer will be taken as indicating that there is something bad which I dare not tell. In short it will be a *scandal* to the Church which I urge you to spare us.

The spirited defense of the Order by Fr. Higgins had some effect, but only temporarily. In June the Bishop made his position clearer:[12]

> My conviction is that your Order, the house, its Services, and its work, should be subject to the Bishop's visitation and authority, as much as the work and services of any Parish or Priest in this Diocese. I believe that the early Fathers' counsel, "Do nothing without the Bishop," covers all Church work in the Diocese. I cannot approve of Orders or houses as exempt from his Authority. If the Bishops have Apostolic Office, they are entitled to its full use. The points at issue are to one, and to many others, very serious. I think that for the present, until we see our way much more clearly, the "incapacity" declared in the Canon should be understood, as it has been hitherto, to cover all official acts of ministry.

Fr. Sargent consulted with Dr. H.R. Percival, an eminent leader of the Catholic party in the Episcopal Church, and received no solace from him. Dr. Percival wrote, "I think he could make you bring letters dimissory or clear out of his diocese. . . . It seems to me that you must try to come to some understanding with Bp. Paret."[13] The problem at this point was that if Bp. Paret accepted the transfer of the three Holy Cross priests into his diocese, he could effectively destroy the ministry and institutional effectiveness of the Order by commanding an unreasonable obedience, there being no canonical protection for religious orders at that time. It seemed altogether likely that this is what Bp. Paret would do, given his antipathy to the Catholic party in the Church. Fr. Sargent wrote to Bp. Paret on July 1, 1895, repeating the course of the controversy, and asking that at least the Order be permitted to officiate in its own House: "If your refusal now covers this we must accept your ruling and prepare at once to leave Westminster."[14]

Bp. Paret was meanwhile considering whether to become the first Bishop of the newly created Diocese of Washington (DC) and replied that he had no objection to private prayers for members of the Order in their own house, and forbade visitors from joining in them, adding, "I could not say or let it be implied that the teachings and methods of the Order have my approval."[15] He decided in the fall to remain Bishop of Maryland, and the question resumed again, this time taking the form of whether Bp. Paret would become Visitor to the Order, with a defined responsibility toward it. Fr. Sargent asked him what he would require of the Order if he were made Visitor, and the Bishop refused to bind himself in any way in advance: "I should expect the full liberty and authority of the Bishop untrammelled by any conditions whatever."[16] In November, 1895, Fr. Sargent sought an interview with Bp. Paret, and, according to a third party, Miss Van Bibber's lawyer, insulted the Bishop. The lawyer was pessimistic, and wrote, "there is no prospect of the relations being bettered."[17] In January, 1896, Bp. Paret and Fr. Sargent apparently reached some sort of understanding, in which the Order, as long as it remained in Westminster, would not officiate in the Diocese in any way, and the Bishop would not press his claim to be Visitor. Fr. Higgins wrote Fr. Sargent in support of the Order's continuation in Westminster, urging the Brethren not to give in: "In all charity to the Bishop, I feel that his desire to get rid of you has taken somewhat the nature of a persecution."[18] And so the matter rested for a year.

In March, 1897, an opportunity presented itself which seemed to offer a solution to the Order's dilemma. St. Andrew's Parish, Baltimore, was without a rector, and extended an offer to Holy Cross to take charge of the parish. Once installed as rector of the parish, the Superior would be relatively free of the Bishop's constraints and the Order could enter into a more regular relation with the Diocese. The relations would no doubt continue to be stormy, as the history of Cowley's Philadelphia parish, St. Clement's, had shown, but the Order's position would in some sense be regularized. A committee of Fr. Allen and Fr. Huntington met with Bp. Paret in April. The Bishop was adamantly opposed to the plan. He said that "he could not approve of their [O.H.C.'s] teachings and he felt himself bound by the vow he had taken at his consecration to guard his flock against what he considered dangerous and erroneous doctrine."[19] The Order had finally heard the Bishop's real objection and further action seemed pointless. The St. Andrew's project was abandoned and O.H.C. continued the rest of its time in Maryland inhibited by the Bishop, confined to its monastery, and having to go outside that diocese to do any active ministry.

Not all outside ministry could be discouraged by Bp. Paret. During 1897 Fr. Huntington encouraged a remarkable woman, Miss Lena McGhee, to found an institution for unmarried pregnant girls called St. Faith's House. Located at first in Hartford, CT, and then in Tarrytown, NY, the House was home to literally hundreds of girls over the years. Fr. Huntington and other members of the Order, especially Fr. Allen, were regular chaplains. Miss McGhee was an invalid who ruled the House from her bed for years. Her view, and Fr. Huntington's, was that these girls needed to be trusted rather than hid away, and so the House was in the midst of a busy town:[20]

> On a main thoroughfare, in a town as big as Tarrytown, no locks except the ordinary lock on the front door which could easily be opened from within, these girls lived with their babies. It was the girls who answered the door when visitors came. From the very start they had to meet the postman, the baker, the butcher. They were sent out on errands into the town. Everybody knew what St. Faith's was, and about the girls. But they were taught to meet the world and to face it, and not to run away from it.

This was a liberal attitude for those times. For years the ministry of St. Faith's was a routine feature of Holy Cross life.

On June 15, 1897, Chapter met to elect a Superior, Fr. Sargent's term having expired. Fr. Huntington received two votes, Fr. Allen one. Fr. Huntington was elected, and entered on a period of ten consecutive years as Superior. Fr. Sargent was made the Novice Master.

During Fr. Sargent's time as Superior a number of men began to display an interest in joining the Order. Fr. Sargent did not really approve of lay members of Holy Cross, and advocated a lighter rule for them, assuming that they were not capable of the mental and ascetical discipline he expected of members of the Order. The first laymen began to arrive in 1896. Fr. Allen remembered two, who came a little later.

Nathaniel Wheaton, "a typical Yankee, shrewd and canny," from Providence, RI, became Br. Paul. William Van Dyke, from Punxsutawney, PA, who had been a Methodist and worked in coal company shops, became Br. Bernard. It was Br. Bernard who became chiefly responsible for the gardening. Fr. Allen remembered some of the efforts to incorporate laymen into the priestly community:[21]

> When the Brothers had spent some time, perhaps a year, as postulants, the question of Habit came up. We decided to give them a grey cassock. Whether a girdle or a belt my recollection does not inform me, but probably a girdle. The next question was to get the cloth. After some inquiries we found a small mill which would weave what we wanted. The Brothers did a good deal of work around the house, though my impression is that we usually had a cook. Sometimes

they went with a Father for a Mission. . . . Both Brothers worked in the colored Sunday School connected with the Parish Church.

Br. Paul had a mental breakdown and was sent to the Shepard Pratt Asylum, and could not continue. Br. Bernard's physical health broke, he returned to western Pennsylvania, entered the priesthood and had a distinguished ministry there. Fr. Allen commented on these two break-downs: "We thought at the time that the breakdown of these two men was in part due to the intense strain put on them by the Novice Master [Fr. Sargent]."[22]

Many others followed. The Rev'd. William Wirts Mills, from Camden, NJ, stayed just a few months. A little brotherhood from the Church of the Redeemer, New York City, arrived, consisting of Duane Pearson, Allan Cook and Samuel MacPherson. Pearson was mercurial and undisciplined, and soon became involved with a young woman of the town. Cook and MacPherson later went to Nashotah House and were ordained. Cook became a missionary to Japan, MacPherson a Roman Catholic priest. Others came and went as well: a Mr. Lyon, charming, enthusiastic and utterly without discipline; Constantine, "an odd genius, mentally un-balanced"; Br. Thomas from the Brothers of Nazareth, who soon left and joined Bishop Grafton's short-lived Benedictine brotherhood in Fond du Lac; Grant Morton, very capable and tirelessly industrious; Albert Seker, a young man inclined to Romanism; the Rev'd. Colin Bassett, English, from Nashotah, who was ill much of the time. Many of the types who continually present themselves to the monastic life were becoming known to the community. Many came. At one time there were nine men in the novitiate. And for years all of them who came left.

Two left especially vivid memories. Thomas Augustine Dwyer, an Irishman, had tried the Roman Catholic Paulists, was for a time a Unitarian and then a Shaker, was immensely clever, and took charge of the housekeeping and sacristy work.[23]

His taste in decoration led him to wonderful displays, as for instance white cloths for altar frontals with artificial violets wrought into letters and words. After he left there were stories about him. His honesty and truthfulness were not to be relied on. . . . But withal he was an entertaining companion and we took many long walks, in which he always had adventures to narrate. We finally dismissed him and he went from us to Father Paul James at the Society of the Atonement at Graymoor, near Garrison. He could not stand the Mother Superior and the visions everyone had save himself and we next heard of him at a Dominican monastery, having returned to his starting point in the Roman Communion. He appears later in Methodist Meeting Houses delivering abusive lectures on the Roman Catholic Church.

A strange character.

The second novice vividly remembered was Fr. Paul himself, the founder of the Society of the Atonement, the Graymoor Friars. At the time he entered the novitiate at Westminster, the Rev'd. Louis Wattson was Rector of Holy Cross Church, Kingston, NY. He had a conviction that he was called to found a Franciscan Society of the Atonement in the Episcopal Church, in three parts, with friars, sisters and lay tertiaries. With his close associate Sister Lurana he had made a beginning, but Fr. Wattson felt he needed solid training in the principles of the Religious Life. Fr. Sargent had been a classmate at General Seminary, and so he made application to Holy Cross. He was accepted as a postulant, but his clothing as a novice was made contingent on his remaining the full two years of the novitiate. In April, 1899, he was accepted as a novice, but remained only five months more, leaving Westminster on October 2, 1899.

Fr. Paul's time at Westminster was not happy. Fr. Sargent disapproved of his vision for the Society of the Atonement, telling him, "I don't believe you have a vocation to found one religious order, let alone three."[24] Wattson's vision was to unite the Anglican and Roman Catholic Churches. But his intention was to bring Canterbury back to Rome, not to effect a mutual reconciliation, and his unhappiness led him inevitably to the Roman obedience. A letter written while at Westminster shows his frame of mind during his time in the Holy Cross novitiate:[25]

> As to loving our Anglican mother—that shall be rightly measured by the extent we spend and are spent in her service, by how much we suffer on her behalf. If tomorrow we could restore to her all that she had lost of Catholic faith and worship and holy living—would we hesitate to go to the stake for her? God sustaining us, I believe we would gladly become martyrs for her sweet sake. In will and intention have we not already offered ourselves a living sacrifice to God to help bring again from Babylon the captive Daughter of our people?

The biographies of Fr. Wattson speak of Fr. Sargent heaping "daily humiliations of deriding Fr. Wattson's aspirations"[26] and Fr. Wattson being "subjected to penances and trials of every kind."[27] It is clear that Fr. Sargent had his doubts about Fr. Wattson, but difficult to believe that his course was made any more difficult than that of other novices, for Fr. Sargent's method was clearly one of excessive rigor. One thing speaks well for Fr. Sargent's course: the men who did persevere were all exceptionally strong and capable men, bringing to the Order energy and achievement far beyond its numbers. But not until 1900 did novices arrive who would eventually complete their novitiate training and remain in the community.

All the uncertainties of life in Maryland under Bp. Paret caused the Order to cast about for alternatives. There was talk in December, 1897, that Fr. Huntington would be elected Coadjutor Bishop of Central New York to succeed his father, but he decided not to pursue that path. In February, 1898, the Order was offered charge of St. Alban's Church, Erie, PA, and missionary charge of the southern deanery of the Diocese of Indiana, both of which were declined. Later the Bishop of Chicago offered his Cathedral to the Order, which was also refused. In August, 1898, a proposal was defeated in Chapter to remove temporarily to the suburbs of New York City. For the first time a proposal was offered to Chapter to transfer the chief residence of the Order to the neighborhood of a large city, and a resolution was adopted that the Order[28]

consider opening a school for young lads, such school to be placed under the care of a secular principal, he himself, however, being responsible to the Superior (or his representative in the community) who shall be head of the school.

In these two proposals can be seen the germ of the next generation of the Order: a main house located near a city, and educational work. Both would happen within six years. The Order's discussions were far from idle.

Two formative decisions were taken by the Order in the autumn of 1899: the habit was adopted, and the first steps were taken to acquire the property that eventually became the monastery in West Park, NY. For some years Fr. Sargent had been dissatisfied with the original habit of the Order, which had since the beginning been a black cassock, black cord (or girdle) and the black ebony cross received at the time of Life Profession. Here Thomas Dwyer's experience of ecclesiastical detail became useful. Various habits were looked at in pictures, but no action was taken until, as Fr. Allen recalled,[29]

Dwyer had been away for a little vacation and on his return he brought an Augustinian habit which he had secured in some way from an Augustinian, perhaps by some subterfuge. It was the black habit: tunic, pellice and scapular. Fr. Huntington was Superior and white material was procured and Mrs. La Motte was instructed how to make a habit according to the sample of a size to fit Fr. Huntington.

The habit was white for home and black for travel. The Chapter adopted it Sept. 15, 1899, and it was worn for the first time officially on Christmas Day, 1899.

Late in September or early in October, 1899, Fr. Huntington conducted a service at Holy Cross Church, Kingston, NY. He was asked to dine with Judge Alton B. Parker at his home, Rosemont Hall, in Esopus, NY. Fr. Huntington mentioned that the Order wished to find a suitable place for a monastery, and the Judge told him of a piece of property for sale on the west bank of the Hudson. Fr. Huntington objected that he did not want to locate on the Hudson River: "It was the highway of fashion." But Judge Parker assured him that the *west* bank was in no way fashionable:[30]

> Before taking the train to New York the following morning, Judge Parker drove Fr. Huntington to the spot. It was neglected and overgrown with bush and thicket. Making their way with difficulty through the undergrowth of a copse, they came suddenly into the open and the view of the river and mountains burst on them suddenly, quite captivating Fr. Huntington by its beauty.

Fr. Huntington asked Judge Parker to negotiate for the property and returned to Westminster. But a neighbor, Mr. Neidlinger, also wanted the property and was prepared to pay as much as $4000 for it. Judge Parker acted quickly, not waiting for a response from Fr. Huntington, and negotiated sale of part of the property to the Order. The owner would have no dealings with the Order directly, and so the sale was arranged through a legal blind, Judge Parker shielding the real intention of the purchase. On Oct. 5 the Chapter approved purchase of twenty-three acres east of Highway 9W for $3000. Fr. Allen made a fast trip to see the property at West Park, and on Oct. 9 the Chapter decided to purchase the rest of the parcel. "By a singular coincidence, three gifts of $1000 each had come to the Community, so there was money to pay for that much in hand."[31] In little less than a month the future course of the Order had become clear.

That winter two men, soon joined by a third, arrived who would have a profound effect on the history of Holy Cross. Shirley Carter Hughson was 32 years old, scion of an aristocratic South Carolina family whose collateral branches included Robert E. Lee. A graduate of South Carolina College in Columbia, he wanted to study law, but necessity drove him to journalism, and he wrote for the *News and Courier* of Charleston, SC. His father was a Baptist minister, but the son never joined the Baptist Church; he was baptized in 1892 into the Episcopal Church of his mother's family. After six years of journalism he entered the University of the South at Sewanee and then Johns Hopkins University, where he received his M.A. in 1893, publishing an authoritative history on "The Carolina Pirates and Colonial Commerce, 1640-1740." After editing a collection of Shelley's letters, he entered General Seminary in New York, graduating in 1896. He began his ministry at the mission to black people of St. Mark's Church, Philadelphia.

Frederick Herbert Sill was the son of a prominent Episcopal priest, Thomas Henry Sill, who had been a friend of Holy Cross since its earliest days and an ardent supporter of Fr. Huntington's social ministries and of CAIL. Twenty-five, he had graduated from Columbia University in 1894 and from General Seminary in 1898. He began his ministry as a curate at Mount Calvary Church, Baltimore, with which the Order had a long and close association.

They were joined one year later by William Francis Mayo, who became the sixth member of the Order. Mayo was 39 years old, from Peoria, IL. After receiving his B.A. in 1884 from Racine College, he attended General Seminary, graduating in 1888, and had a successful ministry in Macomb, Kewanee and Quincy, IL, and for five years was General Missionary to the Diocese of Quincy before he joined Holy Cross in Westminster.

Fr. Sargent's methods may have been exacting, but these three men thrived on them. Fr. Hughson has left a picture full of the rigors of their training, but also with an impression of the devotion and humanity of those novitiate days at Westminster:[32]

During the greater part of four months of my postulancy and two years of my novitiate, I occupied a cubicle so small that I could sit at the narrow drop-shelf which did duty as a desk, and reach anything in the room. The length overall was but a few inches more than that of a single cot which covered just half of the total floor space. A broad dormer window, such as one finds in old attics, occupied almost the entire end of the cell, affording ample light and air. Sweeping and dusting were reduced to a minimum, and it required only the briefest space of time every morning to put things in apple-pie order. And the place was clean, you may be sure. We had Fr. Sargent for our Novice Master, upon whom we used to practice the virtue of Christian charity, forgiving him from our hearts for what seemed to our youthful spirits a very nagging policy. From the summit of the years, one realizes with grateful memories how it was exactly what we young cubs needed. He had, I think, the most charming social facility I have ever known. Had he lived in the world, he would have been the most delightful host that society could boast.

Indeed, to Fr. Hughson, Westminster was like a monastic Vale of Arcady:

No one who lived at the Westminster house a generation ago will ever forget the all-day hikes he [Fr. Sargent] used to organize among the high folds of those glorious Maryland hills, through the vistas of which shone the gleaming peaks of the Blue Ridge, set in lofty outline against the bluer sky, twenty miles away to the west. On these junkets, of which there were always two or three each summer, we carried the life of the monastery chapel with us. Offices were sung at the proper hours in deep woodland dells, to the accompaniment of the pleasant sound of running water; or in some shady corner of the ripening fields, sweet with the fragrance of a thousand flowers, while the birds joined us in the happy praises of God. Passers-by sometimes wondered at the strange melodies which came to them from the deep of the woods or dropped from the height of some adjacent hill. Had our Maryland neighbors been endowed with a little more wholesome sense of poetical superstition than usually flourishes in this age, who knows what strange legends might have grown up in the countryside of unearthly visitants chanting among the woodland hills! . . . The adjacent roads were thoroughfares to nowhere, and there was little coming and going to break in upon the tenor of one's thought and meditation. But such fair surroundings are found where men love to cultivate simple beauty. The unique thing about Westminster was the life within the walls. Religion there was indeed "right well kept." Since those days I have visited not a few monasteries of the Christian world, and I do not hesitate to say that nowhere have I ever found a stronger current of monastic devotion than that which was kept in steady flow by the little group of men who were making the first beginnings of an Order in this obscure establishment. . . . Westminster was not very accessible, pocketed as it was on a spur of a small country railway, but it was this spirit in the house which sent its influence far afield, and made men beat a pathway to its doors.

But attractive as the Westminster house was to Fr. Hughson, it was now entirely too small, and fundraising for the new monastery at West Park swung into high gear. For the next two years appeals were made, friends were contacted, Judge Parker actively solicited funds, and the building project slowly emerged. The community had many meetings to determine what was desired: a separate house for retreatants? indoor toilets and plumbing? electricity? In what style was it to be built: Tudor? Romanesque? Gothic? After much discussion a plan was formed. Henry Vaughn, who had designed the Holy Cross Mission buildings in New York was contacted in November, 1900, and declared himself delighted to design the new monastery. Some sense of the community discussion may be gathered from Vaughn's statement to Fr. Allen on Dec. 10, 1900: "At first I am going to use my own judgment as to the style of architecture, and afterwards, if you please, will change the style to either Elizabethan, Palladian, Italian, Renaissance, Medieval, Baronial, Romanesque, or Colonial, as you may think best."[33]

In April, 1900, Fr. Huntington had finally begun to write his Rule. He expected initially to write only a temporary one to replace Dod's modified original, and wrote to Lena McGhee at St. Faith's House, "I hope to get it sufficiently in shape to answer for the next three years. Then it will have to be worked over and it will be a matter of weeks rather than days."[34] He was reelected Superior in June and continued working on it until September, when the first draft was the topic of a general discussion of Chapter. The Rule and an accompanying Constitution were finished by the following summer, and Fr. Huntington submitted it to Bishop Grafton, who had founded the Sisterhood of the Holy Nativity and had been a founding member of the Cowley Fathers. Grafton was enthusiastic in his praise:[35]

> The three vows are unfolded in a most spiritual way and the spirit of your dedication breathes through every part of it. The cross to us wayfarers is what the Beatific Vision is to the saints. This Rule brings this out and makes the cross, the Ladder, or Royal stairway of our approach to God. The cross is at once the Beacon from whence the Light (as from Gideon's Broken Pitchers of clay) streams into the world, it is the source from which the River of Life flowing from the Eternal comes to humanity. Your Rule not only binds you to it, but brings its efficacy into every action of your life. It is a beautiful Rule, and full of what I humbly think, divine inspiration.

In August, 1901, the Chapter met again to consider changes in the Rule and on Oct. 24, 1901, both Rule and Constitution were adopted.

Fr. Huntington retained Dod's tripartite division of the Rule into Prayer, Penance (which Huntington called Mortification) and Good Works. He connected each with one of the three vows: Prayer with Obedience, Mortification with Chastity, and Good Works with Poverty. He was not shy about borrowing. Many of Dod's phrases are sprinkled through the text, as are quotations from Fr. Benson, especially from Benson's *The Followers of the Lamb*.

The Rule breathes Huntington's spirit. It tries not to choose between prayer and action, but sees them inextricably intertwined, action arising from prayer. Mortification is not a denial of the flesh, but a weapon against Satan, "for the Evil One must tremble at every act of faith which is performed in the power of the Holy Ghost."[36] Good works have no independent life of their own, but are "the fruits of that Tree of Life to which we have been nailed in our Profession."[37] Prayer is the central act of the monk, and prayer issues in holiness, but not holiness in a static sense: "Holiness is the brightness of divine love, and love is never idle; it must accomplish great things. Love must act as light must shine and fire must burn."[38] To Fr. Huntington there was nothing unnatural about the Religious Life. Rather, the Religious Life puts life back into a relation with God which it should have possessed from the beginning. So, despite the rigor of the ascetical program the Rule laid out (and it was not less rigorous than Dod's original plan), the purpose of the Rule was not so much to produce perfection, which had been Fr. Dod's intent, but to produce love, and love embodied in the here-and-now: "If we are gaining in the life of prayer, of intercourse with God, we shall find that we are growing more simple and unobtrusive and charitable and edifying in our intercourse with others."[39] Even the vow of chastity, which can be seen as the hardest, least humane, of the vows, is to be an opportunity for love: "Physical purity derives all its grace and beauty from its being cultivated for the love of God. If purity and asceticism are built on pride and minister to pride, they are not good, but evil."[40] Indeed, moderation in approaching the ascetical life is necessary for spiritual health: "We are to find in our Vow of Chastity a constant barrier against all that would defile us in flesh or spirit, and we must strive not so much after great austerity as after a steady living of the crucified life."[41]

Fr. Huntington's vision of governance was similarly one of moderation. In a structure not unlike that of the American government, he envisioned an executive, the Superior, and a legislature, the Chapter, neither having absolute authority, but the Superior deriving his power from the members themselves. The vow of obedience is to be worked out concretely in the relation between the members and the Superior, and is to be the occasion of grace: "Nor is the occasion for the exercise of these virtues, together with others, such as gentleness, long-suffering, generosity, confined to those in a position of subordination; those in charge will have ample scope for the same."[42] The Superior in Fr. Huntington's vision is not an abbot. He is elected for a term, and is bound absolutely by the decisions of the Brethren in Chapter. But he should possess a unique charism: "He is to be the living illustration of [the Order's] spirit, the embodiment of its Rule.

And this is but to say that he must be the representative of Jesus Christ, whose likeness in each of its members it is the purpose of the Community to create."[43] The Incarnation itself, nothing less, is the true goal of Fr. Huntington's Rule. In this he comes close to the theology of divinization of the Alexandrian Fathers, whose thought so closely underlay the life of the earliest Desert Fathers.

If the Superior is not an abbot, neither is the Order precisely a Benedictine community in Fr. Huntington's thinking. It is not envisioned as a complete counter-society, but rather as a fellowship united by divine love in monastic observance. But it is also not simply an apostolic community, existing for a specific purpose in the world or in the Church. Neither the apostolic nor the Benedictine way is rejected in the Rule. The monastic life is to be lived for the present and for the future, and makes the community able to work and plan for the unknown. In this, Huntington's Rule is at its most American, and breathes a frontier spirit. The Rule does not envision a life enclosed, a future of quiet repose, but one of action: "We must remember that a Religious Order has to be ready for new and unexpected opportunities of service at a time when human enterprise at home and abroad presses on to new fields of effort, while the Church often lags behind in the race."[44]

The cross stands at the center of everything, of work, prayer, community life and the healthy development of the individual. It is not a symbol of the unrecoverable past, but alive, "as full of love and power today as in the Upper Room, in Gethsemane, or on Mount Calvary."[45] A Holy Cross monk's dedication is to the fact of a present reality, and his work is to make that present fact known through his life. The community life itself is centered around the cross, and identifying it with the ancient symbol of mystical contemplation, Jacob's Ladder, Fr. Huntington makes the significance of the monastery clear: "Our house is a house of God, let us strive to make it for ourselves the Gate of Heaven."[46]

Fr. Huntington's legacy to the Church and to the Order in his Rule is a vision of an American, Anglican, twentieth-century monasticism. He does not see those qualities as self-contradictory, but affirms the necessity of the monastic life for the present, seeing monasticism as integral to healthy ecclesiastical and secular life. His vision grew from the roots of Anglo-Catholicism, was tempered by twenty years of experience, and was nurtured by social activism. For him monasticism, and vowed life, are not private devotional exercises, but powerful tools for the Kingdom of God, and essential for the mission of the Church and for the full development of the human personality in the modern world. The monastic life is not for every person, but its presence as a lived option of human community is necessary for the fullness of human society. The Rule seems dated in its language, but its affirmation of the possibility of the real life of God incarnating itself in modern life and among modern men make it of enduring and wide significance.

As the Rule was written, debated and rewritten, the progress of fundraising for the new monastery was disappointing. Many wealthy Episcopalians declined to support such a radical institution as Holy Cross, either because of its monastic ethos or its social views.

Sometime in 1901 the Anglo-Catholic leader, Dr. H.R. Percival, Rector of the Church of the Incarnation in Philadelphia, recommended that the Order take over the Church of the Transfiguration near the University of Pennsylvania and transform it into a monastic-collegiate church. Fr. Huntington saw opportunities for ministry in the proposal, but he rejected it on the grounds that "College men are very irresponsible, and College life is very engrossing,"[47] and not enough students would present themselves to make the venture worthwhile.

The spring of 1902 brought the Life Professions of Frs. Hughson and Sill. The Chapter elected them to membership in the Order on April 1, 1902, and they were professed together on May 3, bringing the membership of the Order to five.

By June the plans for the new monastery were far enough developed and enough money had been received to lay the cornerstone at West Park. Fr. Huntington invited Bp. Potter to attend, since West Park was in his diocese, thinking that Potter would welcome the return to his diocese of the Order he had fostered. The Archdeacon of Orange County was asked to lay the cornerstone. But the Rector of the local Episcopal parish, the Rev'd. C.R. Dickinson of Ascension Church, objected violently. The parish church was adjacent to the proposed monastery, and Dickinson somehow feared that the monastery would interfere with the life of the parish, and so prevailed on the Archdeacon to withdraw his official blessing from the event. But worse, Bp. Potter wrote to Fr. Huntington, coldly approving the Archdeacon's refusal. He then withdrew any impression that he might support the Order as he had in the past, in what may be the saddest letter existing in the Archives of the Order of the Holy Cross:[48]

Once you were the head of a Brotherhood engaged in the service of the poor. Now, I believe yours is a "contemplative" brotherhood, and you a roaming preacher. I must own that neither your aims nor life interest us.

If their experience with Bp. Paret had not convinced the members of the

Order that there was little encouragement for them in the official leadership of the Church, then this must have. Bp. Potter was almost their oldest and most powerful supporter, and he had consigned the Order he nourished to ecclesiastical oblivion. But despite the opposition, the cornerstone was laid in June, 1902, and the building begun.

The temptation to turn away at this point seemed strong to Fr. Huntington. In July he received a call to become the Rector of the Church of the Advent in Boston, the premier Anglo-Catholic parish in America. He did not instantly refuse. In October his father wrote him:[49]

> So far as I can see, your past experience and your present arrangements point rather to the calling of an Evangelist than of a Pastor. You seem to think that the work at the "Advent" would not be much in the pulpit. That I think would be a reduction of your opportunity and your ministry. Either place would be, in one sense, large enough, but you would reach and touch more souls where you are, or have been, than within the limits of any Parish.

He refused the offer, but with what ambivalence we do not know.

On Jan. 20, 1903, William Francis Mayo was elected to membership in the Order, and on Feb. 24 was life professed, bringing the membership to six. In September Fr. Huntington was reelected to a third consecutive three-year term as Superior. But Fr. Sargent, who since the end of his single term as Superior had been Novice Master, was defeated after several ballots by Fr. Hughson.

The time was drawing near to think of the move to West Park, and the question arose of what to do with Miss Van Bibber's house. It seemed to belong to the Order outright, and so in December, 1903, the Chapter voted to open a boys' school in the house, keeping the property in Westminster for the Order's work and a second monastery. Miss Van Bibber had died and her will stated that the house was to remain for the use of the Order of the Holy Cross alone. The boys' school would be impossible, and the Order tried to have the house turned over to the All Saints Sisters, but to no avail. After the Order moved to West Park, the property reverted to the parish church.

The building progressed at West Park. By mid-April it was time to move. And so the still-small Order, doubled from three to six in twelve years, packed up furniture, books, the holy vessels and ornaments of the chapel, and the myriads of small objects which make daily life possible, and set off for the Hudson Valley.

The house the Order loved so dearly was used by the parish, sold into private hands, and eventually torn down. On its pleasant site is now a parking lot.

5

Schools and Crisis (1904-1914)

More than six hundred people gathered at West Park on May 19, 1904, for the dedication of the new monastery building by Bishop Cortlandt Whitehead of Pittsburgh. The first monastery to be built for Anglican monks since the dissolution of the monasteries in 1534, the four-story, white-dormered brick building, vaguely Dutch in feeling, accommodated chapel, cells, guest rooms, kitchen, stables, refectory, library, common rooms and offices under one roof. Indoor plumbing was omitted as an unnecessary luxury, but a few months' experience soon taught otherwise, and within a year the building was fitted with bathrooms. Electricity came much later.

The move to West Park released a burst of expansive energy. Fr. Sargent's Tennessee connections and Bishop Quintard's warm interest in the Order, together with Fr. Hughson's southern background, drew the Order to Tennessee. The Episcopal Church had established the University of the South in Sewanee, and the Community of St. Mary had a convent and girls' school there as well. The Diocese of Tennessee, which had acquired property and had begun planning to open a boys' school there, contacted the Order to see if it might be possible for Holy Cross to operate the school.

Immediately after the dedication of the new monastery, Fr. Hughson set out on an investigative tour of the Tennessee mountains. From May through August he lived with mountain families, preaching when he could, and discovering what the possibilities were for evangelistic work. He was entranced with the beauty of Tennessee:[1]

Picture to yourself a mountain wrapped in dense fog, which in an hour is swept away by the onrush of the torrent of rain, and which itself in an hour yields to a flood of sunshine that changes the forest-clad heights into glittering battlements which hang above

93

valleys whose vivid green is relieved here and there by the soft red of the upturned soil.

And no less attractive were the people he met there. To Hughson, they seemed scarcely changed since the Revolution, fierce in their independence and unapologetic in their culture, so different from the cities and farms of the East and coastal South. He found in them a natural piety to equal (he thought) the great ages of Christian spirituality, lacking only the education to express itself:[2]

> My host told me something a day or two since which would have gladdened the heart of "The poor man of Assisi." We were sitting in front of his cabin in the glow of the sunset, when two doves flew overhead into the woods hard by. "You hear," he said, "of the hunters killin' 'most everything on the mountain, but you never hear of anybody killin' a dove. They claims that God made 'em and put 'em here, and that they was the first to find dry land in the time of the flood. So nobody ever kills 'em."

As the summer wore on, Fr. Hughson became more and more convinced that the Order should direct its efforts to evangelization of the mountaineers. His affection for the strong, independent mountain people of Tennessee was soon transmitted to the whole Order.

In the winter of 1904, Fr. Allen made a trip to Sewanee to obtain independent impressions of the possibilities for the Order's work there. His report led the Chapter on March 3, 1905, to authorize the Superior to "acquire property to carry on Mission work at or near Sewanee." A letter from Fr. Allen six days later explains the Order's intentions:[3]

> There are three lines of work that open up before us: 1) The mountain mission work; 2) The work for the Sisters of St. Mary; 3) The work in the University & Seminary and in association with this an influence making itself widely felt in the South.

Interestingly, there is no direct mention of running a school in Allen's letter, the Chapter resolution or Hughson's letters of the time. Rather, the emphasis is on mission work among the mountain people. This is the context in which St. Andrew's School was undertaken. As to the Order committing itself to new work when it was still very small, Fr. Allen simply brushed such thoughts aside:[4]

> The fact that two have come to us gives us the ability to send away two and yet maintain the number we had in Westminster, when the first two novices came. And the fact of giving them generously in

response to what we trust is a call of God may bring a blessing in kind—another inflow of novices, on the scriptural principle that he that watereth shall himself be watered.

And he was right. Very soon promising young men began to present themselves to the novitiate at West Park.

In September, 1905, the Order took over the small beginnings of what was then called St. Andrew's Industrial and Training School for Boys, begun by Fr. William Stirling Claiborne, the Rector of Otey Memorial Chapel in Sewanee. Fr. Allen and Fr. Mayo were the first to arrive, and in a simple two-story frame farmhouse the first class of St. Andrew's School assembled, eight boys ranging in age from nine to fifteen years. There was a farm to provide food, producing feed for livestock and both white and sweet potatoes.

From the beginning the boys did the work of the school, carrying wood and water, cleaning up the kitchen, doing the farm work, and of course playing games. One poignant detail caught Fr. Allen's attention: "At seven they have foot washing, for as the boys go barefoot it is important that they wash their feet before going to bed."[5] In March, 1906, the cornerstone for the Mission House, the first building to be built for the school, was laid. By April, there were eleven boys.

The poverty of the boys who first came to St. Andrew's was extreme. One thirteen-year-old in the first class had been plowing in the fields since he was eight. Nevertheless the Order asked tuition, $4.50 a month (later lowered to $2.00), both to maintain the dignity of the boys' families and to raise the funds necessary to run the school. The second Christmas, in 1906, brought two young fellows who had walked barefoot across the mountain to apply for admission. They were welcomed and shortly given a warm bath. The next morning, however, they were gone, and left word that they did not propose to stay and "be pizened with pipe water."[6] But the generosity of those mountain boys was as great as their poverty. A visiting priest remarked on Christmas Eve in 1906 that he had no present under the tree:[7]

Instantly Andrew spoke up: "I will give you mine." And sure enough, that evening, when he got out his presents he came over and insisted that our guest should have one of the best of them.

Very soon it became evident that practical as well as academic training was needed, and the curriculum was expanded to include farming skills. A night school for men was begun in the fall of 1906: "The grade of the work is about the same as it is in the school with the small boys, although we have some men nearly 60 years old.''[8] Indeed, St. Andrew's provided primary literacy training for the first time in that remote mountainous part of Tennessee.

The Order formally adopted the school as a "work of the Order" in April, 1906, and the diocese deeded the property to Holy Cross. A fund was established for buildings, but it was partially wiped out by the failure of the Bank of Winchester in the spring of 1907. Fr. Allen was replaced by Fr. Hughson, Fr. Lorey arrived in 1907 after his Life Profession, and Fr. Erskine Wright, a secular priest, joined the staff to teach. Soon there was a sizable faculty and staff to teach, run the farm, and take care of the needs of the school; and Fr. Mayo especially began to do more and more mission work, going from farm to farm, usually on foot, slowly building up the Christian life in the mountains. By February, 1908, the school had doubled the size of the original building and cottages had been built for some of the non-monastic staff; by that fall, the number of boys had grown to thirty.

The South was not the only area into which Holy Cross ventured in that burst of energy after the move to West Park. Fr. Sill dreamed of a boys' school as Fr. Hughson did, but in the Northeast. In March, 1906, just as the work at St. Andrew's was becoming established, Fr. Sill proposed a school that would charge a moderate tuition to make a Church school education possible for boys from families of modest means. Fr. Sill recalled how his school idea began:[9]

> One night, I think it was my birthday, March 10th, Father Huntington and I were holding a mission in St. Louis at Christ Church Cathedral when an opportunity came for a long discussion on the proposed school. He was very much interested in it and warmed up to the establishment of such a school. I had a copy of a paper I had prepared which told of the purpose of the proposed school and an outline of the need for financial help. I hurried to the printer. I meanwhile had several envelopes prepared with the addresses of people I thought would give for such a school. I mailed these in St. Louis. I asked for a reply by Easter. When I reached home . . . I expected to find my mailbox jammed full of answers to my appeal. Instead I found just a few letters. The total amount given was $200, although I had announced that the needs of the school for different buildings would be $250,000. The trouble was that I had not asked for money.

It was the last time Fr. Sill made that mistake.

The word about the school went out; Fr. Sill began receiving applications from boys who wanted to attend, and the search for a site began. At first it seemed well to locate in Tarrytown, NY, because of the proximity of the Order's work at St. Faith's House, but that proved impossible. Then Howard and Bertha Thayer, friends of Fr. Sill and of the Order, wrote to him about a sleepy little town on the Housatonic River north of Danbury, CT, near the New York line. Fr. Sill and Mr. Thayer went out to Kent, looked over several locations, and finally rented from Mr. Clarence Fuller a farm called Schagticoke just south of town for $40 a month. Trustees were organized, three masters were engaged (Lloyd Holsapple from Yale, Eben Haley from Bowdoin and Johns Hopkins, and Theodore Hobie from Princeton), the house was made ready by Fr. Sill and two or three women, and on Sept. 1, 1906, eighteen boys and the staff of the new school sat down to a codfish dinner that "smelled so strong you could almost smell it as you crossed the bridge."[10] As the staff planned the schedule of studies that first night, the boys appeared in their bathrobes to say that they would back the staff in anything they did for their welfare, and then for the first time gave the Kent cheer, which Fr. Sill had taught them earlier: K-K-K-K, E-E-E-E, N-N-N-N, T-T-T-T, KENT!

Athletics and academics soon began, and attention turned to the need for more permanent facilities. Schagticoke was far too expensive to purchase, but Miss Lizzie Fuller had a piece of land with a house on the west side of the Housatonic she would sell for $6000, half mortgage and half cash. Fr. Sill set off immediately for New York, took a room at the Murray Hill Hotel, and began to raise money the hard way, calling every friend and contact he had. "It was tough work. Some were cordial. Some were the reverse."[11] But before long he had raised the $3000 and bought the land from Lizzie Fuller. By February Kent School was well enough established to incorporate, and fundraising began in earnest for proper facilities.

In accordance with the Order's original intention that the headmaster not be a member of Holy Cross, Mr. Holsapple was the first headmaster. But he left before the school year ended, and the trustees elected Fr. Sill headmaster for one year, with the Superior's permission. Fr. Sill, soon known as "Pater," remained headmaster for almost thirty-five years, indelibly imprinting his personality on Kent, and becoming one of the most celebrated headmasters in America. The school grew rapidly, buildings arose almost yearly, more and more students came, until by 1916 there were 10 masters and 161 boys.

Fr. Sill's fundraising abilities were legendary: he had a gift for touching the right chord in the heart of his listener. Fr. Whittemore recalled a story from the founding of South Kent School in 1923, a separate but closely related school in which Pater was keenly interested:[12]

The best story I know about Father Sill is the way in which he secured the first ten thousand dollars for South Kent School. The latter was founded by two Kent alumni who needed the money to buy a certain farm and enlarge and remodel its buildings. At just this time, it happened that a woman in Washington made repeated petitions to Pater to admit her nephew to Kent. The reply had been all along, that there was no room. At last came a letter in which the good soul asserted that she was praying three times a day about the matter. To which Father Sill replied substantially as follows: "My dear Miss so-and-so, You say that you are praying three times a day that I will admit your nephew to Kent. Well, I am praying three times a day for ten thousand dollars." He proceeded to explain just why the money was needed and wound up by saying, "If you will answer my prayer, I'll answer yours." A check for ten thousand dollars arrived by return mail.

But fundraising was only preliminary to Fr. Sill's real goal. He envisioned a school in which boys would not only learn academics and athletics to prepare them for college and professional life, but also the value of physical labor. The first couple he hired to help at the school did not show up, and so from the first the boys began to make their own beds and to do much of the work of the school, something which boys of their social class were not then accustomed to do. What economic necessity dictated to St. Andrew's, monastic simplicity dictated at Kent, and the "Self-Help System" was born. Such a thing seems commonplace now, but it was an important step in breaking down the very real class barriers which existed even for children in the first decade of this century. And as Kent produced more than its share of leaders in business and government, Fr. Sill's methods and goals had a wide impact.

By 1908 both St. Andrew's and Kent were well established. The Order had, in a very short time, tripled its institutional responsibilities. A group of (by then) nine monks between them ran two schools and a monastery, and carried out the constant work of mission, even while the two schools and the monastery were being built. At any given time half or more of the Brethren might be away preaching or teaching, raising money for the schools, visiting St. Faith's House, or doing one of a dozen other things to further the monastic life or the Gospel. Their work load was enormous, and at times it must have seemed that only the novices were ever "at home." (The continual coming and going now characteristic of every Holy Cross monastery, with virtually every member of the Order preparing for some work or returning from it, was evident from the earliest times.)

The rapid growth of responsibilities and membership of the Order was not without cost, however. At the Chapter meeting in September, 1906, Fr. Huntington was reelected Superior and Fr. Sargent was elected Novice Master. Fr. Sargent, however, immediately resigned, stating that "his idea of the Religious Life is not in sympathy with that of the Order."[13] Fr. Allen and Fr. Huntington were asked to confer with Fr. Sargent and assure him of the confidence of the community. After the meeting, which did not convince Fr. Sargent to change his mind, Chapter reconvened and Fr. Huntington was missing. Soon a note was received in which Fr. Huntington tendered his resignation as Superior. The Chapter voted to affirm its support for him, and he took the chair again, but Fr. Sargent persisted in his refusal to accept the office of Novice Master, and Fr. Mayo was elected in his stead.

The records do not tell much of what lay behind this extraordinary sequence of events. Some factors were present which may give some background, however. Fr. Sargent, as soon became apparent, was becoming more and more convinced that the Roman Catholic Church was the true church, and he was aligning himself with the extreme Anglo-Papalist party in the Episcopal Church. Fr. Huntington's father, Bp. Huntington, to whom he was extremely close throughout his life, had died two years earlier, followed soon after by the death of George Huntington, Fr. Huntington's brother. Grief may have influenced Fr. Huntington's willingness to carry on. The small community was no doubt exhausted as well as exhilarated by its recent growth. Fr. Sargent clearly wanted the Order to move in a more Benedictine direction of stability. Perhaps Fr. Huntington and Fr. Sargent, who were both emotionally sensitive men, reached a point of overloaded misunderstanding and accumulated mutual annoyances, and gave vent to their grievances. Perhaps Fr. Huntington was again exhausted; indeed, he left soon after Chapter for a trip of several months in Europe, which may confirm that fatigue was part of the reason for the contretemps. Certainly the Order in 1906 was experiencing not only growth but stress.

Fr. Huntington returned home from his European trip in the summer of 1907. He offered his resignation as Superior a second time in September, 1907, and this time the Chapter accepted it. Fr. Allen was elected Superior, entering on a tenure which lasted until 1915. Fr. Huntington was elected Novice Master. But a year later he resigned even that office, ostensibly because he was elected Chaplain of the Eastern Province of the Community of St. Mary, which required him to be absent from the monastery much of the time. Although the Community of St. Mary was undergoing a crisis at this time and demanded much of Huntington's attention, it would seem that the real reason he resigned his office in the Order was his sense of "deficiencies for the office in mind and heart," as he put it at the time.[14] Whatever he meant by this, in 1906-08 Fr. Huntington was drawing away from the Order, seeking to shed responsibilities he had borne for many years. Perhaps he sensed that the newer members needed more room for their own vocations to grow, or perhaps he felt pushed aside in some way. Certainly he was undergoing a crisis of faith. The result was that he abstracted himself from the affairs of the Order, at least as a central figure, for several years.

Fr. Allen again brought to his stewardship of the community his quiet patience and homely, prayerful wisdom. The years following, up to the outbreak of the First World War, were years of quiet growth for the work of St. Andrew's and Kent. Buildings were built, more and more students arrived every fall, the staff of dedicated secular priests and lay people surrounding the monks at the two schools grew and grew. And the life of the monastery grew as well. Six men made their Life Professions in the Order between 1907 and 1914, doubling the size of the community.

The three men life professed in 1907 were as different as men can be. Fr. Roger Brooke Taney Anderson was twenty-nine at the time of his Life Profession on March 1. He was a descendant of Roger Brooke Taney, fifth Chief Justice of the U.S. Supreme Court. A graduate of Johns Hopkins and General Seminary, he was ordained deacon by Bp. Paret of Maryland and priest by Bp. Lawrence of Massachusetts, and had been curate of St. John's, Roxbury, MA, before he joined the novitiate. From a wealthy family, with uncertain health but possessed of an amiable, easygoing attractiveness, he was an effective preacher, administrator and writer, and soon rose to prominence in the Order as Novice Master and Assistant Superior.

He made several trips to Europe for both health and vacation, and on one trip in April, 1912, he was thrust into the midst of the disaster of the sinking of the *Titanic*, which sank at 11:59 p.m. on Monday, April 12. Fr. Anderson was sailing on the *Carpathia,* which reached the scene at 4:00 a.m. the next morning and picked up some seven hundred survivors and headed back for New York. Fr. Anderson was pressed into service to bury at sea the bodies of three young sailors and a young man who had died of exposure while waiting to be rescued. At the request of the captain of the *Carpathia* he conducted the burial service for those who went down with the *Titanic* as the *Carpathia* passed over the spot where the great ship had sunk just a few hours before. Fr. Anderson continued his trip on another ship after the return to New York, and returned to Holy Cross in September.

Fr. Louis Lorey, 47, was professed on Oct. 2. A native of Boston, he had had a private school education when he joined the Brothers of Nazareth in the 1880s (while the Brothers were associated with Holy Cross). He spent seventeen years in the O.B.N., leaving only when the community dissolved. He joined the novitiate of Holy Cross and was ordained deacon and priest by Bishop Weller of Fond du Lac after private study. As Br. Louis he had been very effective at St. Andrew's Cottage for boys on Long Island. He continued that ministry most of his life in the Order at St. Andrew's School, where for years he was in charge of the domestic life of the boarding boys at the school.

Fr. Lorey was short and fat and bald and wore a skull cap. He had a simple, generous nature but also had a temper; Fr. Whittemore remembered how these two characteristics worked together:[15]

> He meted out hard punishments to the St. Andrew's boys, or a smart cuff on the ears, often without much justice. But, with equal disregard for their deserts, he invited them to have a snack with him, the next moment, in the monastery kitchen. This kind of impulsive, arbitrary treatment seems to be what boys, the world over, best understand.
>
> I can see him now—the shape, and not much more than the size, of a tea cozy—hustling the urchins along like a mother hen with her brood. He looked like the images one sees sometimes of a jolly-faced, paunchy little monk.

And his preaching was completely in character. It didn't matter at all what the ostensible subject was:

> He began his sermon with Adam and went through to Revelation, omitting very little by the way. It was chatty, amusing, filled with simple love and devotion and spiced with shrewd comments on human nature. It won your heart to hear him.

Fr. Lorey had a passion for flowers:

> He was the kind of gardener that could casually drop a few seeds in the ground, and, lo and behold, a few weeks later a garden bloomed. I think it was that way with his sermons.

Fr. Harvey Officer was professed with Fr. Lorey. About 34, a graduate of Harvard and General Seminary, he had served churches in Minnesota and Princeton, NJ, before joining the novitiate. Fr. Officer's gifts, very much like those of Fr. Anderson, marked him for administrative posts, and he, too, at various times was Novice Master and Assistant Superior. Fr. Officer worked with Fr. Herbert Kelly, the founder of the Society of the Sacred Mission, a men's religious community in the Church of England, in the early days of the young Christian movements which led to the establishment of the YMCA. He was often away preaching, like Fr. Huntington and Fr. Anderson, and like them was never permanently stationed at one of the Order's schools.

The next Life Profession, on March 1, 1910, brought to the Order Fr. Jesse MacVeigh Harrison, 32, from Hannibal, MO, the birthplace of Mark Twain. He had an M.A. from the University of the South, a law degree from Washington University, and had been graduated from General Seminary. Ordained by the missionary Bishop Tuttle, he joined the Order almost immediately after ordination. He was a passionate scholar who worked tirelessly but rarely published.

In 1913 two more men were life professed. Fr. Edwin Clark Whitall was from New Jersey and received his theological training at Nashotah House. He was 35 when he took his vows and remained in vows longer than any other member of the Order's first century except Bishop Campbell, who remained in vows for fifty-five years.

Br. Abishai Woodward was the first layman life professed in Holy Cross. From Cambridge, MA, he was 37 at his profession, and had been a nurse, trained at Bellevue Hospital, before he joined the Order. He was a turbulent personality, capable of great depths:[16]

> Brother Abishai had a large and expressive face which mirrored his fast-changing moods. In repose, however, it bore the marks of great suffering. Apparently, he had lived a wild life in his earlier days and his victory over himself cost agony. I remember seeing, as a novice, a massive nail-studded cross which the Brother was said to have worn for a long time next to his skin.

He was, as a nurse, the infirmarian of the Order. Invariably solicitous at the outset of an illness, by the third day in bed he was urging the patient to be up and out.

The turmoil within the Order in 1906-07 was matched by conflict in the wider Church. The first decade of the twentieth century was crucial for the Anglo-Catholic party in the Episcopal Church. In the last decades of the nineteenth century the "more advanced" of the Anglo-Catholics, as they called themselves, had begun to adopt ceremonial and teaching which was more and more adapted from, even identical to, that of the Roman Catholic Church. There was increasing talk of the Pope as the head, not just of the Roman Church, but rightfully of the Anglican churches as well. How this jurisdictional arrangement might be exercised was never clearly spelled out, but the doctrinal gap widened between Anglo-Catholics and other parties of the Episcopal Church.

Two closely related events rocked the Anglo-Catholic party in 1907-08: the adoption of the "Open Pulpit" canon by the General Convention in 1907 and an exodus of leading Anglo-Catholics to Rome shortly thereafter, called the McGarvey Secession after its instigator. The Order was more than peripherally involved in both events, and their proximity in time to the stressful internal events of 1906-08 in Holy Cross is probably not coincidental.

In October, 1907, the General Convention of the Episcopal Church met in Richmond, VA, and adopted, after much modification, an amendment to the canon law defining ministerial duties which gave the bishops the right to permit "Christian men who are not ministers of this Church, to make addresses in the church on special occasions."[17] This seemed innocuous enough. The Bishop had to give permission, the speaker had to be Christian, and could only speak on special occasions, and so the use of the pulpit could hardly be said to have been "opened" in any routine or indiscreet way. In fact, the canon provided the bishops with a tool to *control* the indiscriminate opening of pulpits. But soon after its passage some elements of the Anglo-Catholic party saw in this canonical change a threat to the catholicity of the Anglican position. It seemed to them to give approval to the ordination and ministry of Protestants, and to admit them and their teaching on a basis of equality with episcopally ordained clergy. Fr. Sargent himself led the first charge in the church press with an article in *The Living Church*.[18] But his concerns were mild in comparison with what followed.

The group who saw the Open Pulpit issue as critical was led by Fr. William McGarvey. He was the Rector of the Church of St. Elizabeth in Philadelphia, head of a small quasi-monastic community of priests dedicated to clerical celibacy called the Companions of the Holy Saviour (founded in 1896), a liturgical scholar of note (Holy Cross used his ceremonial for low mass) and Chaplain General of the Community of St. Mary. The Companions had strong connections with Nashotah House and informal connections with most, if not all, of the Anglo-Catholics in the Episcopal Church.

Immediately after the General Convention the Companions committed themselves to six months to formulate a response. Rumors began to fly that the entire Anglo-Catholic wing of the Episcopal Church might submit to Rome: five hundred or more priests, several hundred parishes and all of the religious orders. In February, 1908, two of the Companions teaching at Nashotah resigned, and with five seminarians submitted to Rome. In March, 1908, at about the time Fr. Huntington became Chaplain to the Eastern Province of the Community of St. Mary, Fr. McGarvey resigned as Rector of St. Elizabeth's; in May he and many of his associates renounced the Anglican Church and their ordinations and became Roman Catholics. In June, Mother Edith, Mother General of the Community of St. Mary and three Sisters became Roman Catholics. The Society of the Atonement, founded by one-time Holy Cross novice Fr. Paul James Francis, followed a year later, in October, 1909.

The crisis in the Community of St. Mary was severe, and Fr. Huntington's guidance was severely needed. He and Fr. Hughson, who was Chaplain of the Southern Province of the Community of St. Mary in Tennessee, must have had their hands full for months after Mother Edith's departure. The wholesale defection of the Companions of the Holy Saviour and the Society of the Atonement, and Mother Edith's leaving, reinforced the fears, dormant for some years, that the religious orders were the Roman foot in the Anglican door. This was an important factor in the passage six years later of the first Episcopal canon law on religious communities, which most of those communities found entirely unacceptable.

Fr. Huntington himself reacted very strongly to the Open Pulpit controversy. In an article in the *Holy Cross Magazine* of April, 1908, entitled "The Plan of Campaign," he affirmed that "The American Church has not compounded with heresy, has not committed apostasy, has not abandoned the Catholic tradition of apostolic order and the succession of a valid ministry of the Word and Sacraments."[19] But then he posited a "definite and concerted *plan* to destroy the essential character of the Church in this land." He pointed to no persons or parties, but asserted that "the whole scheme has originated with those spiritual agencies which have ever been striving to deceive and overcome the rulers of the Church." He advocated spiritual weapons against these spiritual agencies: prayer for the Bishops, for the spread of the Church, for penitence, and for willingness to suffer. In July he replied to strong criticism of his stand, particularly that the issue had been blown out of proportion. He revealed that the real issue for him, and doubtless for many others, was not just the implied recognition of the validity of Protestant orders, but the admission of the new winds of modernism and liberalism beginning to blow through the churches:[20]

> We wrestle not against flesh and blood, we are not contending against our brethren, however mistaken they may be. We are warring for a living God, for an historic Christ, for spiritual realities which are the

heritage of our brethren just as much as they are our own. We are struggling to keep distinct "a household of faith" into which all the families of man may enter if they will, and know one another in a brotherhood which God has created by making them his sons and daughters in his well-beloved Son.

His fear was that modernist theology would dilute this vision, would remove the direct and historic relation of God and people:

Beginning with man instead of God [the religion of the day] emphasizes all that comes from man, all that originates in man, until God becomes a shadowy and impersonal influence, a "divine element" in human nature. And the Church becomes a general tendency in the stream of human affairs, a congeries of denominations within "the pale of civilization"; its distinctness gone, so that no one is *in* because no one is *out*, it fades away into an atmosphere or an attitude, "all door and no house."

The passion with which this is asserted is one with the passion displayed by McGarvey, and soon by Fr. Sargent in his journey of conscience which these events set in motion. Fr. Huntington's reaction may be taken as typical of the Anglo-Catholic vision of the day. It is passion for a vision of mankind invited to join the historic Catholic Church and to live by the unquestionable words of the Lord recorded in the unassailable Gospel record, in Scripture unfailingly conveying God's own Word to his world. The vision was generous. But a tone of defense creeps in. This is not the joyful full-blooded battle cry of the Catholic who has discovered the key to human society, to life, in the full Catholic faith. It is rather an admission that the world and much of the Church have left that faith behind. Indeed, concerns symbolized by words such as "return," "recovery," and (in Huntington's own word) "distinctness" reveal a reactionary tone now evident in Anglo-Catholic discourse. Somehow the Anglo-Catholic vision has moved from a world-embracing expansiveness to a concern for ecclesiastical rightness. The Open Pulpit may have been the watershed for the Anglo-Catholic movement.

In a letter to Fr. Huntington's biographer, Vida Scudder, Fr. Sargent, then long a Roman Catholic, wrote:[21]

He [Fr. Huntington] asked me, just before I left Holy Cross [in 1909], "Will you tell me *just why* you are leaving?" I answered as briefly, that, for one thing, I thought the Movement had failed. He said only this, "So do I," and that was our only positive discussion on the subject.

Fr. Huntington never abandoned his conviction that the original Anglo-Catholic vision was the vehicle for the Kingdom in his time. Unlike Sargent, he remained an Episcopalian, and seems to have understood the worthlessness of defensive theology, for his apologetic tone never again reaches the stridency which the Open Pulpit debate evoked. The Anglo-Catholic movement may have failed, in Fr. Huntington's judgment, but certainly not in the minds of many of the rest of the Order, who remained steadfastly committed to the Anglo-Catholic cause.

Fr. Sargent's crisis of faith had its climax in 1909, but it had begun years earlier. In the earliest days of his association with the Order, and even before, he had shown a tendency towards a self-conscious catholicism. His constant method was to refer any question, and practice, to a catholic "ideal." Indeed, much of his inability to work with Bp. Paret in Maryland came from his assumption that there was a catholic ideal to which to appeal, which somehow inexplicably excluded Bp. Paret as an authoritative figure. And as the years passed this tendency grew.

By the summer of 1908 Fr. Sargent had moved even closer to leaving both the Order and the Church, so Fr. Allen sent him on a trip. He spent the fall and winter of 1908 visiting other Anglican religious communities in England. His comments on other communities and on Anglo-Catholic figures shed light on the Religious Life of the time. In November he was at the Society of the Sacred Mission in Kelham, and reacted to Fr. Herbert Kelly's vision of religious community: community, school and associates all together, producing a wonderful, natural catholicism without preciosity:[22]

> The House of the S.M. is an extraordinary place. I told Fr. Kelly that I was constantly alternating between a sense of shock and admiration. He enjoyed that and said, "I knew you would be shocked and some of my own household are. Fr. Huntington was not!". . . . He has set before himself the ideal of making these young men perfectly normal and natural and there is as little self-consciousness in these cassocked youths as I have ever met. They are human and manly and clean and lovable. . . . When I told them something laughable, they roared and shouted and stamped, and gave three cheers when I left. Certainly I felt that Fr. Kelly has somehow struck the note, and that another man, less of a pioneer than he, will systematize and regulate. The obedience is military, the personal liberty very large, and while the family·life is a weak point, mixed in as they always are with Associates, there is a spirit of harmony and good temper everywhere. The fare is plain and the life is rough.

Fr. Sargent found Cowley more difficult, however:[23]

Last week at St. Edward's House Mr. Slaters, bound for India that night, and Dian Singh, an Indian boy, appeared. Fr. Clark, S.S.J.E., was leaving for India that same night. As he left the recreation to say good-bye for two years they shook hands with cold formality as if he were going to another county. The Fr. General accompanied him to the station and Fr. Waggett was suddenly moved by an afterthought to propose that they follow Fr. Clark to the door. When they came back and told them that, one might suppose he was to return the next day and that in America we should all have fallen on his neck. They are queer folk, the English, without imagination and sympathy, and S.S.J.E. is, for Religious, uncommonly cold.

But he found holiness and joy at St. Peter's, London Docks, in the ministry of Fr. Wainwright, one of the greatest of all the Anglo-Catholic social priests:[24]

Fr. Wainwright, dear old Fr. Wainwright, is so unlike them, open-hearted and light and lovable. He put himself out to go to the underground with me Sunday evening to send me on my way to a Church where I was to preach (St. Mark's, Marylebone Road) and when I left him I found that he had bought me a return ticket. I think it is his loving experience and deep sympathy for the poor that has developed all the sweet and amiable qualities that make him so attractive. Going to the Wapping Station Sunday evening and returning about 10—we met on our return—everybody along the way knew and greeted him. One little fellow, about six years old, ran up, caught his cloak, and without a single word all the way hobbled along to the station. . . . The poverty and squalor are pitiable. At the Children's Mass on All Souls Day I did not see one child decently dressed. Most of the girls come hatless because they have not hats and some of the boys and girls go barefoot all winter. They fetch with them a meagre parcel of food, for their breakfast, I think in some cases, and the poor little things look hungry and often eat their scraps in Church. In a number of cases women come up to the Clergy-house daily for bits of food left from the plates in a large hospital nearby—"and fight like animals for it," the Vicar said.

Fr. Sargent found the Benedictine nuns at West Malling, Kent, installed in an ancient abbey. They sang the Divine Office in Latin to plainsong, and he reported "a strange sense of companionship this night in this quiet old spot, where peace really seemed to abide—the true Benedictine *pax*."[25]

At Caldey Fr. Sargent met the remarkable Abbot Aelred Carlyle, the founder of the first men's Anglican Benedictine community and one of the most bizarre and colorful characters in the history of the Anglican Religious Life:[26]

> He has a wonderful charm in dealing with his Brethren and with all he meets. Their piety is very simple and natural and all seems quite unstudied. In Chapel at Adoration night before last they sang hymn after hymn, said intercessions, etc., and the Abbot in his beautifully clear, resonant voice gives one almost a thrill when he speaks. . . . His one special criticism [of Holy Cross] offered very kindly is that we do not make enough of old and established forms in Religion. He would like more outward deference paid to Superiors—"A Superior should be often very approachable, and at times his authority and *unapproachableness* should be felt, even if uncomfortably." I find the life here very attractive. It is very real and entirely lacking in anything artificial. The Abbot feels that America must sometime have the Benedictine life, the contemplative, and that it will probably grow out of an existing community.

Abbot Aelred was taken with Fr. Sargent as well. Immediately after Sargent left Caldey, Aelred wrote Fr. Allen to ask that Fr. Sargent be allowed to stay at Caldey for at least a year and become the Novice Master for the nascent Benedictine community.[27] But Fr. Allen, perhaps sensing the extreme instability of Abbot Aelred, and the fantastic, almost illusory character of his enterprise, declined. Nevertheless, Fr. Sargent felt more and more drawn to the Benedictine life.

He returned to America in December, 1908, full of plans for guest house work, for building "proper monastic buildings" with cloisters and garths, for starting another school, at West Park, for including Associates and Oblates in community life, for starting a theological college, for enlarging the magazine.[28] The Order, however, was struggling to maintain what it had already undertaken, and Sargent reentered the work of preaching and prayer at West Park. But by August, 1909, his doubts about the Anglican Communion had redoubled, and he began pouring them out in long letters to Fr. Allen during August and September.

He tried to get Holy Cross to join the Society of the Atonement in converting to Rome:[29]

> I can conceive it possible—I conceive it more than possible—that our Community, the most efficient instrument of the Holy Spirit in our Church today, might set out and take the lead and point the way to

Reunion. A Uniat movement in our Church is a suggestion that has met with favor amongst some in authority in the Roman Church. Rome needs and wants to have the help of the English race. Some real approach on our part, the Anglicans, may mean much to her in suggesting that she look into herself that anything amiss may be reformed. Rome will never surrender one single point in her doctrine or authority, but the occurrence of an English movement in upon her life may affect great things in her moral temper. Dear Father, we may put all this aside with a snide or a sneer and hug our Anglicanism to our hearts. And we may face the prospect of bitter accusation, unpopularity and loss of friends, but—unless it is an idle dream and not a heavenly vision I am contemplating—our Order may do a wonderful thing for God and for his Church if we will act now.

But where Fr. Paul James Francis succeeded in bringing the Atonement Friars to the Roman Catholic obedience, Fr. Sargant failed in his bid to convert the Order of the Holy Cross *en masse*. No notice of his initiative appears in any official acts of the Order. Fr. Allen in his steady and sensible way kept the Order on course, and by October Fr. Sargent made up his mind to go. He sailed for England on the H.M.S. *Baltic* early in October, made his way to Downside Abbey where he recieved instruction, and then to London where he was received (without being rebaptized) into the Roman Catholic Church on Nov. 6, 1909.

Sargent's action drew comment from many quarters. A typical reaction came from Fr. Herbert Kelly, S.S.M. Sargent's action intensified Fr. Kelly's own anguish at the seeming lack of vitality in the Anglo-Catholic movement:[30]

> My own belief is that the old-fashioned Catholicism, Catholicism of the Oxford Movement, is quite played out. . . . What we have got to do is offer men a law of thought of which 'the consent of antiquity' is one great factor, a guide to truth, not a substitute for it. . . . The Church of England stands for intellectual honesty—the faith that maketh not ashamed, readiness to learn. This is the principle on which we stand. Unfortunately, with the amazing and astounding intellectual sloth of the English mind, we have never in fact carried it out. The Church stands for the principle, you might say, of my favorite text: "They shall all be taught of God." Whereupon she curls herself up, and purrs herself to sleep like a cat before a fire.

Yet for Kelly the answer was not to submit to an even more authoritarian structure by becoming Roman Catholic.

Fr. Hughson's reaction was typical of the Order:[31]

It is a call to us to greater faithfulness to the Church on our part.
I do not pretend that at this time there does not come an hour of
temptation to be discouraged at the way the current has set these recent
years. But I thank God I am always able to say "It is mine own
infirmity." The Church in our time has never been in so dreadful
a state as that which prevailed when St. Ambrose was made Bishop.
. . . I suppose those who look for temporal results must be
disheartened. But those are God's affairs, not ours. Ours is to be
faithful. If we remember that the Holy Ghost is guiding the ship, we
shall know that we can weather any tempest that might blow.

On Jan. 1, 1910, Fr. Allen presented the situation of Fr. Sargent to the
Order in Chapter, noting that he had "abandoned the Order and the
Communion of that part of the Catholic Church which he has served as
a priest for nearly a quarter of a century."[32] The Chapter voted to expel
Sargent.

But Henry Rufus Sargent did find his home as a Benedictine. He was
ordained a Roman Catholic priest, became a monk of Downside Abbey
in 1914, and was the founder in 1919 of Portsmouth Priory, later St.
Gregory's Abbey, in Portsmouth, RI, a monastery of the English Benedictine Confederation. As Fr. Leonard he led an exemplary life as a
Benedictine monk and died in 1944.

The importance of Fr. Sargent's crisis for the Order of the Holy Cross
cannot be overemphasized. At a very early time it confronted the Order
with a fundamental question which every Anglo-Catholic had to face
sooner or later. Authority, the claims of the Papacy on the Church, is
the constant theme of the ecclesiology of Anglo-Catholics. In Fr. Sargent's
crisis the Order faced the question of becoming Roman Catholic and
rejected it. From that point on there was no question that Holy Cross was
a completely Anglican community. And paradoxically, that position made
it easier for the Order to express its Anglo-Catholic convictions to the
Episcopal Church, in its stands on canon law, in Fr. Hughson's writings,
in the constant preaching and teaching the Brethren were engaged in, in
the social work growing from Fr. Huntington's earliest days and the
Order's experience in New York City.

The year in which Fr. Sargent's crisis was finally resolved also saw the
publication of the first major book by a member of the Order. Perhaps
the title of Fr. Hughson's book reflected the turbulent state of Anglo-
Catholicism in 1910: *The Warfare of the Soul*. It is almost an antimodernist
tract. In it Hughson describes the Christian life as one of constant struggle

against temptation, the training of the virtues, and finally the battle itself, followed by victory and the indwelling of the Holy Spirit in the victorious soul. Fr. Hughson's work is completely unaffected by contemporary psychology, and he posits a theory of personality which differs little from classical and medieval psychomachias. For Hughson, the self can will (with the help of grace) to do the right thing; the world can be adequately described as being the battleground between personifications of good and evil forces; and the Christian life is fundamentally a personal, not a social or communal, matter. Indeed, to read this book is to anticipate the thought world of all his books to come. The book found a ready audience, and continued in print for many years as a classic description of the soul's struggle for virtue unaffected by the revolution wrought by Sigmund Freud.

Fr. Sargent's defection hit Fr. Huntington very hard. But it was Sargent's criticism of the failure of Anglo-Catholicism which went deepest. Had the Order failed? Huntington had another crisis of health in the winter of 1911-12 which forced him to spend that winter in Florida with Fr. Lorey, similarly stricken. The crisis, however, brought forth from Fr. Huntington the clearest statement of his vision for the Religious Life and for his own Order that he had yet produced. His vision is ambitious, and not primarily interested in an organic evolution of traditional monastic life based on the inner integrity of the community. The community, for Fr. Huntington, is not its own reason for being. Rather, he sees monasticism in the context of the mission of the Church. He intends monasticism to be the agent of the evangelization of the entire society, reaching far beyond the traditional boundaries of sectarian Anglicanism in America.

That winter Fr. Huntington wrote a series of articles for the *Holy Cross Magazine* in which he raised the question "Is there a Need for the Active Work of Communities of Men in America?" Three concerns motivated him: the failure of the Order to grow as rapidly as he had hoped; the failure of other communities of men to arise and grow in the American Church; and the failure of the Church through the bishops to make use of monastic communities of men for missionary work to extend the Church.

The starting point of his analysis is an overview of the first thirty years of the Order of the Holy Cross, which reveals his own disappointment in its failure to grow and become an influential tool for the growth of the faith:[33]

It is just thirty years since the first effort in Community life was made, which later developed into the Order of the Holy Cross. The period of thirty years is reckoned as the lifetime of one generation. As one of those who took part in the first beginning of our Community life, may I not fitly ask how far we have attained what we set before us at the start, at least in the active work of the Order? From the outset we believed that a want existed, a need that God might intend to meet by a Community of men, priests and laymen who had heard His call to a life of separation from individual efforts and achievements, and to a life of corporate energy and community action. We recognized the Church as God's kingdom and the Bishops as the appointed rulers in that kingdom. We dreamt of gathering a body of men, all of one mind and heart, which would be, in the hands of the Bishops, a weapon in their warfare against worldliness and sin and an instrument in their extending and strengthening of the kingdom. That was our dream. Rather, that is our dream, for it remains still unfulfilled.

He finds that there is no consciousness of the need of the ministry of men's communities in the American Church, and lays the cause at the door of congregational parochialism. The Episcopal Church does not conceive itself as a Church for the nation, as does the Church of England, but rather more as a sect for the likeminded:[34]

We must overcome what seems almost like the evidence of our senses —the impression that the Episcopal Church is simply a voluntary association of persons who enjoy a certain form of religious worship, and who enjoy particular historical associations.

The mission the Episcopal Church conceives for itself is that of opening and maintaining discrete congregations, and in that mission there is little room for a general mission of the Church to society at large. He asks, "If the real responsibility of the Episcopal Church is to convert America to the Catholic Faith, and to bring its sons and daughters into union with God by Baptism and Holy Communion, is not something more required than the individualism of the parish system?"[35]

He then lays out his program. Suppose there were two hundred (lay and ordained) men in three or four communities, vowed for life and "really in earnest," thorough community men seeking to realize themselves through the action of the Community, with the bishops making active use of them. The result, according to Fr. Huntington's vision, would be a revived sense of corporateness in the Church; a greater elasticity and mobility in the Church's mission than is possible under the parish-dominated system; a consistency and unity of teaching and purpose in the ministry derived from common training and community ideals which would make the Church's message clearer to the nonbeliever; a growth of spiritual centers for the Church in the various community houses throughout the country; and a growth in related Church institutions around the community houses, providing centers of Christian work of many types. He is not unmindful of the possible dangers of such an enterprise—an *imperium in imperio,* religious communities becoming powerful within the Church, and on the other hand, the control of religious communities by diocesan bishops of varying dispositions. But he brushes these considerations aside with a challenge:[36]

'The proof of the pudding is in the eating.' The Bishops want men who will work in difficult and discouraging places, men who will keep on working when there are no visible results, and they want a continued supply of such men so that when one falls out another will take his place. If a community will furnish such men, and in addition, be prepared to conduct a thought-out plan of campaign, a Bishop will not be disposed to raise difficulties about the methods by which the men have been trained or the code that keeps up their morale.

He finds in the revival of monasticism the possibility for such a movement, full of spiritual power leading to evangelization, not just of the small part of the nation which is drawn by natural inclination to the Episcopal Church, but of the whole society. Its power lies in the virtue of common action:[37]

The virtues of the monastic state are, indeed, the virtues which characterize the Christian life everywhere,—humility, otherworldliness, obedience, self-sacrifice, purity, love. But that which distinguishes the monastic ideal is that, according to it, these virtues are no longer practiced by each individual, living his own life, doing his own work, but they are practiced by a number of individuals who have abandoned themselves to live and act in common, as a single, unified body, moved by one impulse, guided by one will.

It is clear from this series of articles that Fr. Huntington's vision of the monastic life was a large and comprehensive one. He looked for not a small, inward-looking, doctrinally pure Anglo-Catholic clerical society, but a large and growing and disciplined and effective corps of missionary monks whose effect on the Episcopal Church and on American society as a whole would be electric. The strength of such a group, its cohesion and positive energy, would, to Huntington's mind, redirect the individualistic parochialism of the Episcopal Church and make that Church the instrument for the conversion of the whole nation. A broad vision indeed! No wonder, after thirty years, when only nine had presented themselves where he had hoped for a hundred, he was discouraged. Yet he continued for the rest of his life to do the ministry he dreamed others might do as well, and as he did so, gradually the Order grew toward a consummation of his vision.

At the same time he was pleading for the mission of monks, Fr. Huntington brought together Lena McGhee of St. Faith's House and the Rev'd. William T. Manning, Rector of Trinity Church, Wall Street, to establish a national Episcopal work for unmarried teenage mothers. The resulting organization was named the Church Mission of Help, founded in 1911, and although Huntington characteristically refused to be its head, he was universally recognized as its founder. His own attitude to those whom the mission would help reflects his deep social concern and absolute refusal to patronize:[38]

> More and more it becomes plain that those to whom we minister . . . are not nearly so responsible for injuries done to society as society is responsible for cruel wrong done to them. It is not these poor girls who are most to blame. We ourselves are the actual 'offenders'; the girls are, many of them, only the victims of our neglect and injustice, of the false standards we have set up and the debasing or disheartening conditions we have suffered to persist. . . . The questions raised by the Church Mission of Help go down to the roots of our social life. We shall never find their solution unless we are prepared to face the truth at any cost.

And the truth was that in an age before birth control, when millions of near-destitute immigrants were streaming into America, broken homes and children forced into adult roles far too early in their lives were common. Sexual abuse of children and child prostitution were constant features of American life in the early part of the twentieth century. The enormous number of girls and women given a new start by the Church Mission of Help is by its very nature uncountable. Miss McGhee's sense of urgent social need, Fr. Huntington's vision and persuasive power, and Dr. (soon Bp.) Manning's wise use of the Church's resources combined to form one of the most effective social service agencies in the Episcopal Church's history.

But not all the Order's relations with the official Episcopal Church were as happy. Several times the General Convention had discussed religious communities with an eye to providing canon law to regularize their status in the Church. As a result of Dr. Muhlenberg's foundation of the ministry of deaconesses, their formal status in the Church's ministry had been provided for. In 1877 the Convention came close to passing a canon on sisterhoods (there being then no religious communities for men in the American Church) but failed. The subject had been broached several times since, but never brought to successful conclusion.

In 1913, however, the General Convention did pass a canon on the Religious Life, extending the formal recognition of the Church to religious orders if they undertook to obey the canon. The Canon (Canon 22) "Of Religious Communities" seems to have been written in response to the defections of various communities (the Society of the Atonement being one) and individuals from the Anglican to the Roman obedience. Hence it says nothing about the nature of religious vows or community life, of the work which the community might be called to do, or the reason for its being at all. Nor does it provide any help for questions such as ordination or lay participation in the political life of the Church, questions important to religious communities since they exist outside the parish structure of the Church.

What the canon did do was to establish an absolute control of communities by diocesan bishops. The rule and constitution of a religious community had to be approved by the Bishop and could be altered only with his approval. No house of the community could be established without the diocesan bishop's approval, and he could withdraw that permission after establishment. Any chaplain to a women's or men's lay community was to be subject to the direct control of the Bishop (obviously referring to McGarvey and the Community of St. Mary). Worship was to be governed solely by the *Book of Common Prayer* "without alteration, save as it may be lawfully permitted by lawful authority." The goods and real estate of the community "shall be held in trust for the community as a body in communion with the Church." A visitor was to be appointed who would see to it that the rule and constitutions were observed, and to receive appeals.

Not all of this was objectionable. But the religious communities as a whole were not consulted in the construction of the canon, and the restrictions it placed on them were far more stringent than those placed on any other Church institutions. The canon seemed designed to control and limit, rather than to foster the growth of religious communities.

The Order of the Holy Cross objected to three aspects of the canon. First, there was the question of permanence. What guarantee was there that a bishop, having given his permission to a community to locate in his diocese, would not have his permission overturned by his successor, or do so himself, making impossible permanent foundations requiring substantial financial investment? There was no guarantee of permanence, and every reason to think that a new bishop would not feel bound by his predecessor's decisions unless bound by canon law.

The second objection had to do with the integrity of the community's inner life. If the bishop did not approve of the rule and constitution of a community, it appeared he had the power to change them arbitrarily or to disband the community altogether. The Order's experience with Presiding Bishop Lee, Bishop Paret, Bishop Potter in his later years, and the hostility of many other bishops, had taught it to be wary of bishops, for not all, by any means, approved of the Religious Life.

The third objection was to the loss of control over goods and property. In a practical sense this provision of the canon made it impossible for a community to retain independent control over its own affairs, and in introducing outside trustees, opened the door of temptation to the unscrupulous.

The Chapter considered the new canon and in August, 1914, decided not to seek official recognition from the Church under it. Fr. Allen explained in a public letter:[39]

> In the present condition of affairs, the status of a Community that secures recognition in the Diocese of New York [where the Order's main house was located] will be a peculiar one. It will have changed its Rule and Constitutions in all points required by the Bishop. It will have pledged itself to make no further changes without his consent. The Corporation of such Community will have deeded all its property, with endowments, etc., to the diocese—resigning forever all voice in their legal control; and in return will have received an "official recognition" which may be revoked as soon as a new Bishop enters upon the see. . . . Under these conditions, the Order of the Holy Cross feels that there is but one course that can be regarded as wise,— namely, to follow the counsel of the Bishops who advise our not asking for recognition under the canon.

Most other religious communities acted likewise, and so until a new and more satisfactory canon was passed by the General Convention in 1976, sixty-three years later, most religious communities remained outside the formal structure of the Episcopal Church. They found in their free but unrecognized status the latitude to pursue their ministries and institutional development until the Church as a whole had a code based on a more sympathetic understanding of the Religious Life.

James Otis Sargent Huntington
In this photograph taken soon after his Life Profession in 1884, Father Huntington, then thirty years old, is wearing the original habit of the order—a black cassock and cincture with the distinctive black ebony Life Profession cross of the order.

The Reverend Doctor George Houghton
The Reverend Doctor George Houghton, rector of the Church of the Transfiguration ("The Little Church Around the Corner"), New York City, was spiritual director for the new order from 1881. He acted in a similar capacity for the Sisters of Saint John the Baptist and was well known as a spiritual guide and friend of the religious life.

Bishop Frederic Dan Huntington
The Right Reverend Frederic Dan Huntington, Bishop of Central New York, was Father James Huntington's father and was celebrant for the 1884 Life Profession eucharist in the chapel of the Sisters of Saint John the Baptist at their convent in New York City.

Bishop Henry C. Potter
The Right Reverend Henry Codman Potter, Assistant Bishop of New York, received Father Huntington's vows in 1884. With this act, Father Huntington became the first Episcopal priest to take the threefold monastic vow in an American religious community.

Holy Cross Church in New York City
Holy Cross Church, circa 1884-85, near the corner of Fourth Street and Avenue C in New York City's Lower East Side was an impressive brick and stone gothic structure designed by Henry Vaughn.

Holy Cross Monastery, Westminster, Maryland
Holy Cross Monastery in Westminster, Maryland (1892-1904) with its vegetable garden was located on the corner across the street from the Episcopal Church of the Ascension.

The monastery chapel in Westminster, Maryland
Many of the furnishings in this chapel of the monastery in Westminster, Maryland, are still to be found in and around the present chapel at West Park, New York.

The first monastery, West Park, New York
More than 600 people gathered at West Park, New York in 1904 for the dedication of the new Holy Cross Monastery. Designed by Henry Vaughn, the four-story brick building facing the Hudson River and vaguely Dutch in feeling was the first of the four connected buildings in the present complex.

The first chapel at West Park
This is the crowded chapel in the 1904 monastery in West Park, New York. The two side chapels on the right were used for daily celebrations of Low Mass.

Saint Andrew's School in Tennessee

Saint Andrew's School for Boys near Sewanee, Tennessee, was founded by the order in 1905. Begun as a school to train mountain boys in the industrial arts, it evolved into a college preparatory boarding school.

The first nine members of the order

The first nine members of the order photographed in 1909 are, seated left to right: Fr. Hughson, Fr. Huntington, Fr. Allen, Fr. Sargent, and Fr. Mayo; standing: Fr. Sill, Fr. Anderson, Fr. Lorey and Fr. Officer.

The community, circa 1922

The community (circa 1922) were, left to right, front row: Fr. Mayo, Fr. Sill (behind), Fr. Baldwin, Fr. Hughson, Fr. Huntington, Fr. Allen and Fr. Harrison; middle row: Fr. Lorey (partially obscured), Fr. Anderson, Fr. Tiedemann and Fr. Whittemore; back row: Fr. Whitall, Fr. Gorham, Fr. Smyth, Fr. Orum and Fr. Campbell.

Old Saint Mary's Church, Bolahun

Old Saint Mary's Church as it appears today. The small wooden church was built circa 1924, soon after Holy Cross Mission was established at Bolahun in Liberia, West Africa.

Father Shirley Carter Hughson

Father Shirley Carter Hughson was to provide the contrast to Father Huntington that would mark the order's character even to this day. These two powerful and charismatic men personified the two great traditions of the Anglo-Catholic movement in the order. For Father Huntington, monasticism was evangelical and social; for Father Hughson, it was contemplative and personal. Father Hughson was the author of numerous tracts and books on spiritual life, and was known as an authority on prayer and spiritual direction in the United States and throughout the Anglican communion.

The founding Saint Helena Sisters
The founding sisters of the Order of Saint Helena (1946) are, left to right: Sr. Mary Teresa, Sr. Jeanette, Sr. Mary Florence, Sr. Ignatia, Sr. Hannah, Sr. Rachel, Sr. Marianne, Sr. Josephine, and Sr. Frances.

Mount Calvary Retreat House
Father Karl Tiedemann welcomes guests at Mount Calvary Retreat House in Santa Barbara, California, circa 1954. Father Tiedemann established Mount Calvary as a retreat center and western work of the order in 1947.

Old refectory at West Park
Standing for grace at supper in the refectory of the 1904 monastery at West Park, N.Y., are, left to right, Br. Aidan (Companion OHC), Fr. Francis Parker, Fr. Whittemore (Superior), Bishop Campbell, Fr. Whitall, Fr. Harrison (in the reader's pulpit), Fr. Tiedemann, Fr. Baldwin and Br. George, circa 1947.

Bishop Campbell and Father Kroll
Two former superiors, Bishop Robert E. Campbell and Father Leopold Kroll, wash dishes in the pantry at Holy Cross Monastery, West Park, 1952.

1958 chapter photograph of the community
The community gathered for the Annual Chapter of 1958 in West Park are, left to right, front row: Br. Dominic Taylor, Bishop Campbell, Fr. Turkington (then Superior), Fr. Atkinson and Fr. Gunn; second row: Fr. Harris, Fr. Bicknell, Fr. Whittemore, Br. George and Fr. Hawkins; third row: Fr. Baldwin, Fr. Stevens, Fr. Tiedemann and Fr. Bessom; top row: Br. Michael, Fr. Whitall and Fr. Taylor.

High Mass at Holy Cross Monastery
The liturgical reform movement in the order moved from this 1960 Solemn High Mass ceremonial at Holy Cross Monastery in West Park to a more simplified and corporate celebration of the community's eucharistic worship. In the early 1960s the substitution of a community eucharist for the individualistic private celebrations had a most powerful social and psychological effect on the order.

Holy Cross Monastery, West Park
Holy Cross Monastery in West Park, New York, is located on the west bank of the Hudson River, 80 miles north of New York City. St. Augustine's Chapel and the "middle house" were designed by the famous Gothic Revival architect Ralph Adams Cram and were added to the original 1904 building in 1921.

Father Lincoln Taylor
Father Lincoln Taylor's actions in his first days following his election as Superior in 1960 foreshadowed a generation of change and dynamic growth for the order. Fr. Taylor was a truly contemplative man, whose life was characterized by a blend of deep love of silence, nature and prayer, and a willingness to move, to risk and to trust others.

Father Connor Lynn
Father Connor Lynn brought a restless energy to the office of Superior. A tireless traveler and innovator, his nine years as Superior were characterized by constant movement, growth, change and challenge to the community.

Holy Savior Priory
The main house of Holy Savior Priory at Tower Hill Plantation in Pineville, South Carolina, serves as guesthouse for the rural retreat work of the order established in 1975.

Absalom Jones Priory
The present classic New York City brownstone row house at 455 West 148th Street in Harlem was purchased in 1977. The six members of the Community living at Absalom Jones Priory in this urban setting are employed in a variety of works and assist several parishes in the area.

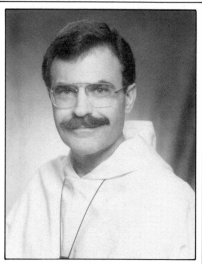

Father Clark Trafton
Father Clark Gregory Trafton was elected Superior in 1981. He was the principal revisor of the Constitution *and* Custumal *of the order and had first proposed to the community that it consider adding the* **Rule of St. Benedict** *alongside the Rule of Fr. Huntington.*

Holy Cross Priory, Toronto
The order opened a house in Toronto, Ontario, Canada, in 1973. Holy Cross Priory on High Park Avenue in Toronto ministers in local parishes and focuses its counseling, retreat and conference programs within the Canadian church.

1984 Centennial Chapter

In the community photograph taken during the 1984 Centennial Chapter, are, left to right, front row: Fr. Clark Trafton (Superior), Br. Paul Hayes, Br. Augustine Brown, Br. Boniface Adams, Fr. James Robert Hagler, Br. Orlando Flores, Br. Leonard Abbah, Br. William Brown, Fr. Christian George Swayne, Br. Paul Lauer and Br. Brian Youngward; second row: Dale Horton (postulant), Fr. Joseph Parsell, Br. Cecil Couch, Fr. Romuald Brant, Br. Samuel DeMerell, Fr. Dominic Wilson, Dom Robert Hale, OSB Cam., Fr. David Bryan Hoopes, Br. Eduardo Bresciani, Fr. Adam McCoy, and Br. Stephen Miller (novice); back row: Fr. Nicholas Radelmiller, Fr. Roy Parker, Br. Stephen Christopher Harrell, Fr. Thomas Schultz, Br. Timothy Jolley (almost hidden), Br. William Sibley, Br. Ronald Haynes, Fr. Bede Thomas Mudge, Fr. Raymond Gill, Fr. Douglas Brown, Fr. Allen Smith, Br. Reginald Martin Crenshaw, Fr. Richard Vaggione, Fr. Carl Sword, Br. Terry Williams (novice) and Br. Michael George Stonebraker.

Centennial Service of Thanksgiving

The great Centennial Service of Thanksgiving was held at the Cathedral Church of St. John the Divine in New York City with fourteen bishops and members of thirteen Anglican religious orders joining the large congregation on Saturday, June 2, 1984. In the photograph, the Most Reverend John M. Allin, presiding bishop of the Episcopal Church in the USA, at left, and the Most Reverend Edward Scott, Primate of the Anglican Church of Canada give the final blessing at the centennial eucharist. At right, the sacred ministers of the eucharist are, left to right, Br. Michael, subdeacon, the Superior, Fr. Trafton, celebrant, and the Assistant Superior, Fr. Smith, deacon.

The Decision for Mission (1915-1929)

✠ In addition to factual history represented by accurate chronologies and documents, there is a mythic history which represents fundamental truth. For many years the Order of the Holy Cross depended on such thematic myths for its historical self-understanding. The alternation of Fr. Huntington and Fr. Hughson as Superiors has assumed such a mythic capacity for Holy Cross, balancing each other in their personalities and agendas almost as yin and yang. Fr. Huntington was Superior from 1915-18, Hughson from 1918-21, Huntington again from 1921-30 and Hughson from 1930-36. The years 1915-36 were shaped by the alternating superiorships of these two powerful personalities.

Fr. Whittemore, in his unpublished memoir "O.H.C.," aided this mythic process by deliberately contrasting Fr. Huntington and Fr. Hughson, mainly to Huntington's advantage:[1]

I think most people reacted as I did with regard to these two big men. In a deep, supernatural way, we loved Father Huntington. We trusted him and knew that any considered action of his would not only be just but wonderfully generous. But to others beside myself there was the marked impression that he was aloof and awe-inspiring. With Father Hughson it was different. You could not be at all sure that he would be generous or selfless. On the contrary, he was often selfish, arbitrary, downright cantankerous and contradictory. There were times when one felt, in matters great or small, that one could drown him cheerfully! A bit later on, one turned to him in some difficulty and found him more sympathetic and outgoing than anyone else possibly could be. To sum it up, he was intensely "human," warm, colorful. One loved him today as intensely as one had been tempted to hate him yesterday.

Of course, they had some things in common. They were both saints.

They were both possessed of extraordinary ability. They were both gentlemen. But Father Huntington was a gentleman of New England breeding whereas Shirley Carter Hughson was from Charleston, South Carolina, of close kin to General Lee.

Because they were both saints (and because, for that matter, they were gentlemen) their sharp conflict never degenerated into personalities. Except for that, their differences were so marked and so long-enduring that it would be no exaggeration to call them a feud. . . . For years on end, their practice, their policies, their whole outlook on life were diametrically opposite. It is to the very tension between them, as well as to the positive principles for which each stood, that our Order owes a vast deal of the richness and strength of its background.

As much of the Order's history for a generation was built on the competition of these two men, and as that competition is the background for the other events of the period, Fr. Whittemore's development of this theme becomes essential for an understanding of these years:

Father Huntington was philosophical. Father Hughson was practical.

Father Huntington was forward-reaching, looking for enriching change and development, interested in the future. Father Hughson was an historian, interested in the treasured experience of the past.

Father Huntington stood for liberty, Father Hughson for authority.

If Father Huntington's instinctive reaction to any project or idea was "Yes," Father Hughson's was as characteristically "No."

Father Huntington's ideal for the Order was that of a family, Father Hughson's that of an army.

You could always reason with Father Huntington. He welcomed suggestion or criticism. You could never reason with Father Hughson. He instantly became controversial, concerned not so much to get to the truth of the matter, but to beat you in argument. Should you see his point and agree, he would actually shift to the side you had started out on and argue as hotly for that point of view as he had just now argued against it.

Conflict and competition, politics and personal alliances, differing theologies of monasticism and mission and society, all characterize this long and seminal period of the Order's second beginning. For that is what it was. A different generation of men arose, and the parties clustered about the two great men reoriented the Order to foreign mission, as well as to promoting Anglo-Catholicism and a hyperascetic life drawn from the revival of research and study on the history of the monastic life in the larger Church.

His election as Superior in September, 1915, marked the return to leadership of Fr. Huntington after his self-imposed absence of eight years, during which he gained fresh strength. It also saw Fr. Hughson's emergence as a force in the internal life of the Order, for as Novice Master he trained the entire next generation of leadership. After almost thirty-five years of leadership of the first three members of the Order, the next generation was taking charge.

As if to signal his rise to prominence in the Order, Fr. Hughson published *The Fundamentals of the Religious State* in 1915. It can be read as a manifesto of his program for the Order, as it set forth in almost legal detail the way in which he thought the Religious Life should be led. It was derived from the sources of the past, beginning with the evangelical counsels of the Lord and continuing through the whole tradition from Anthony to Richard Meux Benson, S.S.J.E. Hughson gloried in the book's orientation to tradition, claiming that "there is not a statement or opinion in the book that is original."[2] His aim was to link the traditional sources of the Religious Life with current Anglican theory and practice, and to demonstrate that the Religious Life of the Anglican Churches, far from being a new thing, was congruent with ancient models. But in order to produce a consistent theology of the Religious Life, Fr. Hughson obliterated the differences between ages and cultures, and produced an ideal of the Religious Life which was very much his own.

Fr. Hughson's point of view is well contrasted with Fr. Huntington's. Fr. Huntington envisioned a missionary monasticism, thoroughly at home in its own culture, open to the future, winning the contemporary world to faith through holiness. Hughson saw that holiness, or perfection as he preferred to call it, as the end of the monastic life in itself. For Huntington, monasticism was evangelical and social. For Hughson, it was contemplative and personal.

Fr. Huntington's term as Superior from 1915-18 was relatively uneventful. The two schools grew, and so did the Order. Three men made their life commitment during that term, all trained by Fr. Hughson.

Liston Joseph Orum, known as Br. Francis until his ordination as a priest in 1920, took his vows on Sept. 14, 1916. Only 24 years old, born in Texas and reared in Selma, Alabama, Orum was a romantic soul. A poet and passionate lover of nature, he had an uproarious sense of humor, and told of his initial reception at West Park to Fr. Whittemore:[3]

It was before my time [wrote Fr. Whittemore], so I did not see the gawky youth, wearing somewhat countrified clothes, when he arrived on the evening train and was given a late supper, alone, in the Refectory. But I can imagine his appearance—rendered all the more remarkable by the arched eyebrows swung high on his forehead which gave one the impression of constant surprise. The task of serving his meal fell to an old friend of the Order who happened to be making one of his frequent visits to Holy Cross. He was a good soul but a little lacking. "Are you coming to try your vocation?" he asked, surveying the strange apparition at the table. "Yes" replied Liston. "Well," sighed the waiter, "with God all things are possible."

Fr. Orum was devoted to King Charles I, and tried frequently at Chapter to have his name added to the calendar of saints observed by the Order, and each time was defeated. His entire working life in the Order was at St. Andrew's School, where he was Prior from 1923-24.

Frs. Robert Erskine Campbell and Karl Ludwig Tiedemann were life professed together on St. Thomas Day, December 21, 1917. Campbell was the son of Fr. Erskine Campbell, who had attended Bishop Huntington's St. Andrew's Seminary in Syracuse. The younger Campbell was 34, a graduate of Columbia and General Seminary. He had worked for the Order at St. Andrew's School from 1909-10 and from 1911-15 had been headmaster, until he joined the novitiate. An impressive, articulate conservative, he was marked from the beginning for leadership.

Tiedemann was 27, a graduate of Washington University in St. Louis and General Seminary, and entered the novitiate immediately upon ordination. A midwesterner, he was gifted with enormous cultural breadth and a uniquely expressive bass voice, impressive and memorable in speaking. Where Campbell was short, Tiedemann was enormous, with a great mane of dark hair combed straight back, and deep, piercing eyes.

The Chapter of August, 1918, elected Fr. Hughson Superior. The other candidate was Fr. Officer. What part Officer's disappointment may have contributed to his later troubles is not clear.

Fr. Hughson was determined to bring a new spirit of Anglo-Catholic witness and discipline to the Order, as well as a new spirit of outreach and mission. He continued to act as Novice Master as well as Superior, and so the next three men professed in the Order bore the mark of his training even more effectively than those before.

Alan Griffith Whittemore, 28, known as Pudge, was a New Englander, born in Boston to a clerical family, educated at Hoosac School, Williams College and General Seminary. He began his ministry in a rural mission in Maine. Affectionate and trusting, he was also realistic and strong.

Much later, considering what had led him to the monastic life, Fr. Whittemore remembered his contact with the Holy Cross Fathers in school. As a boy, he loathed confession:[4]

Father Sill, O.H.C., used to visit Hoosac from time to time to hear the confessions of any who cared to make them. His room was on the second floor of the rectory and was reached by a back staircase. I often have thought that no one ever climbed Pike's Peak with greater difficulty than I had, getting myself up those stairs to confession. It is simply the fact that I kept up the practice that makes me feel that my religion was not wholly unreal. . . . I had seen a great deal of the Holy Cross Fathers, and rightly or wrongly, I felt that the monastic life affords the most complete opportunity of giving oneself to God. Always my philosophy had been (and still is) that you cannot have too much of a good thing.

James Henry Gorham, 27, was professed with Whittemore on Feb. 12, 1919. From an old line Stamford, CT, family, whose interests included Gorham silver and Church publishing (the Edwin S. Gorham Co. later merged to become Morehouse-Gorham), Fr. Gorham attended Trinity School in New York, Princeton and General Seminary. He entered Holy Cross immediately upon ordination. Fr. Sill was his cousin, and Fr. Whittemore described Jimmy's family resemblance:[5]

Father Gorham was, so to speak, a reproduction in miniature [of Fr. Sill]. Their impulsiveness, their generosity, their complete lack of affectation or self-consciousness, these were not the only things. The resemblance extended to posture, to the very way in which, as they sat, they clamped their hands on their thighs. . . . [Fr. Gorham's] sermons were straightforward and exceedingly good. One of them made an especial hit with us at Holy Cross; about David dancing before the Lord. Jimmy liked dancing and—I say it with all reverence —he liked the Lord. He had a simple, natural affection for Jesus. Indeed, he was a little suspicious of things esoteric. I remember him confiding to me once that he wasn't sure that he put much stock in "supernatural love." As a matter of fact, there was a real streak of very tender mysticism in him.

Joseph Henry Smyth, professed Nov. 25, 1919, another clerical child, from North Carolina, attended General Seminary before receiving his B.A. in 1925 at Ripon College. He had been an assistant at St. Luke's, Newtown, PA, for a year before entering the novitiate. In his early years in the community he allied himself with Fr. Tiedemann, both of them ardent ritualists and supporters of Fr. Hughson.

Fr. Hughson's program bore fruit in the men it trained, most of them strong and influential men. But it also carried a cost. Fr. Hughson's concept of obedience was not Fr. Huntington's. Br. Abishai, a mercurial temperament who was much attached to Fr. Huntington, found himself more and more at odds with the community under Fr. Hughson, and by March, 1919, had left the monastery and let it be known that he no longer considered himself bound by his vow. Fr. Huntington and Fr. Allen were asked to persuade him to return, but he refused, and so in April the Chapter expelled him from the Order. His vow was not dispensed until 1923. However, he returned to the community and was restored to profession in 1924.

During the course of World War I, both Fr. Anderson and Fr. Whitall enlisted as chaplains of the American Expeditionary Force. This had not disturbed Fr. Huntington greatly; in fact, there is no mention of it in Chapter before 1919. But in October, 1918, shortly after Fr. Hughson became Superior, a notice appeared in the *Holy Cross Magazine* which clearly set forth the new Superior's concern for the discipline of the community:[6]

> Fr. Anderson and Fr. Whitall are still at their posts in France, but their remaining there seems very doubtful. The last ruling of the military authorities in regard to chaplains is that at the end of three months no chaplains will be recognized, or even given access to camps, hospitals, etc., abroad other than chaplains in the regular army under military orders. Such a chaplain has, of course, no option as to where he shall serve. He may be ordered to Alaska, or some other place far removed from the scene of the present strife. By no means would we depreciate the importance of such a chaplain's ministry, but it is quite another question whether or not one of our number shall be thus permanently isolated from the Community, and from the life to which he has given himself.

Fr. Whitall returned swiftly to the obedience of the community. But there was disagreement between Fr. Hughson and Fr. Anderson. The Superior reprimanded Fr. Anderson, and in October, 1919, Fr. Anderson appealed that reprimand to Chapter. There was an attempt to release Fr. Anderson from his vows, which failed. The Chapter voted to sustain the Superior's action, but there was division in the community. The nature of the disciplinary action against Fr. Anderson is now lost, but Fr. Hughson was clearly willing to use his office for what he considered the discipline of the community's life.

The most agonizing of these cases was Fr. Harvey Officer. A brilliant preacher and a gifted administrator, he had increasing difficulty with the vow of chastity. Early in 1921 he was arrested in a New York subway station for propositioning a man, was convicted and jailed. Fr. Hughson and the community did not act hastily, however. The Order spent more than eight months considering action. Only after Fr. Officer was deposed from the priesthood in July by Bishop Manning of New York did the Chapter expel him from membership in the Order. In an age when pastoral sensitivity to homosexuality was almost nonexistent in the Church, let alone the secular world, Fr. Officer's struggle was long and difficult, and his trauma intense. It meant the end of his bright career. An Associate of the Order who knew him said many years later, "He was the most brilliant preacher the Order ever had. If he had lived fifty years later, his life would have been much different."[7]

The monastery consecrated in 1904 had by 1916 become too small. Containing in a single building chapel, kitchen and refectory, cells and guest space, offices and library, it sufficed for five monks and their work, and the novitiate, but not for twelve, with a novitiate bursting at the seams. In August, 1916, the Chapter authorized an expansion of the monastery, but not until five years later were the new buildings finished.

Given as a memorial to industrialist and architect William Masters Camac by his widow, the new portion of the monastery was designed by the famous Gothic Revival architect Ralph Adams Cram. The new chapel exhibited a faint North Italian or Lombard character. Cram wrote:[8]

It is the sort of thing you may find in Syria, Greece, Italy, Spain, the Rhineland. . . . These little churches were built of local materials, in the simplest form, with round arches, timber roofs, a semi-circular apse and where they can afford it, a few columns used to support a clerestory wall. . . . The principal architectural feature, if it can be called such, is the lofty campanile which, more than any other portion of the building, carries a certain North Italian quality.

The chapel was joined to the original monastery building by a cloister and a two-story building which came to be called the Middle House, with offices and sacristies on the first floor, and on the second, a chapel and cells for the growing novitiate. Carried away by enthusiasm for his medieval creation, Cram forgot to include a bathroom for the novitiate.

Fr. Hughson, the Superior, saw to it that the consecration service was virtually a who's who of the Anglo-Catholic world. He was himself the principal celebrant; Bishop Manning of New York, the Order's Visitor, was the consecrator; the preacher was Fr. Frank Vernon of St. Mark's, Philadelphia; and participating in the service were (besides other members of the Order) Fr. Mabry of Holy Cross, Kingston, NY, Fr. Schlueter of St. Luke's Chapel, New York, Fr. McClenthen of Mount Calvary Church, Baltimore, Fr. Baker of Christ Church, New Haven, and Canon Winfred Douglas, already making his mark on Church music.

The most significant decision made by the Order since its move to West Park and the establishment of the two schools was taken at a special Chapter on March 28, 1921. Bishop Reginald Weller of Fond du Lac had invited the Order to take the parish of St. Peter's, Ripon, WI, as a location for a house of the Order. The discussion in Chapter ranged far wider than Ripon, however, and the community decided to move both into foreign and domestic mission at the same time. The resolution of Chapter read: "The Chapter recommends the Superior establish a Branch House of the Order in the foreign field, and another Branch House in the Parish of Ripon, or at some other place within three hundred miles of Chicago."

There were sixteen active members of Holy Cross when this decision was taken. If both houses were established, it would mean that on the average there would be three monks for each of the Order's houses, plus the Superior. This tendency to divide into small units is constant throughout the history of the Order. But what is more remarkable is the way the discussion moved from a domestic concern to a foreign one. This was a deliberate decision for mission, which fell within both Fr. Huntington's concern for evangelization and Fr. Hughson's vision of the ever-expanding Church Militant.

The article announcing the decision in the May, 1921, *Holy Cross Magazine,* invoked a spirit of adventure:[9]

> It was the unanimous feeling of our Chapter that it was time we were making another adventure for God. As was the case fifteen years ago, there may be those who think we are rash. Perhaps we are. We have not troubled ourselves to consider that question. "Safety first" is not our motto, as it has never been the motto of any high enterprise that man has undertaken for God.

Fr. Tiedemann and Fr. Smyth were dispatched immediately to Ripon, where they intended to set up a monastery on the lines of West Park, "where our brethren, both clergy and laity, may come freely for spiritual refreshment and retreat."[10] But the first letter Fr. Tiedemann sent from Ripon, published in the *Magazine,* spelled trouble. He dwelt at length on the buildings, and especially the high-church paraphernalia of the parish, the statues, and the naming of different rooms for saints. The only references to mission in the letter are of a three-day retreat soon to be held, and the "goodly number" who "find their way to daily Mass." What lacked was a dynamic vision of an attractive and outreaching center for the Midwest. What was present was exaggerated concern for the ritual aspect of religion.[11]

Before very long Fr. Tiedemann was elected Rector of St. Peter's. The Bishop's intention had been that the Order should have the parish, yet there was (and is) no provision in Episcopal canon law for an institution such as a religious order to hold a rectorship. It can be conferred only on an individual. Fr. Tiedemann's conception of his role as rector led him to conflict first within the parish and finally within the Order. This conflict need not have ended Holy Cross's ministry in Ripon if the Order itself had held the rectorship, and could have replaced Fr. Tiedemann when that became desirable.

The Order's plan to make St. Peter's a center for mission throughout the Midwest, translated as it was into Fr. Tiedemann's strident ritualism, met opposition within the parish. Not everyone at St. Peter's was delighted by the Bishop's invitation, and after the Fathers arrived and the honeymoon came to an end, serious divisions in the parish appeared and eventually became public in the Church press. Fr. Tiedemann and Fr. Smyth continued, with briefer stays by Fr. Gorham and Fr. Hawkins, but by 1924 it was clear that Holy Cross's midwestern house was in serious trouble. Fr. Huntington paid a visit to Ripon in the fall of 1924, and after returning to West Park, determined that the work there could not continue. On January 1, 1925, a special Chapter was held which supported his decision. But Fr. Tiedemann and Fr. Smyth continued in disagreement, refusing to obey the Superior's order to return to West Park. On February 16 the Chapter met to consider their request to be released from vows, but failed to act because a quorum was lacking. On July 24, after attempts at reconciliation, Chapter met and received this telegram from Frs. Smyth and Tiedemann:

> Letters received. We have not changed our views, we cannot violate conscience. We have formed our own Community. We respectfully renew our request that we be released not only from our Vows, but from all obligations to your Order.

Chapter expelled them both.

Their community was short-lived. The next year Fr. Tiedemann sailed for Oxford, where he was at Keble College for two years. Fr. Smyth remained in Wisconsin as Vicar of Berlin and Omro until 1927. Fr.

Tiedemann returned to the Order in July, 1930, soon after Fr. Hughson was elected Superior. Fr. Smyth returned thirty-five years later, in 1960, after a career as a parish priest and having married and raised a family.

The failure of the Ripon project had two long-lasting effects. The Order has not yet been able to establish a permanent monastery in the Midwest. And for many years the thought of permanent direction of a parish in America was anathema to the community.

The second area in which the Chapter of 1921 had decided to look for mission was "in the foreign field." The Order wanted to go where the Gospel had not yet been preached, and where the Episcopal Church had some responsibility and the possibility of jurisdiction. Conversations with the National Council of the Episcopal Church and correspondence with various missionary bishops narrowed the possibilities to Liberia and the Philippines. The response of Bishop Overs of Liberia was so enthusiastic that the decision was taken to go to Liberia, to open the interior of that land to the Gospel.

There was also a group in Philadelphia contemplating a similar venture, and so forces were joined for the first expedition. On January 14, 1922, Fr. Herbert Hawkins and two members of the Philadelphia group, Frs. Barnett (of St. Mark's, Manayunk, PA) and Hazzard (of Wrightstown, PA), set sail on the *Baltic* to Liverpool, changing there for the *Appam,* arriving Feb. 4 in Freetown, Sierra Leone. It was not until the 1960s that the Liberian government built a direct road from Monrovia to Lofa County, so for generations all the Holy Cross travel to the Liberian Mission was through Freetown.

The little party made its way to Bo, Sierra Leone, on the 2′6″ narrow-gauge railway, and at Bo were met by two priests from the Diocese of Liberia, and continued by rail to Pendembu, the end of the line. Engaging porters there, they set out for Liberia, reaching Masambalahun on Feb. 22, and Kolahun the next day. Bishop Campbell later wrote:[12]

> Father Hawkins records that in every town where they stopped they would tell the Chief and people why they had come, not failing to inquire whether a mission station would be welcomed. The answers were all in the affirmative, apparently, though sometimes more polite than convincing. The Paramount Chief Fofi of Masambalahun seems to have extended the most cordial invitation for the strangers to "sit down" in his jurisdiction.

From Kolahun in Bandi country the small band "tramped eastward through the dense forests and over the high hills of the Buzi, or Lomas as they are properly called."[13] They stopped in all the principal towns,

Vezala, Voinjama, Zigita and Pandemai, and in every place up to Zigita they received a cordial welcome. The reception cooled from that point, however, and they turned directly to the capital, Monrovia.

After consulting with Bishop Overs in Monrovia, the Philadelphia group claimed the most promising site, in Pandemai, where three houses already stood available for the missionaries. Bishop Campbell dryly remarked that "Father Dwalu was dispatched at once to Pandemai to 'hold the fort' till Father Barnett and his companions could come. Be it said to the lasting praise of Father Dwalu that he held on for nearly twenty years, for the expected missionaries never materialized."[14] Holy Cross eventually assumed care of the mission at Pandemai.

To Holy Cross, Bishop Overs gave the care of five peoples, Bandi, Kisi, Loma, Mende, and Mandingo. Fr. Hawkins returned to Masambalahun early in April, sending carpenters, sawyers and building supplies ahead while he went to Freetown to establish banking and business contacts. Late that month the Bandi Paramount Chief, Fofi, together with his Speaker, Njave Manjo, and the Liberian District Commissioner, Mr. Ledlam, met for some days to discuss the mission, and on Tuesday, May 2, agreed to establish the mission in Bandi country. The monastery to be built was named for the saint of that day, Athanasius.

The land granted to Fr. Hawkins for the mission was the site of Mbola's Town, or Bolahun, uninhabited since a tribal war in 1910 had destroyed it. Fr. Hawkins said the first Mass in Bandi country on May 7, and building was started.

But the requisite permits had not been obtained, and the government in Monrovia put a stop to the new mission, thinking that there might be trouble afoot. The priests after all had come through Sierra Leone, and were doing new things in the corner of the country near the English and French colonies of Sierra Leone and Guinea. In July Fr. Hawkins traveled to Monrovia, at last had an interview with the Liberian President, Charles D. B. King, and on August 4 the necessary permits were issued, assuring the legality of the mission.

In September Fr. Robert Campbell and Mr. Harold Manley, an architect and builder, arrived in Freetown, traveled to Pendembu by rail, and trekked to Bolahun. Campbell remembered that journey, typical of so many the Fathers would take over the years:[15]

Stopping at every halt, the train crew would alight to pass the time of day with acquaintances and friends, and women and children would walk up and down in front of the car windows selling oranges, bananas and goodies of various sorts for the passengers to buy. . . .

We entered bush, ever more bush, especially after we had left what is technically known as the "colony," and had gotten in the protectorate, where native laws and customs hold.

The trek to Masambalahun took four days and required many porters and bearers. The white men were expected to stay in their hammocks, slung between the shoulders of two bearers, unaccustomed as they were to day-long hikes in tropical climes.

Slowly the first buildings began to take shape, and the curiosity of the Bandi people about the newcomers, at first intense, gradually waned. It did not take long before people with illnesses presented themselves, and a rudimentary medical practice grew up. Typewriters, razors for shaving, paper, tin cans all fascinated the people of Masambalahun. Time passed and Christmas arrived, "for us the strangest Christmas ever," wrote Bp. Campbell. Chief Fofi's sister had died and[16]

even while we were eagerly opening [presents] the wailing began. Women sitting on the ground tossed handfuls of earth aloft to fall on their heads. Others all over town rent the air with their doleful cries. Yet, hardly had the interment taken place when the dancing began. The sharp, rhythmical snap of beads woven about a gourd and always played by women; the hollow "talking" of fanga drums carried under the arms of the men; the clapping of hands in unison while in a loud voice the leader would recite the virtues of the deceased, broken by a mighty chorus at intervals, "Our sister has gone away. We cannot see her." This continued almost without interruption for a week, so that on New Year's Day they were ready for the funeral feast. Sacrifices of chickens, rice and palm oil were offered to make certain that the departed was "satisfied,"—i.e., no longer angry. A cow was killed and untold bushels of rice cooked. The pagans washed all this down with copious draughts of palm wine, while the Moslems fared better with unadorned water. We were sent a cut of the cow, a present most acceptable, for real meat like this was scarce. But it did show that, white strangers though we had come into their midst, now we were accepted as an integral part of their tribal society.

This statement of satisfaction that the mission was "accepted as an integral part of their tribal society" indicates the true spirit of the mission. There was to be no denigration of native customs, no forced conversion, no arbitrary replacement of indigenous customs with the new ways of the white man. Rather, the Fathers offered what they had: education, medical and agricultural knowledge, and the Gospel, in the conviction that the real value of these gifts would be discerned by the people themselves and incorporated into their own society.

Frs. Campbell and Hawkins were not the only members of the Order to be fired with zeal for the African mission. Fr. Allen, who turned 71 in June, 1921, became convinced that he was called to the mission, and that he should end his days in Africa. In a moving letter to Fr. Huntington he described his decision:[17]

My thought is that if the Order has any special reason for accomplishing Mission work it must be because of the [Religious] Life. My vision is to establish the Religious Life in Liberia—to plant it and for this purpose to send me to keep up the Religious Life. Someone will have to be at the headquarters and maintain the Religious Life. And that can be myself, as well as anyone else. The very thought thrills me—makes me young again. . . . What difference does it make whether one dies in Africa or America? Indeed a death in Africa might do more for the cause than a long life. It seems to me that for me life is just beginning.

Neither Fr. Huntington nor Bishop Overs was so easily convinced. But Fr. Allen was not to be denied. Bp. Overs at first turned him down flat because of his age, but Fr. Allen persevered, as the Bishop later recalled:[18]

Fully convinced that he was divinely called, he left no stone unturned to attain his purpose. On nine different occasions he came to see me. He reasoned; he argued; he begged; he appealed. When I told him he could not live six months in that climate, he replied, "What of it? If I stay here I may live ten years, but a priest seventy years old is not wanted much in this country. If I can go to Africa and work six months for those poor people in the Hinterland, it would be better than living ten years here in practical retirement."

But I still turned a deaf ear to his entreaty. One day he informed me that he had come to see me for the last time. He had used every means at his command to convince me that he must go to Africa. It looked as if he had failed. Just before he left he turned to me and said: "One day you and I will stand before the judgement seat of God. Then the Lord will say to me, 'Father Allen, did I not call you to go to Africa?' I shall answer, 'Yes, Lord.' Then he will say, 'Why did you not go?' I shall answer, 'There stands the Bishop. Ask him.' "

Bishop Overs gave his blessing to Fr. Allen. He sailed for England, spent several months at Livingstone College, London, taking a course in tropical medicine, and arrived in Liberia on June 10, 1923. He reopened Fr. Hawkins' dispensary, closed since Fr. Hawkins had been sent home with a case of blackwater fever. Bp. Campbell remembered Fr. Allen's early ministry in Bolahun:[19]

> Since he was always kindly, humorous, careful, the Father's skill was recognized at once. So greatly did the number of patients grow that we saw the necessity of building a special native house for the medical department. . . . No matter whether dressing those dreadful tropical sores, or extracting an aching tooth, or dispensing epsom salts, Father was always deliberate and sympathetic. He prayed for each sufferer as he ministered healing. No wonder the people loved him. No wonder that through Father Allen's personality and effective deeds of mercy the last vestiges of suspicion and opposition to the mission, like a cloud before the morning sun, melted away.

The early months of 1923 saw the building of the first monastery and the establishment of the first school at Bolahun. Mr. Harold E. Manley had answered the Order's call for helpers at the mission. Skilled at all kinds of building design and construction, the first buildings began to rise after the rainy season of 1923. The monastery was in western style, the school buildings in the indigenous round house style.

The first pupils of the new mission arrived on Sept. 1, 1923. The young boys were named Fodi and Langama, and they arrived dressed in their country gowns and carrying the sleeping mat and rice they had been asked to bring. The teacher was Mr. Tom Hunter, temporarily at the mission from Sierra Leone. Fr. Harry Stretch, an Episcopal priest from New York, arrived in Jan., 1924, and took charge of the school, which soon grew far beyond the capacity of buildings and teachers.

A third event in that first full season of mission ministry, 1923-24, took place shortly before the Church of St. Mary was dedicated. On Feb. 1, 1924, William Morlu was baptized. He was the first of the Bandi to receive baptism, and the first person to be baptized at the mission. As a child he had been sold into slavery in Sierra Leone and later managed to escape, learned English in Freetown, and became the first interpreter for the Holy Cross Fathers.

By the summer of 1924 all the essential elements of the Holy Cross Mission had been established at Bolahun. Church, monastery, clinic and school were all running well. In two short years an incredible amount had been accomplished, largely through the will and faith of Frs. Hawkins, Campbell and Allen. Mr. Manley and Fr. Stretch, the first of a long line of dozens of secular helpers, had arrived and begun working. And the regular rotation of Holy Cross monks began. From 1924 the story of Bolahun becomes one of the regular extension of the ministry of the Gospel in wider and wider circles, through medicine and education as well as preaching, and before long Bolahun became what in fact it was to have been: the Christian center for the nations of that place.

One year later, in the summer of 1925, Fr. Campbell was called back to the United States and was appointed Prior of St. Andrew's School, where he had taught before joining the Order. Bishop Overs had grown gradually weaker from illness, and tendered his resignation as Bishop of Liberia in time for the House of Bishops at General Convention that fall to elect his successor. Meeting at New Orleans from Oct. 7-24, the bishops looked about for an able priest who could withstand the constant danger to health that the Liberian climate provided. Fr. Campbell had already survived three years in Liberia's hinterland with no noticeable ill effects, and had proved himself capable in his work to establish the Holy Cross Mission. The House of Bishops elected, and the House of Deputies confirmed, him as the sixth Bishop of Liberia in their New Orleans session.

It was an unprecedented act. Never before had the Episcopal Church elected a monk to the episcopate. Bp. Campbell was consecrated on St. Andrew's Day, Nov. 20, 1925, at the Cathedral of St. John the Divine in New York City. The Presiding Bishop, Ethelbert Talbot, was assisted by the retiring Bp. Overs and Bp. Gailor of Tennessee, who also preached. Five other bishops were in attendance. Bishop Campbell, who perhaps thought his role in Liberia was to be confined to the beginnings of the mission at Bolahun, now found himself in charge of the whole Church in Liberia.

In the 1920s a new movement arose to disseminate the Anglo-Catholic message: the Catholic Congresses. The greatest of these without doubt was the London Congress of July, 1923, attended by almost 16,000, and the occasion of many stirring speeches, among them the memorable cry of Frank Weston, Bishop of Zanzibar:[20]

You have your Mass, you have your altars, you have begun to get your tabernacles. Now go out into the highways and hedges and look for Jesus in the ragged and the naked, in the oppressed and the sweated, in those who are struggling to make good. Look for Jesus in them; and when you have found Him, gird yourself with His towel of fellowship and wash His feet in the person of His Brethren.

This Congress gathered together what was probably the greatest collection of Anglo-Catholic churchmen and scholars in the history of the Anglo-Catholic movement. Papers were read by P. N. Waggett, S.S.J.E.; Charles Gore; K. E. Kirk; J. K. Mozley; W. H. Frere, C.R.; G. A. Studdert-Kennedy; and Francis J. Hall, among many others. The general topic of the Congress was "The Gospel of God," and it is a measure of the respect in which Fr. Huntington was held that he was invited to give the second address of the Congress, on Sin, sandwiched between Fr. Waggett on Creation and Bishop Gore on the God of the Prophets.[21]

Fr. Hughson became very active in the Catholic Congress movement in the United States, and ultimately an officer of its continuing body. The first American Catholic Congress was held in Philadelphia in 1924, with as many Holy Cross men present as could attend. The following year it was held in New Haven, in 1926 in Milwaukee. As time went on, the Congresses became less frequent, and ultimately the organization responsible for them dissolved to reform itself as the American Church Union in 1936. The Order, through the enthusiastic participation of Fr. Hughson, always held an honored place in the Union until the days of liturgical and monastic reform and experiment in the 1960s.

Fr. Hughson's ideals were clearly enunciated in his statements to the Congresses. In 1925 at New Haven he stated the uncompromising catholicity of the Anglican ministry:[22]

This Church, true to the Catholic trust reposed in her, regards . . . a Protestant minister as a layman pure and simple. There is only one valid Christian ministry, and that is the Catholic ministry of the Apostolical Succession which this Church enjoys, and which the Protestant does not have, and, generally speaking, does not want, and declines to receive. This Episcopal Church, and every officer of it, be he High, Low, or Broad, refuses peremptorily even to consider any ministers serving at her altars except those who have this Catholic and Apostolic succession.

And at the Third Anglo-Catholic Congress in London in 1927, in an address on the practical implications of the doctrine of the Holy Eucharist (which was the topic of the entire Congress), he made this extreme statement of devotion to the Lord in the eucharistic elements:[23]

Wherever God is, there he is to be adored. God dwells in the Blessed Sacrament, therefore in that sacrament he is to be worshipped. And this worship is no modified thing, to be hedged about with cautions and inhibitions. Do we expect to fall down in utter adoration before the Eternal Trinity if by God's grace we come to that blessed place? Then let us learn now the worship of the heavenly courts, for the identical adoration which is given him in heaven by the saints and angels is to be given him wherever he dwells on his earthly altar. No essential difference can be made between God in the Eucharist and God who dwells on high and uplifted on the throne of heaven.

Fr. Hughson's passion for the restoration of Catholic doctrine, worship and practice in the Anglican Church was fully as strong as Fr. Huntington's for social justice flowing from the love of the Gospel. It would be a mistake to oppose the two great men, as though Fr. Hughson had no social conscience or Fr. Huntington was no High Churchman. Hughson's was the social conscience of a southern conservative, more responsive to individuals than to the implications of systems. And wonderfully responsive he was, as hundreds of spiritual directees would testify. Huntington's churchmanship was that of the convinced Catholic Christian, for whom Bishop Weston's cry was truth itself: the Church propels its members to serve Christ in his people. Where Hughson would find God in the eucharistic elements, and fall down in adoration before them, Huntington would locate the holy in the creation so loved by its Creator. At times exasperated by each other, nevertheless these two powerful and charismatic personalities personified the two great traditions of the Anglo-Catholic movement in the Order of the Holy Cross. The Order's own character was not complete until it had been marked by its second great personality, Shirley Carter Hughson.

During all the other activity of the 1920s the life at West Park continued, and St. Andrew's and Kent grew. The priests of the Order were constantly in demand as preachers, and as often as not West Park appeared to be populated by novices, guests and helpers, everyone but the monks.

A newsletter written by Fr. Huntington in November, 1922, conveys a sense of the busy community and an incident from Fr. Huntington's youth:[24]

October brought us a succession of almost perfect autumn days. I wish that more of us could have been here to enjoy it but there have been a good many absences. Fr. Hughson gave a mission in Carthage, N.Y., and he and Fr. Whittemore have just completed a very successful mission at St. John's Church, Newport, R.I. Earlier in the month, Fr. Whittemore gave a mission at the Onondaga Reservation near Syracuse. He found the Indians extremely responsive and interesting. When my father went to Syracuse, Captain George was at the head of the Reservation, a stately Indian six feet six inches tall. He told my father of carrying a message in his youth a hundred and twenty-five miles in one day. My father asked him what he did the next day, and, with an Indian Umph he answered, "Ran back again." Fr. Harrison was in Buffalo for a week. He had Br. Sidney with him. They gave a mission at St. Andrew's Church for Fr. Harrison Rockwell. Fr. Anderson has been in Geneva, N.Y. and I think that his mission has gone well. I heard from Bp. Brent shortly after it started. I went to St. Paul's Church, Flatbush, for a mission to children for Fr. Wallace Gardner. I liked the looks of things there very much. I had between eighty and one hundred children every afternoon. Last Saturday, at Letchworth Village, I presented eighty children for Confirmation. Bp. Shipman confirmed them and was as nice as possible and really interested, I think. He gave each child his or her name immediately after the words, "This thy child." Mrs. E.H. Harriman came over to the service and William Rhinelander Stewart, the president of the State Board of Charities, came.

A 20-year-old visitor in May, 1922, was charmed by what he found at West Park:[25]

Dear Father,

Where do you think your son and heir is writing this from?—a monastery. Seeing as I had no girl for the dance and as I wanted to look this place over before I finished the year, I decided to spend Sunday down here at Holy Cross, a few miles below the college [St. Stephen's, later Bard].

How different this is from what the world conceives a monastery to be! The buildings are of brick and look like two or three college dormitories. As I came down the road I saw a few black-gowned fellows digging and throwing up earth lustily all the while shouting to each other in exquisite slang. They are the new men or "novices" and seem about as religious as the Beach combers. There are about twenty of these young men who are training to become regular monks. There is only one monk on the place. The rest have all gone off preaching. After I rang the door bell, a fellow ran down, showed me into a waiting room, then into a "cell" and invited me to play basketball with them.

So charmed was he in fact that Joseph Harold Bessom eventually joined the community, becoming one of the Order's greatest missionaries in Africa.

The large novitiate produced a strong crop of new members for the Order. Fr. Herbert Hawkins, who was sent to Liberia even before he was life professed, took his final vows on Holy Cross Day, Sept. 14, 1923. An Englishman with a background as an accountant, he received his B.A. from Columbia and his theological training at the Kansas Diocesan School of Theology. He held various cures in Kansas before he joined the novitiate in 1920. Even as a young man he was firm and uncompromising in his theological positions and in his personal habits as well. After helping to establish the Bolahun Mission, Hawkins returned home in 1923, and again in 1926, with a severe case of blackwater fever. He left the Order in 1932, and returned in 1945 after marriage and a clerical career.

The same year John Sears Baldwin was life professed, on St. Thomas Day, Dec. 21, 1923. Son of Professor Charles Sears Baldwin of Columbia, he was one of only two members of the Order trained at Kent (the other being Fr. Packard). He was graduated from Columbia in 1916 and studied for the ministry privately. Fr. Baldwin was a tireless missioner with a lifelong interest in ministry both to children and to the armed forces.

Charles William Webb, Jr., was from Anderson, SC, and had attended Clemson and the University of the South. Made a deacon in 1925, life professed August 4, 1925, he attended Nashotah House and was priested in 1929. He was not an exceptionally gifted man, except in singing. Fr. Whittemore's description of him indicates how Webb's easygoing personality grated on Whittemore's Puritan soul, and is a good example of the small interpersonal tensions which often loom large in the monastic world:[26]

I have said that his work in choir was his most conspicuous contribution to our life, but it was not the deepest. The deepest was his careful keeping of the Rule, combined with leisureliness in regard to other things. There is, I am sure, a wonderful atmosphere of peace at Holy Cross. But one reason why it is so solid and real is that it is bought at a price. In other words, most of us get through the work of at least two men. It is there before us and has to be done and we are conscious from morning to night of a sense of pressure. It is the unremitting effort to be recollected and calm in the midst of so much activity, and, especially, to throw oneself heart and soul into the Chapel worship when one's mind is beset with distractions, that produces the impression of a deep and genuine tranquillity. Father Webb's lack of tension came easier for the simple reason that he, unlike the rest of us, was without big burdens.

Some of the brethren thought he was lazy. Perhaps he was, but he was always ready to do the jobs which were given him. If they were not numerous, it was due to his lack of ability. He was never in demand as a preacher and, despite good intentions, he did things in a heedless way resulting in snarls which had to be disentangled by someone else. His typing was inexpert and his handwriting so immature that he could not be used much even for copying.

Consequently, outside his periods for meditation, spiritual reading, etc., he found ample time to read magazines and to wander around the place with an old and rather noxious pipe in his mouth. He did not seem unhappy or at a loss for something to do. And it was strange that a person who loved the piano so much was quite content when no piano was available.

This fascinating passage not only describes Fr. Webb, but gives a vivid entrance into Fr. Whittemore's own inner life as well: busy, pressured, intense, constantly calling himself back with effort to the work of prayer, seemingly tranquil but seething underneath, heedful of duty, competent in many things, overworked and envious of someone so obviously at ease with himself. No better portrait of the brilliant and utterly self-controlled Whittemore exists.

On August 4, 1926, the second layman to be life professed in the Order took his vows. Sidney Taylor, known as Br. Dominic, was 42 years old. A native of New York City, he had attended public schools there. As different as he could be from the first layman in the Order, Br. Abishai, Dominic was a secure, deeply pious, humorous and holy man. Much of his long life in the Order was spent at St. Andrew's. Fr. Turkington remembers their annual train trip back to West Park for Chapter. It was the custom to walk from the station to the monastery, and as they started down the steep hill to the monastery, Br. Dominic would solemnly intone, "I went down into the garden of nuts to see the fruits of the valley" (Song of Solomon 6:11, KJV). His commitment to the community was so deep that he would joke about its idiosyncrasies.

William Edward Harris, known as Brother Edward until his ordination as a priest in 1945, was born and educated in Blackheath, England. Thirty-two years old, he was life professed on Holy Cross Day, Sept. 14, 1928, and served several tours in Bolahun as well as teaching Latin at St. Andrew's. He wrote a light hearted account of his experiences in Africa called *Plenty How-Do from Africa*.

Fr. Francis William George Parker, known affectionately as Fanny, was born in Boston, received his college education at Racine College and attended Nashotah House. Before he entered the Order he was Vicar of

St. John's Church, Shawano, WI. Forty years old at the time of his Life Profession on Nov. 1, 1929, he spent much of his ministry at St. Andrew's School.

For forty-four years after Fr. Huntington's profession in 1884 not one member of the Order had died. The men who joined in those days were young; most were in their thirties when they made their life vows. Fr. Huntington was 30; the oldest were Fr. Mayo and Br. Dominic, both 42. Even so, forty-four years is a long time without the intervention of death, even in a young man's community like Holy Cross in its early days.

When death first arrived, it was unexpected. Fr. Orum, one of the youngest members of the community, professed at 24, died suddenly on Nov. 30, 1928. He was only 36. But before he died, the devotee of King Charles had his day of triumph. Fr. Whittemore recalled:[27]

> The red-letter day of Fr. Orum's life was on the occasion of the great procession held at St. Andrew's one year on the Feast of St. Charles, a procession which caused reverberations not only in the Church papers but in the national, secular periodicals as well. Photographs were produced of the elaborate procession with the Bishop of Tennessee in attendance and one of the fathers splendidly vested and carrying a relic of St. Charles on a cushion. Where this relic came from, originally, I have no idea. It was, of all things, a hair from King Charles's beard! When the uproar broke out and the whole country, one might say, focussed its outraged attention on St. Andrew's, I remember exclaiming, "If it had only been anything else—a piece of the backbone, for instance, instead of a hair from the beard!" So Father Orum's triumph was short-lived. But the child of St. Charles had had his day of complete exaltation.

The following year two members died. Fr. Lorey, 69, died on July 11, 1929. His life had spanned two Anglican communities. He had been faithful to the end of the community life of the Order of the Brothers of Nazareth, and had found his vocation as a priest in Holy Cross. Devoted completely to the boys at St. Andrew's, and a hearty, simple soul, he left a strong legacy of love and simplicity.

The death of Fr. Allen on March 26, 1929, really marked the end of the early era of Holy Cross. He was the only member of the community who was with Fr. Huntington in the community from before 1884. Superior twice, from 1888-94 and 1907-15, he did not seem outwardly possessed of many gifts; but in his own way he was as important to the foundation of the Order as Fr. Huntington.

His determination to end his life as a missionary was fulfilled. While every other member of the Order assigned to Bolahun came and went in the 1920s, Fr. Allen remained. He was the most stable member of the Order at the mission in those years, and it is largely on his devotion that its credibility with the local people grew. When his small knowledge of tropical medicine was superseded, he looked for other fields. Fr. Whittemore remembered his work to establish a branch of the mission at Porruma:[28]

A visit to Fr. Allen at Porruma was worth the long trek there and back. To begin with, though the village itself is squalid, it is located in quite a pretty place dominated by a gigantic and most picturesque cottonwood tree. Spread out from this tree was a small area cleared from brush and covered with grass for the cattle. Such a sight is unusual in our part of Africa. The irregular field looked almost like a Maine meadow and was very lovely, especially when it was lit by the long, colored rays of the sunset.

It was at the edge of this field and almost under the wide-spreading branches of the tree that the small mission-house was constructed of rectangular mud sides and a thatched roof. Here Father Allen prayed and studied and ate and slept but was quite willing to be interrupted a hundred times a day; as indeed he was, ordinarily. First, a man would come with a cut hand to be treated with iodine. Then Kandekai, the Paramount Chief, would drop in from his near-by hut, to pass the time of day, and, incidentally, to share Father Allen's coffee. After the great man's departure, a trio of little boys would slide in through the door and watch the white man's strange ways with unflagging attention. Perhaps an old woman would be next on the list, with a present of bananas.

Fr. Allen became ill late in 1928 and was brought back to Bolahun. He spent several months growing weaker and weaker, but never losing his self-deprecating humor and humility. Fr. Whittemore was present throughout:[29]

He was a tough old boy and we had several false alarms before his death. One evening, as the doctor left the sick-bed, he told Father Gorham and me that it was unlikely that the Father would live through the night. But, lo and behold, the next morning he sat on the edge of his bed devouring an enormous helping of porridge. (He always had a very healthy appetite and was wise enough to deprecate excessive fasting for himself or others. When Father Gorham and I wanted to reduce our food to native standards, Father Allen finally convinced us that such a procedure would be reckless and wrong for Americans living in the tropics.)

The afternoon before he died, I asked if he would like me to read aloud to him. "Yes," he said. I asked what book, expecting to be assigned Taylor's *Holy Dying* or some such literature. Instead, he asked for *Rip Van Winkle*. And how he chuckled whenever Rip got a lambasting from his wife!

In the early hours of March 26th, 1929, Father Allen died.[30]

He had said all along that he did not want us to use a coffin, but to bury him in a mat, native-fashion, so as (he himself said) "to help the daisies grow." We took him at his word and carried his little body to its grave beside the old St. Mary's at Bolahun, where it lies among the bodies of his African friends.

Fr. Allen's death received much publicity. Fr. Huntington was preaching at the Church of the Transfiguration, the Little Church Around the Corner, in New York City, when he was informed of Fr. Allen's death. He announced the death dramatically from the pulpit, and a reporter who happened to be in the congregation wrote the story, which appeared on the front page of *The New York Times*. And in a long letter to the Kent School *News,* Fr. Whittemore told in enormous detail about Allen's death.

Fr. Allen was far more than a dear, devoted little old man. A man who could in humility direct the charismatic Fr. Huntington for years on end and retain his trust; a man who at 70 would take up Italian to read Dante in the original; a man who at the same time of his life would spend endless hours on his knees rubbing the floor bricks in the new chapel to give them the proper patina of age; a man who then would set out to penetrate Africa's unmapped forests. Such a man could be a saint.

There is a story of one of the early Egyptian Desert Fathers:[31]

Abba Joseph came to Abba Lot and said to him: "Father, according to my strength I keep a moderate rule of prayer and fasting, quiet and meditation, and as far as I can I control my imagination; what more must I do?" And the old man rose and held up his hands to the sky so that his fingers became like flames of fire and he said: "If you will, you shall become all flame."

Fr. Allen was like Abba Lot. He was not communicative of his experiences, but he lived a deeply contemplative life, hidden in Christ. Fr. Whittemore was privileged to witness him in prayer, and his account confirms the holiness and ecstatic union of Fr. Allen's saintly life:[32]

> It was on the occasion of a visit to Porruma that I opened the door of the little mission-house before the Father knew of my arrival. As I stepped into the main room, I saw Father Allen kneeling on the floor of his own little cell. He was perfectly motionless, with hands slightly raised before him and a few inches apart. His lips were parted and the head was tilted back as though he were gazing at some wonderful object above him; but whether his eyes were opened or closed I know not. I have never witnessed anything which gave so deep an impression of utter absorption in God.

7

The Old and The New (1930-1948)

✠ Shirley Carter Hughson was elected Superior at the Chapter of August 5, 1930. He was 63 years old, and in a way his election was a valedictory of an already immensely productive life. His *Warfare of the Soul,* and other books and tracts on the spiritual life, had made him an authority on prayer and spiritual direction throughout the Anglican Communion. His *Fundamentals of the Religious State* was a basic text in the theology of the Religious Life. He was a respected leader of the Anglo-Catholic party, and held an honored place in its counsels. His long ministry to the Community of St. Mary as Chaplain of one or another of their provinces from 1906 on (until 1943) and as their Chaplain General from 1908 until 1918 gave him immense influence over the largest women's community in the Episcopal Church. His time as Prior of St. Andrew's from 1906-14 gave him school experience, and his time as Novice Master of the Order from 1915-20 and then again in the mid-1920s had given him yet another opportunity for spiritual guidance. He was probably the most experienced spiritual director in the Episcopal Church, and at the height of his powers when he was elected Superior.

At the time of his election the Order of the Holy Cross had twenty active members, a figure which would remain more or less constant (at a low of sixteen and a high of twenty-five) until the spurt of growth in the mid-1960s. Fr. Tiedemann had been restored to the community in July, 1930, and two new men had been life professed earlier that year. Fr. Carl Marty was an older man, 43 at his Life Profession. He had been secretary to the Dean at Seabury-Western Theological Seminary and was a gifted musician. Fr. Russell Garvey Flagg, Br. John at the time of his Life Profession until his ordination in 1935, was 30 years old, from Florida. He had spent much of his time in annual vows in Bolahun. Neither Marty nor Flagg spent long in the Order. Marty was dispensed in 1936, and ultimately became a Roman Catholic priest in the Diocese of Scranton.

Flagg stayed until August of 1941. He was never happy in any house of the Order and finally decided he did not have a community vocation. He became a diocesan priest in Illinois and Indiana, finally settling in Texas.

In 1930 the Order was a solid, strong and established institution. Its two schools, St. Andrew's and Kent, were flourishing, with Kent in the heyday of Fr. Sill's remarkable headmastership. The mission at Bolahun was well established, with the new monastery built by Fr. Harvey Simmonds in the two preceding years finally open, the schools and clinic booming, and many native people beginning to respond to the Gospel. The large staff of secular helpers grew and an increasing number of Liberians were being trained for the work of evangelization. The Bishop of Liberia himself was a member of the Order, Bishop Campbell. And West Park was without question by 1930 the most important monastery of the Episcopal Church. Indeed, through Fr. Hughson's little book *An American Cloister,* Holy Cross Monastery was looked on as the premier expression of the monastic life, and *a fortiori* of Anglo-Catholicism, in the Episcopal Church. In fact, by 1930 the Order had an almost unbroken and remarkable record of success in its works, having sustained only a single failure, Ripon in 1925.

The same Chapter which elected Fr. Hughson Superior conferred on Fr. Huntington the official title "Father Founder." He was known from that time on by his title. But he was not pleased by it. To him it seemed inappropriate, since in his understanding of the Order's history, Fr. Robert Dod was in fact the founder, and Huntington his follower. He made this clear in an article he published in 1933 called "Beginnings of the Religious Life for Men in the American Church." Fr. Huntington at the end of his own career remembered his first leader in the Order thus:[1]

> Fr. Dod was the leader in the enterprise. . . . He was still young, a striking figure, tall, handsome, an excellent Latin and Greek scholar, an exceptionally able preacher, a good sportsman, and a man of deep devotion and piety. But the intensity of his experience in many directions had tended to burn up his physical strength and already he was suffering from an asthmatic affliction which was to blight the brilliant promise of his youth.

Huntington was the founder only in the sense that Fr. Dod's health prevented him from continuing. Fr. Huntington did not want the Order to forget its real beginnings in the bestowal of an almost hagiographic honor upon himself.

Fr. Parsell remembered Fr. Huntington's reaction to Hughson's elevation of him to Father Founder:[2] "Fr. Huntington didn't accept that very easily because he never thought of himself as the Founder. . . .

> Fr. Huntington's greatness was that he was not a typical Fr. Founder. He wasn't trying to expound his own ideas. . . . He took other people's ideas and made something special out of them. . . . The Order is his memorial. . . . Fr. Huntington was a man of ideas, always thinking of new ways to do things, but his basic idea of consecrating himself to the service of our Lord is left to us here in the Order.

Huntington was humble, as many monastic founders were not.

Fr. Hughson's conservatism asserted itself quickly in the Order's work and life. No new work was established during his tenure as Superior, even though there is at least one recorded invitation to do so, from the Bishop of Northern Indiana, Campbell Gray, in 1930, and doubtless others in the ensuing six years. The Chapter in 1927 had decided to put the brakes on continual changes in the Rule and Constitution, and had established that no change could be instituted unless it was passed at an annual meeting of Chapter and confirmed at a subsequent meeting by a two-thirds vote, but that subsequent meeting could occur only in 1933 and every sixth year afterwards. In other words, no change could be made in the basic formularies of the Order except in 1927, 1933 and 1939. This would not have been a problem, except that the Rule incorporated even the minutest details of daily life along with the general principles and ideals of the community. There was thus no way of dealing with day-to-day matters and desirable changes in structure as they emerged from year to year. As Fr. Hughson's term wore on, it became more and more evident that this was unsatisfactory, and gradually half the community coalesced around a desire for more rapid change.

Fr. Hughson's term as Superior from 1930-36 was a quietly productive time for the Order and for him. During these years he published two more major books, *The Approach to God* (1932), and *Contemplative Prayer* (1935) as well as several smaller works, establishing himself even more firmly as one of the major Anglican spiritual writers. But his term also saw the building-up of a serious division in the community, brought on by his almost stifling conservatism.

The first sign of this division occurred just one year after Fr. Hughson's election. There were some novices in the novitiate when Hughson became Superior, but shortly after his installation the Order was horrified to discover that for virtually the first time in thirty years it had no one joining. The Chapter of 1931 passed an extraordinary resolution, testimony to its respect for Fr. Hughson's power and authority (it did not direct a new policy, as it could have), but also to the deep alarm felt in the community:[3]

> Whereas at the present time there are no novices in the Community; and Whereas it has been stated that several aspirants have been turned away because of a change of policy as to qualifications of aspirants; therefore be it Resolved that the Chapter humbly requests the Fr. Superior to restate what qualifications are to be looked for in considering possible aspirants, whether laymen or men in Holy Orders.

The debate over laymen vs. ordained members of the community had raged almost since its foundation. The Order of the Brothers of Nazareth had been founded to accommodate laymen in association with the Order of the Holy Cross, then thought of as a community of priests. In fact the first life professed lay member of the Order was the unstable Br. Abishai. Fr. Lorey had had himself ordained specifically that he might join the community. In fact, before Fr. Hughson's term as Superior came to an end, Brothers Francis, John (Baldwin), Charles, and John (Flagg) would all have been ordained priests, leaving only Brothers Dominic and Edward as lay members of the community. A number of men who did not persevere were also sent off to seminary or to private study.

If the policy in the 1920s was (with some notable exceptions) to expect ordination as the normal course for laymen joining the community, Fr. Hughson evidently tightened it to admit only those already ordained or clearly on their way. The community's explosion of concern on this issue seems to have reached Fr. Hughson, because of the seven novices clothed during his time as Superior, two were not in Orders. Still, seven novices in six years is a very small number, and perhaps evidence that Fr. Hughson did not greatly modify his severity.

This issue continued to be of concern to the Order to such an extent that Fr. Huntington, in a statement made as he lay dying in 1935, made a direct reference to it. Regarding the larger purpose of the Order, he said,[4]

> This [the admission of laymen] seems to me—I am speaking now as an individual yet as one who has known the Community from its very inception—thoroughly consonant with the ideal which I have tried to set forth. Our first efforts to incorporate in the Community those who were not in Holy Orders were unsuccessful, but failures are sometimes illuminative. As time has gone on the Community has found place for those not yet in Holy Orders. In doing this it has shown that there are principles quite capable of being grasped and

illustrated by those who are not priests. These principles are those characteristic of the Religious State. They serve to mark the Community as not limited to the Second Order of the Sacred Ministry, they are illustrative of elasticity and yet of stability, of "freedom in the bonds of law." I believe that it would be a distinct loss to the Community if it were limited to those in the sacerdotal office.

While the community seems to have listened to Fr. Huntington on this issue, impediments remained to full lay participation in the Order's life until much later, and in fact, until 1960, only four of the forty-three men life professed remained laymen.

Fr. Hughson made some attempts to assure the continuation of his ideals. He was, of course, very much in touch with his fellow-conservative Bishop Campbell in Liberia. He also brought forward several younger men as possible future leaders. The first of these was Fr. Baldwin, 34 years old in 1930, a priest since 1923. Fr. Hughson made Fr. Baldwin simultaneously Assistant Superior and Novice Master in 1930, a dramatic push forward for Fr. Baldwin. Though a great missioner and tireless preacher, Fr. Baldwin was so indecisive that he would hide in the legalities of the Rule and Constitution rather than decide anything. Nevertheless in 1930 he seemed the young hope of the Order. In 1932 he was sent to Bolahun to act as Prior, replacing Fr. Gorham. In his place Fr. Hughson appointed Fr. Whitall Assistant Superior and Fr. Tiedemann Novice Master, installing two more conservatives in positions of influence. In 1935 Bishop Campbell developed heart trouble which, coupled with malaria and a generally run-down constitution, as well as with letters from some of the brethren urging him to make himself available to be elected Superior, caused him to resign. He returned to West Park and Fr. Hughson appointed him Assistant Superior in January, 1936, positioning him to succeed in the election of 1936.

As there were few novices in the Order under Fr. Hughson, there were few Life Professions. Of the seven novices clothed during his tenure, four went on to Life Profession after the term expired. But only two men made their Life Profession during this term. Both had served their novitiate under Fr. Huntington.

Fr. Leopold Kroll was a child of a missionary priest who ultimately succeeded Bp. Campbell as Bishop of Liberia. Born in Wisconsin and reared in New York and Hawaii, he attended St. Stephen's (later Bard) College, graduating in 1924, and General Seminary. Professed on Christmas Eve, 1930, he later spent much of his ministry in Bolahun. Fr.

Kroll was a strong administrator, bringing from his father's Prussian ancestry a decisiveness which would be seen in his time as Superior.

Joseph Gibson Parsell was from Altoona PA and was at 21 a student at St. Stephen's College. He was graduated from St. Stephen's in 1926 and read privately for Orders, having an excellent education in classics. He was ordained Deacon in May, 1931, took his life vows on Epiphany Day, 1932, and was made priest in May, 1932. During his earlier years in the Order he acted as secretary to Fr. Huntington and ran the *Holy Cross Magazine*. But soon after his Life Profession he was sent out to Bolahun, and spent more than forty years there, more than almost any other white missionary in Liberia, earning, not entirely in jest, his sobriquet "Father Africa" among his friends and brethren. A brilliant, restless man, Parsell combined an extreme pro-Romanism with respect to liturgy and observance with a flexible and sensible devotion to the community. In practical affairs he was pragmatic and unorthodox, and more than once "Uncle Joe" finessed the community, in Liberia and elsewhere, out of difficult waters by his engaging and clever personality.

In 1932 two men asked to leave the Order. Fr. Anderson, who had come to grief with Fr. Hughson in 1919, finally decided to leave the community; after his dispensation in April, 1932, he entered a successful and respected career as a parish priest in Waterbury, CT. Fr. Hawkins decided to leave the Order about the same time, and on the same date as Fr. Anderson was released from his vows, marrying in June, 1932. He held cures in Geneva, NY, New Canaan, CT and White River Junction, VT before returning to the Order after the death of his wife in 1945. A third man decided to leave in 1936. Fr. Marty, increasingly drawn to the Roman obedience, was expelled in May, 1936.

All told, the Order maintained its strength at twenty from the beginning of Fr. Hughson's term to its end.

In the fall of 1930 a young writer named James Gould Cozzens published a series of stories about "Durham" School and its headmaster "Dr. Holt." The school is recognizably Kent and Holt is clearly Fr. Sill. Cozzens entered Kent in September, 1916, a lad of 13, and remained there until his graduation in June, 1922. Fr. Sill and Cozzens had a stormy relationship, and Sill remained a dominant presence to Cozzens for the rest of his life, as Sill no doubt did to many other Kent boys. He was not known as Pater for nothing. Cozzens' first publication was a defense of Kent in *The Atlantic Monthly* of March, 1920. Written in rebuttal to a condemnation of boarding schools in general, Cozzens defended Kent and Sill:[5]

He [Fr. Sill] has endowed American boyhood with a great gift—a gift not yet fully understood by present-day educators, but one which we who have benefitted from it must believe to be the coming school, the true, democratic American school.

Fr. Sill was never a democrat, however, and nobody understood this more clearly than James Gould Cozzens.

In the best of the "Dr. Holt" stories, "Someday You'll Be Sorry," Cozzens gives an accurate and penetrating description of Fr. Sill, even then on his way to being the most renowned headmaster in America:[6]

Doctor Holt was, in fact, a roaring schoolmaster, being a genius himself. His instinct instantly rejected much of the nonsense making up modern pedagogies. He had an inspired knowledge of when to be patient and when to be impatient. His genius was his uncanny gift for grasping what nine boys out of ten thought and felt and intended to do next. He turned hundreds of them out: healthy, honorable, quite intelligent enough to have no trouble with college entrance examinations. A thousand more—many of whom with their names entered when they were born—waited perpetually to get in. "Durham," "Doctor Holt" were great names among the Eastern preparatory schools.

Doctor Holt had a magnificent, solid, convex profile. The type is often small-boned, intellectual, but Doctor Holt's face was like something outstanding and lordly cut from a cliff. His blue eyes, keen, haughty and wise, waited, ready to leap. His tangled blond eyebrows —these were a sandy, strong blond, and similar hairs grew out of his massive nostrils—resembled somehow the illustrations in the fourth-form Caesar, showing a cross-section of the Gallic defenses— ditch, glacis, and a hedge of uprooted trees. Rather round-shouldered, he was not tall enough to have a hollow appearance. He was intensely solid; a considered, terrible energy. Also, he was slightly deaf. This seemed sometimes a stratagem, for whatever it was disastrous or inexpedient for him to hear, he heard. Involved explanations, trembling evasions and artless falsehoods he could not hear. He roared for their repetition—a task beyond many a guilty conscience.

Cozzens' biographer, Matthew Bruccoli, records that Fr. Sill "recognized himself as Dr. Holt and was pleased by the Durham stories."[7] Cozzens continued to be helpful to the school, writing a tribute called "Kent: A New School" in 1933,[8] and a fond reminiscence of Fr. Sill in 1956 after Sill's death.[9]

Fr. Sill was not the only member of the Order who found a place in Cozzens' fiction. In 1936 he published *Men and Brethren,* an ecclesiastical novel set in New York. One of the characters was inspired in part by Fr. Harvey Officer. The novel fictionalizes some of his trauma, and although the character is not a direct portrait, its origins in Fr. Officer were widely recognized in reviews at the time.[10]

Cozzens' tributes to Fr. Sill and Kent only underscore a great truth, that Sill was a great, if eccentric, headmaster. Kent was Sill and Sill was Kent to a very large degree, for thirty-four years. Many distinguished men graduated from Kent, marked by Pater's powerful personality, among them congressmen, prominent men of business, academe and the Church, and a Secretary of State, Cyrus Vance.

Another literary glimpse of Holy Cross work and life in the 1930s is provided by the novelist Graham Greene in his 1936 travel book, *Journey Without Maps.* It is the record of a trip to Liberia in the mid-1930s. His first stop in Liberia was Bolahun, as he entered the country the same way as the Holy Cross Fathers: steamer to Freetown, rail to Pendembu, both in Sierra Leone, and then cross country to the border and to Bolahun.

Greene was not impressed with Sierra Leone or with Liberia, and freely expressed his disapproval of Liberian officials and the (to his mind) unnecessarily primitive conditions of the Republic of Liberia. His dissatisfaction provides an interesting contrast to the fulsome praise of the same regime eight years earlier by Fr. Hughson in his 1928 account of the Liberian mission, *The Green Wall of Mystery.* But Greene respected the work of the Holy Cross Fathers, and recorded his judgment:[11]

It was a two-mile walk up to the mission through the village of Bolahun, through the deep barking of the frogs. The mission belonged to the Order of the Holy Cross, a monastic order of the American Episcopal Church. I dumped my loads outside the long bungalow and waited for the priests to come out from Benediction. I could hear the low murmur of Latin inside; in the darkness only the white eyeballs of my carriers were visible, where they squatted silently on the verandah; everyone was too tired to talk. But the sound of the Latin represented a better civilization than the tin shacks of the English port, better than anything I had seen in Sierra Leone; and when the priests came out and one led the way to the rest-house, his white robe stirring in the cold hill wind, I was for the first time unashamed by the comparison between white and black. There was something in this corner of a republic said to be a byword for corruption and slavery that at least wasn't commercial. One couldn't put it higher than this:

that the little group of priests and nuns had a standard of gentleness and honesty equal to the native standard. Whether what they brought with them in the shape of a crucified God was superior to the local fetish worship had to be the subject of future speculation.

Greene was especially impressed by the utter lack of advantage to the missionaries at Bolahun. This was no capital city, there was no trade to exploit, the people and the situation were as remote and as hostile as could possibly be imagined. It was Christianity powerless, save in the power of its originally revolutionary message:[12]

> One had to remember that background to Benediction in the ugly tin-roofed church. The raised monstrance was not a powerful political symbol: "Come to me all ye who are heavy laden and I will give you commercial privileges and will whisper for you in the ear of a Minister of State." It offered, like early Christianity, stripes from the man in power and one knows not what secret opposition from the priests of the fetish. There were not many at Benediction: Christianity here was still the revolutionary force, appealing to the young rather than the old, and the young were on holiday. A tiny picaninny wearing nothing but a short transparent shirt scratched and prayed, lifting his shirt above his shoulders to scratch his loins better; a one-armed boy knelt below a hideous varnished picture. (He had fallen from a palm-tree gathering nuts, had broken his arm, and feeling its limp uselessness had taken a knife and cut it off at the elbow.)

What Graham Greene saw at Bolahun was the real Bolahun, often obscured by its best friends, even by Holy Cross Fathers themselves in their eagerness to present the best to the world. What Greene saw was the confrontation of primitive Christianity, in its Anglo-Catholic form, with a culture ready and waiting for its liberation. And the only force brought to that confrontation in Bolahun was love, love and what little energy and holy guile the Fathers could muster. Never was there enough money, especially in the Depression when the giving from America dropped first by half and then by two thirds. Never were there enough people on the staff, even with the constant stream of secular helpers and diocesan priests. There was always another mission station to open, another class to be taught, another clinic to run. Even with the addition of the Sisters of the English Community of the Holy Name, from Malvern Link, in April, 1931, there were not enough hands. Bolahun was always a work of faith and hope and creative ingenuity for the Gospel.

Another force was growing at Bolahun as well. The little community there in the early 1930s, Fr. Gorham (sent home with cancer in 1932), Fathers Whittemore, Kroll, Parsell, later Baldwin and others, had to depend on mutual observation and consensus to make the best decisions in an alien culture. Very early, even in the late 1920s, the brethren realized this. When Fr. Huntington sent Fr. Whittemore to Liberia in 1926 it had been his intention to make Whittemore Prior. But he wisely left the decision to the household. Fr. Allen, still alive, voted for Fr. Gorham, on the basis of character. Fr. Whittemore was wise, crafty, a little sly, intelligent, always ahead of whatever was going on. In fact, his nickname in Bandi was "Banangi" (Rascal). Gorham, on the other hand, was preternaturally kind, placid, trusting, and seen to be holy through and through. Allen's insight was to combine these characters through community consensus, and to let Fr. Whittemore's gifts express themselves through Fr. Gorham's guileless nature. It worked marvelously, and when Fr. Baldwin arrived in 1932, the habit of community consensus formed in the previous years was tailor-made to his cautious nature. The habit of community discussion and consensus may not have been alien to the Order in its origins, but real ongoing, day-to-day consensus had its baptism and confirmation in Africa. This new force, so unlike the conservative autocracy of Fr. Hughson, made itself known back home, and formed the nucleus of the new era elected in the person of Fr. Whittemore in 1936.

Back in the United States, Fr. Huntington continued vigorous and active through most of Fr. Hughson's term as Superior, even though he was 76 in 1930. He continued preaching and holding retreats, ministering to the retarded children at Letchworth Village, maintaining his voluminous correspondence. He stayed in touch with the radical movements in the Church, and in particular with Fr. F. Hastings Smyth, founder of the Society of the Christian Commonwealth, a Christian Socialist society. Smyth remembered in 1954 the still-youthful radicalism of Fr. Huntington in the 1930s, a testimony to Huntington's vigor and faith:[13]

Father Huntington interested himself greatly in the affairs of this nascent Society. He found here an element of social reference for which he had striven in his own youth, but which (as he told me) he discovered was not to be God's will within the Vocation of the Order he had founded. Just as I (then in Clinton, N.Y.) would sometimes become greatly discouraged in my earlier encounter with Church authorities and by the dark future which seemed sometimes to lie ahead for any such vocation as I envisaged, Father Huntington had a way of suddenly appearing on the doorstep.

Was Fr. Huntington disappointed in the Order he had founded? Vida Scudder, his biographer, thought so, and so did Fr. Smyth, apparently. Fr. Whittemore, as we have seen, testified to Huntington's exasperation with the conservative Hughson. Huntington may well have reflected on how far from his own ideals the Order had strayed in the fifty-odd years since that autumn in 1881 when he, Dod and Cameron came together for the first time. Perhaps his thoughts strayed to the Lord's words to Peter at the end of John's Gospel: "When thou wast young, thou girdest thyself, and walkedst whither thou wouldest: but when thou shalt be old, thou shalt stretch forth thy hands, and another shall gird thee, and carry thee whither thou wouldest not." (John 21:18, KJV)

But perhaps not. Huntington the radical was also Huntington the founder who immediately turned over responsibility to the next man professed in the Order, Fr. Allen in 1888. He was the man who thought only of the future, never of the past, and profoundly trusted the Spirit in community life. He was the man who had consistently attracted strong, young, bright and able men to his community, and had given them place and responsibility beyond their years and experience. He was the man who had chosen the path of holiness, for whom there was no contradiction between the Beatific Vision and effective political action, between the life of prayer and the life of service. "Love must act as light must shine and fire must burn" was key to his theology and to his life. His was a life of filial trust, to his father and family, to the Church, to the Order, and above all to God. He trusted God, gave his life to the Church, his energy to the Order, and his love to all who came to him, especially to his Brethren.

Fr. Tiedemann was present at his last illness.[14]

He entered St. Luke's Hospital for an operation [June 13, 1935, for an obstruction of the bowel]. At first all went well. Then towards the end of the first week after the operation he failed visibly. The nurses said he could not last through the night. The hospital had most generously given me a room next to him. I phoned Holy Cross that the Founder was dying.

It was at this time that I realized that he had not been born into the Catholic Faith, but that he had had to think his way into it in later years. I asked him, "Father, would you like to receive the Blessed Sacrament tonight?" "Oh yes," he replied. "And Father, would you like to be anointed?" This seemed to puzzle him for a moment. Then he said vigorously, "Yes, yes. Oh, yes."

So he received the last sacraments and sank into unconsciousness.

At 11 p.m. he was able to drink some hot milk. I was sitting in the shadows near the door. As the nurse went out of the room, she whispered to me, "He's looking at you." I went to him with my best of bedside manners and said, "Can I do something for you, Father?"

"Yes," he said peremptorily, "go to bed!"

Two hours before, we had thought he was dying! His first conscious words were to help someone else. That is obedience in action.

He died a week later. Two of us were present [Fr. Chalmers had joined Fr. Tiedemann]. We stood for his passing which took about two hours. "He's praying," the nurse said. Toward the end, Father Schlueter came in. You know his words to Father Schlueter. "I want everyone to know that I care, that I shall always care. That I love them and always will love them. That I am lifting up hands in prayer for them, and will always intercede for them."

His last words said very deliberately sum up his whole life. "I-want-them-all-to-have-joy."

Fr. Schlueter's version of Fr. Huntington's last words is somewhat different:[15]

I knelt at his bedside as he prayed a long prayer of blessing, not just a mere formal blessing. When I felt I could hold no more, I rose to go; and as I went to go, he held out his hand; and I took it. And he said, "Edward, tell them I forgive everyone." Then he added with intense feeling, "Tell them I want to be forgiven." And that he repeated three times; and then very solemnly he said, after a pause: "Tell them I love them; tell them I am praying for them, and I shall always pray for them." And then, dropping my hand and lifting up both his hands as a priest does at the altar, he added: "I am lifting up hands of intercession for them; I shall always intercede for them."

That, I think, was the end of his intercession. That he himself, and all of us, might be forgiven. In fact, I think his passion to understand people came out of this deeper passion, a passion for their forgiveness. With him it was always forgiveness. It was all *Given*. Given of God, freely.

And so, on June 19, 1935, James Otis Sargent Huntington died.

The jubilee of his Life Profession on November 25, 1934, had been celebrated with joy all over the American Church, with hundreds of telegrams and letters to him expressing joy at his fifty years of dedication, his many accomplishments, the countless acts of love and consideration he had performed, his almost single-handed establishment of the Religious

Life for men as a normal part of the Episcopal Church. Now, seven months later, the Church prepared for an outpouring of grief and celebration rarely seen for its leaders.

Fr. Hughson was in Africa, so Fr. Whitall, the Assistant Superior, took charge of the arrangements. The body was brought to the Cathedral of St. John the Divine where it lay in state in St. James Chapel. The watch was shared by the Sisters of St. Margaret, St. Mary and St. John the Baptist. Hundreds of priests gathered as the word spread, and many offered private masses for his soul. Most of the Religious in the American Church gathered, and finally, on July 12, the funeral was held. The Presiding Bishop of the Episcopal Church, James DeWolf Perry, presided. The Brethren were pallbearers and bore his coffin into the Cathedral. Bishop Perry was assisted at the requiem eucharist by Fr. Whitall and Fr. Spence Burton, the Superior of the American Cowley Fathers. There were no hymns, but the organist played "I Know That My Redeemer Liveth" from Handel's *Messiah* and a glorious triumphal voluntary. After the service the body was taken to West Park and interred in the tomb behind the crypt altar, where it still remains, the primary relic of his saintly life.

There is a fine, final irony which would have delighted Fr. Huntington's dry New England humor. Shortly after his profession in 1884 the Presiding Bishop of the Church had denounced his action, seeing in it a reflection of sin, shame and suffering. Some fifty years later, the Presiding Bishop of the Church stood at the head of his casket pronouncing the blessing, and was reported to have said later that Fr. Huntington was "the best loved priest in the Episcopal Church."

Fr. Huntington was followed in death on January 27, 1936, by the mercurial, difficult, hearty and ultimately loyal Br. Abishai. He was 60 years old at his death. Fr. Whittemore's obituary of him serves as a reminder that faithfulness must always be renewed, and is a matter of final commitment, and not merely of consistency:[16]

He stuck to his vocation. There were interruptions and failures, but on each such occasion he repented and rose to renew the fight. He did not give up but won the fulfillment of His Master's promise, "He that endureth to the end shall be saved." And who can tell the struggle Abishai's vocation cost him?

And who can tell the rejoicing in heaven?

The election for Superior in 1936 was perhaps the most exciting, and in some ways the most important, in the entire history of the Order of the Holy Cross. In 1936 Fr. Hughson was 69 years old, and had no desire to be reelected. Bp. Campbell, 51 years old, whom Fr. Hughson had made Assistant Superior, had resigned as Bishop of Liberia and returned to the United States, at least partially in anticipation of being elected to head the Order. Whether Hughson's appointment of Campbell was a directly "political" move or not is not known. For most of its history Holy Cross has viewed its elections of Superiors as above politics in the ordinary sense, and to "run for Superior" was thought to be more than unseemly. Others managed one's campaign. Fr. Gorham managed Fr. Whittemore's.

Several issues had emerged during Fr. Hughson's conservative reign. They seem small now, but each was an indication of the desire of the community to evolve. The most burning, perhaps, was the question of whether or not clericals could be worn outside the monastery when traveling instead of the black traveling habit. Smoking was absolutely prohibited by the Rule except with explicit permission of the Superior, and yet many members did so secretly. There was a prohibition on theatre- and movie-going, particularly galling to New Yorkers who saw in the theatre not a seat of sin and vice but a necessary window on contemporary culture. And most restrictive of all was the six-year rule, which denied even the smallest change except in 1933, 1939, 1945 and every six years thereafter. To those for whom these were issues, and for whom these issues served to crystallize a more modern approach to monasticism than Fr. Hughson would allow, Fr. Whittemore was the leader. Several times Novice Master in the 1920s, he had been sent to Liberia in 1926 and had remained there ever since, was never made Prior, but was in many ways the effective leader of the Mission.

The election for Superior was held on August 4, 1936. It ran six ballots before a decision was made by a single vote for Fr. Whittemore. He was still in Africa, and Fr. Parsell remembered the arrival of the news in Bolahun:[17]

Fr. Kroll and I had figured out when we would get this telegram about the Chapter. The mail came in on Friday but we figured that the last day was Sunday. It took a day's walk and came from Kailahun, and there were two telegrams that came. . . . They came at tea time; it was this time in the afternoon. The first telegram that we got came to Fr. Whittemore from some of his friends congratulating him, so we knew before the official telegram came to Fr. Baldwin. Fr. Baldwin didn't come to tea that day, I don't know why, there was some delay. He was off doing something else. . . . So we went down and we had

Vespers and Benediction—always, it was a Sunday. . . . So we installed him immediately as Father Superior. Ah yah—that was wonderful!

Fr. Whittemore left Bolahun for America on August 23.

When he arrived in West Park, he immediately issued blanket dispensations allowing the use of clerical garb in travel, smoking, theatre, and other "modernizations," pending Chapter's action, which could not be final until 1939. The annual Chapter of 1938 passed four major pieces of legislation accomplishing many of these changes which were confirmed in 1939. The six-year requirement was eliminated. The distinction between lay and ordained members in the matter of prayer time was done away with; to that point laymen had been required to spend only half as much time in private prayer as priests. A new provision was accepted for dispensations, making it easier to provide leniency from the Rule. And the habit was changed, permitting those professed before 1920 to continue wearing the black habit while traveling, all others to wear clerical suits. Fr. Spencer recalled how the opposition to the change in habit dissolved:[18]

When the permission was given, however, only Frs. Hughson and Mayo remained traveling in habits, curiously enough. The rest all immediately shifted and Fr. Mayo himself offered to shift, but he didn't go out enough. It didn't seem worthwhile providing him with clericals and so he did continue, the few times he went out, to travel in habit.

Fr. Gorham's management of Whittemore's election was one of his last acts. Stricken in Africa with a stomach cancer, he had returned to the United States in 1932, and had been at Kent School ever since. He was Fr. Whittemore's dearest friend, and the usually dry-eyed Whittemore wrote this elegy about his death:[19]

I was not with him at St. Luke's Hospital when he died, but was conducting a retreat in Boston.

A day or two ahead, however, I recalled the agreement which he and I had made years before at Bolahun, that the first to get to heaven would pick out "a nice park bench" and be ready to greet the other with a chess-board and box of cigars. With the directness which characterized our dealings with one another, I wrote and reminded Jim of this. The letter arrived in time for Jimmy to chuckle over it on the morning of the day he died.

His last words were to his brother Edward—"Ed, I guess I can't make the grade"—and he fell asleep in Christ.

Jimmy was a chip off the old block as evidenced by the following story about his Mother, who was surely one of the bravest and holiest of women.

I did not see her after Jim's death until I reached New York in time to sing the Requiem at St. Mary's. The Church was packed and there, in the front row, sat his mother, who loved him with devoted ardor.

Before the service began I sat beside her for a moment to put my arm around her and kiss her. And what do you think she said, with her son's coffin resting before her eyes?

"You must visit us a lot. We have an extra room for you now."

Jimmy Gorham was only 45 when he died on January 8, 1937. He is buried at Kent.

Early 1937 saw two Life Professions. Fr. William Chalmers, 29, fresh from Princeton and General Seminary, was a teacher by inclination. He was born in Edinburgh, and spent much of his time in the Order at Kent School, where he ultimately became headmaster. Fr. William Turkington, 32, a Philadelphian, graduated from the University of Virginia and the Virginia Theological Seminary, with a Master's degree from General Seminary. He had briefly been a curate at St. Luke's Chapel, Hudson Street, in New York City, under its Vicar, Fr. Huntington's protege Fr. Edward Schlueter. A man of great personal sensitivity to others, he was a born listener, and would spend much of his ministry with young people.

Fr. Baldwin stayed on at Bolahun for a year while Fr. Whittemore gradually assembled his leadership team. Bp. Campbell continued as Assistant Superior and then in 1938 was sent to St. Andrew's School, where he was Prior until 1947. Fr. Whittemore himself at first took the task of Novice Master, with first Fr. Chalmers and then Fr. Baldwin as assistants. Fr. Tiedemann became Assistant Superior when Bp. Campbell went to St. Andrew's. With the departure of Fr. Baldwin from Africa in June, 1937, Fr. Kroll, an experienced Africa hand trusted by Fr. Whittemore was appointed Prior there, where he remained until 1941.

In 1938 Fr. Kroll decided it was time to build a proper new, large church at Bolahun. Fr. Whittemore agreed, and Frederick J. Woodbridge, a prominent New York architect (and Fr. Baldwin's brother-in-law) drew up the plans. It was to have as little wood as possible, to discourage termites and decay, and was designed with noble proportions: 122 feet by 45 feet, 35 feet high, one of the largest buildings of the time for hundreds of miles around. Fr. Whitall, who knew Liberia from his tour there in 1929-32, was sent back to supervise the building. Bp. Campbell recalled the trying circumstances of attempting to build such a structure in the Liberian bush at the beginning of World War II:[20]

> Sawyers had to cut out rafters, planks, and boards far out in the bush. Laborers had to tote cement, nails and the hollow iron pillars weighing 315 pounds each from Pendembu.
>
> Father Kroll had assembled as many of these essentials as he could before Father Whitall commenced the actual construction within a few weeks of arrival. Then World War II broke out, that tragedy affecting every known land. Priorities, scarcities, supply ships sunk at sea, threatened German invasion from Vichy-held French Guinea, soaring costs of materials—these formed a few of the hindrances to rapid completion of the work. Operations would halt sometimes for weeks on end for lack of materials. It would be an understatement if we should label this a most trying time.

Nevertheless, the building was substantially complete and ready for its first mass said by Fr. Parsell on Saturday, June 13, 1942.

Fr. Whitall was indefatigable in building St. Mary's, Bolahun:[21]

> On one occasion he had one of the iron pillars in place and bolted to the floor within five minutes after it arrived. On another, when the men were setting rafters the Father slipped and fell to the ground from a high scaffold. By some miracle he sustained no injury, but got up with an amused expression and proceeded to climb right back to that same scaffold. The wonder is that he was not killed by the 25 foot drop.

World War II brought many difficulties, but also opportunities of service and adventure. Fr. Baldwin became a chaplain to the U.S. Army from 1942 to 1946, and for the rest of his life proudly recalled his service, even to wearing khaki trousers whenever he could. Fr. Kroll and Fr. Parsell were torpedoed off the coast of Africa. Fr. Whittemore sent Fr. Kroll back to Africa in 1941 after a time of furlough. Fr. Parsell remembered:[22]

> He sent him by way of South Africa. It was the only way to get to West Africa in those days, and he went down the coast when the submarines were shooting at his ship. This was just after Pearl Harbor. He came to Port Elizabeth and then to Capetown and met me there and we came back together after a month together there in Capetown. We got a trip for Freetown, but we only made it about 150 miles off the coast of Liberia and got torpedoed. So together we were five days in a lifeboat and came to Cape Palmas.

Bishop Campbell's account is more circumstantial:[23]

> Right after dinner on Easter Eve, April 4, '42, their ship was torpedoed about 150 miles south of Cape Palmas and sank almost at once. Fortunately all the passengers by moving expeditiously climbed into the lifeboats and thus saved their lives, though losing all their luggage. After the steamer had sunk the submarine rose to the surface and inquired whether the boats had water and food sufficient to see them to land and then slid off in search of further prey. This was a strange Easter for all in those little boats, crew and passengers alike, being tossed about on the boundless sea.

They put to shore, only to discover that it was the Ivory Coast, in Vichy and German hands, and were advised to push on to Liberia unless they wanted to spend the duration of the war in a detention camp. They put back to sea, and eventually came to land at Cape Palmas, were put up by Roman Catholic missionaries there, and, flying to Monrovia, trekked inland to Bolahun, a journey of many days.

The Depression had closed Cuttington College in 1929, where all the Liberian clergy for the Episcopal Church had been trained. For fifteen years there was no organized center for training, but it was done privately. In 1944 Bishop Kroll of Liberia, Fr. Kroll's father, decided to centralize clergy training at Bolahun. For four years Fr. Packard and Fr. Parsell taught the Liberian seminarians, as well as many catechists and evangelists, at the new St. Cyril's Seminary. It lasted until 1948, when the new Bishop of Liberia, Bravard Harris, was able to reopen Cuttington and again combine college and seminary resources.

The years 1939-41 saw three more men take their life vows. Br. George, Frederick Ewald, was professed in August, 1939; from Garden City, MI, he was 28. George had great talent as a bookkeeper, and was a man of extraordinarily deliberate working habits, and ideally suited to conservative fiscal management. He also had a great love of music, particularly of the recorder; wherever he was, he would frequently gather together little amateur performing groups of singers and instruments.

Fr. Bonnell Spencer, 30, from New York City, whose father was an artist and whose mother was a devout churchwoman, had graduated from Williams and earned a B. Litt. at Oxford as well as having studied at General Seminary before joining the Order and taking his life vows in February, 1940. His brilliant mind and powerful, magnetic personality, and his boundless energy, made him almost instantly central to the community. He spent much of his earlier career at St. Andrew's School, and in the course of his life held virtually every office of the community save Superior, before going out to Ghana at the age of 74 to teach at St. Nicholas Seminary. He and Fr. Chalmers helped found an organization for young people called the Servants of Christ the King. These young people were originally associated with Holy Cross, but in 1940 the Society became the youth wing of the American Church Union.

Fr. Bessom, the young man whose 1922 letter found West Park so charming, was life professed in April, 1935, at the age of 38. From a Massachusetts family, he was a graduate of St. Stephen's College and the Episcopal Theological School in Cambridge, MA. His early ministry was in Augusta and Old Town, Maine. He spent most of his ministry from the time of his Life Profession until 1956 in Bolahun, and is greatly revered there. When asked in 1982 who of the old fathers he remembered, Stephen Palima, who had been with the Mission from the beginning, unhesitatingly said, "Father Bessie," as he was known.

All was not gain in these years, however. Fr. Flagg, finally realizing that he did not fit in any house of the Order, asked to be dispensed in August, 1941.

In March, 1940, Fr. Sill suffered a severe stroke. His effectiveness as headmaster at Kent was immediately diminished, and the ability of the community to carry on at Kent was called into question. Up until this time the other members of the Order stationed at Kent were accepted more as Fr. Sill's "relatives" than as the owning and controlling agency of the school. The Board of Trustees, even though made up of Holy Cross members, had acted as a rubber stamp of Fr. Sill's policies. But suddenly, with Fr. Sill's health declining, the question of the future of Kent School as a work of the Order became prominent.

Kent was not like St. Andrew's. St. Andrew's had not had a single dominating personality at its center for its whole existence, but had seen a regular progression of Holy Cross Fathers and Brothers come and go, establishing it without question as a Holy Cross school. But Fr. Sill's brilliant, energetic, engaging, penetrating and altogether unique character as headmaster made him seem indispensable to Kent. So much was this true that the Order as such was, while important to Kent, seen largely as a dependency of Pater. As early as 1909 the Chapter had directed Fr. Sill to bring Kent School more in line with the Order's direction, and on several occasions thereafter similar attempts had been made. But all dissolved in the face of Sill's charm, ability and determination.

Now, however, Fr. Whittemore was determined to make Kent a Holy Cross school. He had already sent three of his best men there to bring a strong Holy Cross presence to the campus. Fr. Spencer, Fr. Chalmers and Br. Dominic attempted to establish themselves, only to find the faculty and Fr. Sill hostile to their attempts to reassert Holy Cross control over the school. Fr. Whittemore had intended to make Fr. Chalmers the Novice Master, but that was abandoned when it became evident that he should carry on as headmaster. Fr. Chalmers was caught between loyalties to Whittemore and to Sill. Fr. Spencer recalled Fr. Chalmers' change:[24]

> Fr. Chalmers became more and more convinced that the only way to run the School was for him to become as much like Fr. Sill as possible, so that by the fall of '40 Fr. Chalmers was almost a small edition of Fr. Sill, or a large edition, about twice as tall, actually, of Fr. Sill, and Fr. Sill, through Fr. Chalmers, was still running the situation very strongly. And Fr. Chalmers felt himself very strictly under a tension of loyalties. As Headmaster of the Schools he felt he had to be loyal to the School and what the School wanted, faculty, alumni, and so on, and on the other hand of course, as a member of the Order, he was under the Superior. And he found himself in a state of conflict as Fr. Whittemore kept working and working to get some sort of control of the School.

Fr. Whittemore saw that the Order must both control the policies of the school and be able to lead the monastic life there in its own building if there was to be a future for the Order at Kent. The first was really already impossible of realization, as the effective control of the policy of Kent had long since passed into the hands of alumni and faculty, whose connection with Holy Cross was in most cases tenuous. The second ran into the active opposition of staff and faculty, as it meant the Order moving the school's bursar out of the house it wanted to occupy on the campus.

Fr. Sill continued to oppose Fr. Whittemore throughout the winter of 1940-41. In February, 1941, Fr. Whittemore finally wrote Sill of his displeasure, requiring his obedience:[25]

> I believe, then, that along with your wonderfully generous and fruitful work with souls and along with your genuine and touching devotion to the Order, there has been a strong element of self-will; and that this has existed from the very inception of Kent.
>
> You yourself have told me, more than once, that there was much self-will in your attitude toward the Father Founder; as, for example, the way in which you mailed those first letters about the School from St. Louis, "that very night, before he could change his mind."
>
> I have not said so before, and it wrings my heart to say so now, but I firmly believe that all these difficulties I have had with Alumni and other friends of the School derive from the fact that you built

up the impression (however unwittingly) that you and Kent were in a real sense independent of the Order's authority. I do not say that you ever asserted this in so many words. Indeed, I know that you have often stated the contrary. But actions speak louder than words. . . .

How came it that on several occasions other people outside the Order have been amused at your technical submission to its authority and laughingly doubted whether you would agree to leave Kent if you were told to do so?. . . .

I want the Order to go on at Kent. With full knowledge of the danger involved, I have given you three of our best men—two of them very young men—with the hope that God will bring things to a right and wholesome issue. I still retain that hope. But I would infinitely prefer that the Order should withdraw completely than that a situation should continue which I myself (and, I believe, almost all my brethren in the Order) have regarded as anomolous.

Whittemore asked Fr. Sill directly to write to the alumni and set forth the true case of things: that Kent was a work and school of the Order of the Holy Cross, and that the Superior intended to work with the alumni and faculty to make it an even finer school, but a Holy Cross school. Sill did as he was asked, but his efforts did not avail. Fr. Chalmers was made Headmaster before the fall of 1941, and there things rested for the time being.

Fr. Whittemore's term as Superior ended in August, 1942. He was doubtless reluctant to act in such a weighty matter as the closing of the Order's work at Kent so near to the end of what might, after all, be his only term as Superior. Another man might feel and act differently. But on August 4, 1942, he was reelected Superior on the first ballot for a second six-year term. He worked through the fall of 1942 and the spring of 1943 to bring about a satisfactory resolution at Kent. Fr. Whittemore was absolutely determined that Kent should be under the control of the Order of the Holy Cross, just as St. Andrew's had always been. But his efforts were in vain. He announced his intention of closing the Holy Cross work at Kent at the Chapter of August, 1943, and was sustained in his decision by the majority of the members of the Order. That he had not premeditated this action is made clear in one of the most bizarre episodes in Holy Cross history, an abortive attempt to remove Fr. Whittemore by committing him to a mental institution. Fr. Spencer's vivid memory gives some of the urgency of the moment:[26]

During the Long Retreat before Chapter [in August, 1943] I was making a meditation out on the cloister and Fr. Turkington was out there also and he called me over and said, "Have you heard what is going on?" and I said, "No, what's going on?" And he said, "Well, certain members of the Order. . . ." I think it was actually Fr. Chalmers himself in the case of Fr. Turkington, who at that time was stationed at Kent, thought that of course Fr. Turkington would be on the Kent side and so he went to him and said that they were going to bring up in Chapter the resolution asking Fr. Whittemore to go off somewhere for mental assistance, because obviously he was making impossible decisions and was clearly incapable of being Superior. And they had planned somehow or other to get him to resign, or get him to be removed. . . . Fr. Turkington was wildly furious about it and so immediately was I. Fr. Turkington said that Fr. Hughson was supposed to be also a part of this business of getting rid of Fr. Whittemore. I said, "That does not sound to me like Fr. Hughson," so Fr. Turkington agreed to go and see Fr. Hughson. Well, when he saw Fr. Hughson, Fr. Hughson said, "Oh, so that's what they were talking about. I couldn't understand what the world, so I didn't pay much attention, they said something or other, and I said, oh yes. Well, I think it would be good for him to get a little rest or something. But of course we can't do anything like that." So he was completely on the side of Fr. Whittemore immediately and Fr. Baldwin, who was the only Kent alumnus in the house (Fr. Packard at this time was in Africa), immediately of course backed the Superior. Of course the Superior was the Superior and he would back the Superior and so on. Fr. Turkington and Fr. Hughson and Fr. Baldwin and I were among those who strongly backed the Superior throughout this crisis.

What happened was that when Fr. Whittemore, who was told of this during the retreat, came to the first morning Chapter, and as we began the appointments he immediately announced that in view of the situation that he had been informed of, what was happening within the Order, it was clear that Kent was pulling the Order apart, and that therefore we could no longer go on and work at Kent. So he was closing the house as of then. . . . And he turned to Fr. Chalmers and said, "I'll give you another year as acting headmaster because of the situation and need to get another headmaster, but I want you back at West Park as of this time next summer." . . . And then, having said this to Fr. Chalmers, there was a sort of stony silence and then he turned again and he said, "You will be back then next summer, Fr. Chalmers?" And Fr. Chalmers said, "Yes."

The dissident Brethren appealed to the Bishop Visitor, Bishop Manning of New York, but he refused to intervene. They called a special Chapter, which required a petition of one-third of the members of the Order, but were unable to accomplish anything by it.

The Order's work at Kent (though not, of course, the school) was closed on September 30, 1943. Kent has remained a great school, one which the Order is proud to have founded and fostered. Fr. Chalmers remained as headmaster, ultimately requesting to be dispensed from his vows in 1945. He joined the Oratory of the Good Shepherd, a society for secular priests under vows but not living in community. In 1949 he resigned from Kent to become headmaster of the Harvard School in Los Angeles, where he had a distinguished career.

Fr. Whittemore's motivations in all this turmoil were clear. He did not wish the Order to continue to be used as a dependency of the headmaster of Kent, but rather to make the necessary bond of obedience between the Order and its members clear in their work. He wished that a school which used the name of the Order should in fact be the Order's school. And he would not permit the community to be torn apart by factionalism for the sake of a single work of the Order. His course demanded strength and courage, and while the Order lost Kent, it could be argued that it was really Fr. Sill's school, and only accidentally the Order's. Whittemore kept the Order together, and established the absolute priority of monastic obedience for its members.

At the same Chapter which reelected Fr. Whittemore in August, 1942, two members of the Order were life professed. Br. Herbert Bicknell was from Rhode Island, 30 years old, a graduate of New York University. He taught at St. Andrew's School for much of his time in the community, and eventually went to General Seminary, graduating in 1961. He was ordained, and returned to St. Andrew's. Fr. Alpheus Appleton Packard, a graduate of Kent, St. Stephen's and General Seminary, was a parish priest in New York State, and Rector of Holy Cross, Kingston, NY, before he joined the Order. He was 37 at the time of his profession, an indefatigable writer of poetry, articles and tracts, and a man of regular habits bordering on compulsion. It is said that in his earlier days he would swim in the Hudson, taking exactly the same number of strokes going out as coming back each time. When he made his meditation on the Long Cloister at West Park he would take just a certain number of steps, wheel about, and repeat that number, in a precise and unvarying pattern.

Two more men were life professed the following year. Br. Sydney Atkinson, 28, a Canadian from Hamilton, Ont., was professed in August, 1943. He was ordained in 1953 after education at the University of the

South and private study for the priesthood. He was a cheerful man, with administrative and pastoral ability in abundance. Fr. Vern Adams, 38 at the time of his Life Profession in October, 1943, grew up in Colorado, and attended St. John's College in Greeley, Colo. He held parishes in New Mexico from 1935 until 1940 when he joined the novitiate. He spent much of his ministry in the Order in the West, first at Nixon and then at Mount Calvary. His sense of humor was dry and piercing, but always kind.

In 1942 the Order received an invitation from the Bishop of Nevada, William Lewis, to minister at St. Mary's Mission, Nixon, NV. Bishop Lewis was at the beginning of his long episcopate in Nevada, and wanted to bring in some new energy. Nixon is the principal town of the large Pyramid Lake Paiute Indian Reservation north of Reno. Fr. Tiedemann was sent out to open the work, and soon had established himself in a solid ministry there. Various members of the Order joined him, and it was not long before Fr. Tiedemann began his itinerant preaching and retreat-giving all over the West, for which in time he became famous.

During the course of the work at Nixon, which lasted until 1946, Fr. Tiedemann convinced the Order that it should open a monastery in the West. The Chapter of 1921 had authorized a western monastery, but to the eastern eyes of those years, Ripon, Wisconsin seemed west. Now Fr. Tiedemann, perhaps wishing to redeem his part in the Ripon fiasco, began looking in earnest for a suitable site for the new western monastery of the Order. At first he favored Nixon itself. Indeed, it is pretty much geographically central to the western states. But geography is one thing in the West, and population and transportation are another. The population has always been predominantly on the coast, and there he went in search of a site.

The Board of Directors of the legal corporation of the Order in January of 1946 authorized $12,500 to the Superior to establish the western monastery. Fr. Tiedemann began looking. Sites were found outside Sacramento, then in Pacific Grove on the Monterey Peninsula, but it was not until he reached Santa Barbara that Fr. Tiedemann found what he was looking for. Mr. Raymond Skofield had begun to build a large Spanish Colonial hacienda for his family on the ridge of one of the highest hills in Santa Barbara. The work was begun in the 1920s, when he was at the height of his prosperity, and he envisioned a great center for entertaining his friends, especially the Rancheros, an exclusive riding fraternity. They would gallop up the hill, he thought, thunder into the great central court of the hacienda, dismount, and be feted in grand style in the magnificent halls of his new house. But the Crash of 1929 intervened, and while Skofield recouped some of his wealth and continued to build during the

1930s, he gradually abandoned his plans. The house stood structurally complete, but an unfinished shell, until Fr. Tiedemann found it.

The Skofield property was perfect for Fr. Tiedemann's taste. Romantically situated, the highest house in Santa Barbara, with a forty-mile vista along the seacoast, it commands the terrain. And the architecture appealed to Tiedemann's sense of the past. He hated what he called "The Goethick" and adored the Baroque, and where better than Santa Barbara to build, at last, a monastery to his own taste. It was big enough for a retreat ministry, and for the community. And Mr. Skofield's price was reasonable.

The house was purchased on October 16, 1947, for $47,500. Tiedemann went to work immediately to finish the interior, using Skofield's detailed plans to produce windows and doors, walls, moldings and cornices, everything in accordance with the original design. And he began a concerted program of canvassing the grande dames of Santa Barbara and its wealthy suburb Montecito for furniture and art. It is said that Fr. Tiedemann never came away from tea empty-handed. This is no doubt an exaggeration, but his untiring efforts to realize his dream produced a monastery of unique beauty and unparalleled situation which has since been the site for countless retreatants, in their moments of decision, of joy or of distress.

Two deaths occurred during Fr. Whittemore's second term. Fr. Webb, only 49 years old, died on May 4, 1944. He had spent much of his time at St. Andrew's School, and when illness forced him back to West Park, he brought back his dog with him:[27]

> During his last year at St. Andrew's he adopted a most unprepossessing mongrel and obtained reluctant permission to bring it with him on his transfer to the Mother House. What a nuisance that dog was! Whenever the Angelus or the De Profundis was rung he howled dismally. After which, when the doors were open in summer, he made his way into Chapel, where he did not go quietly to somebody to be stroked, but back and forth in a way which distracted and irritated everyone but "Webbie." Father Webb's devotion to him was rather pathetic; as when a passing truck ended the dog's own troubles.

Fr. Whittemore's own reaction to Webb was recorded earlier. Fr. Webb's life was one of unrecorded faithfulness, hidden as many monastic lives are.

Fr. Mayo died on May 25, 1946. He was 85 years old, forty-three years in Life Profession. Fr. Mayo had many endearing characteristics, and Fr. Whittemore called him "Brother Juniper" for his impish ways and small pranks and utter unselfconsciousness. Fr. Whittemore tells many stories of Fr. Mayo. One may illustrate his character:[28]

Father was so zealous in adding to the community intercession list and so persevering in his petitions that, at times, the Community spent the better part of its daily fifteen minutes in offering Fr. Mayo's private intercessions. One became intrigued with the question who is "Mary, whose great-aunt has just died of typhoid fever" and just what heinous crime was committed by "Walter, who has been confined in prison for fifteen years and who is the only son of his aged mother"—the latter petition being followed, for many months, by "His mother, in dying condition."

It seems that Father Baldwin, possibly to escape from too restricted a use of Father Mayo's suffrages, devised a scheme for various days of the week and month whereby we prayed for a range of broader objects; such as, for example, the works of the Church at large and the welfare of its various branches, or a right adjustment of the relations between capital and labor, or of international affairs.

It so happened that, on one page of this compendium was a list of various professions, followed by a list of the jurisdictions of the American Church. One list was to follow the other, but to economize space, was typed in a parallel column.

What was the enchanted amazement of the brethren when Father Mayo, whose turn it was to conduct Intercessions, began to pray as follows, with the utmost solemnity and a short pause between petitions:

For the dentists in Alaska (pause)

For the carpenters in the Panama Canal Zone (pause)

For the firemen in Western Massachusetts (and so on, to the bottom of the page, with Father Mayo serenely unconscious of the agonizing efforts of his brethren to suppress their laughter.) Each new and gloriously combined petition almost annihilated them.

Time took its toll on Fr. Hughson as well during these years. Fr. Whittemore had wanted him to act as Novice Master in 1945, but it was too much for him. The day-to-day running of the monastery at West Park was frequently delegated to the senior Father present, who often was, of course, Fr. Hughson. On Holy Cross Day, September 14, 1945, he was dispensed from this duty at his own request. On November 30 he was relieved of his duties as Novice Master. But he continued to write and counsel those who came to him. In his old age (he was then 75 years old) he had mellowed, losing nothing of his remarkable character but the shaprness of his will. Those who knew him in those days remember a man of deep understanding, wisdom and knowledge, great patience (learned the hard way) and, most of all, the knowledge of God which comes only from experience and the spiritual work of a lifetime. He was, by all accounts, a saint.

Fr. Whittemore's most brilliant accomplishment was not his reform of the Order, nor holding it together during the crisis of 1943 over Kent. It was the foundation of the Order of St. Helena. At Margaret Hall School in Versailles, KY, there had been for many years a convent of the Order of St. Anne, operating the school. The Order of St. Anne is a Benedictine community which leaves wide discretion to individual convents, but which demands of them a strict obedience, which makes difficult an openness to contemporary life and culture. Many holy women have found their lives in the Order of St. Anne. Nevertheless, the nine Sisters at Versailles wished to change their customs and found it difficult. Fr. Whittemore was called on by their Superior, Mother Rachel Hosmer, a remarkable woman of penetrating intelligence and strong character. They counseled for many months, and finally decided to break away from St. Anne and form their own community. On November 8, 1945, they voted to adopt the Holy Cross Rule, and a modified form of the habit, and to accept the Superior of the Order as their own Superior, an arrangement which lasted until the 1970s.

The new life which the Versailles Sisters chose brought them wider horizons. They established their first House outside Kentucky in Helmetta, NJ, and later transferred their Mother House to a graceful red brick convent in Vails Gate, NY. Their works have taken them to Liberia and the Bahamas, and to Ghana; and they have established convents in New York City, Augusta, GA, and Seattle.

As Fr. Whittemore himself did, in their worship and life they pursue a combination of contemplative quiet and order, even withdrawal, with the most radical concern and involvement with the contemporary world possible. They were the first community of women to embrace the ordination of women in the Anglican communion, and yet they retain diversity of opinion on even that subject. They are the most Anglican of women in their dedication to consensus rather than authoritarianism. Their own journey, at first with Holy Cross, and then independently, has paralleled the journey of women in North American culture in an uncanny way. In many ways the Order of St. Helena is Fr. Whittemore's most enduring legacy.

Conservatism and Change (1948-1966)

✠ In August, 1948 Bishop Campbell was elected Superior to succeed Fr. Whittemore. The Bishop had spent the preceding nine years at St. Andrew's, where he had presided over a steady expansion of the school. Immediately upon his election, Bp. Campbell assigned Fr. Whittemore to the mission at Bolahun.

Bp. Campbell was a study in conservatism. He was just short of his 64th birthday at the time of his election, and had already had two careers, as teacher and headmaster of St. Andrew's, and as a missionary bishop. As a retired bishop he delighted to assist at confirmation and other ceremonial occasions, and took great pains to suit his vestments and actions to the churchmanship of the place he was called on to visit. He was convinced that he was of royal descent, and belonged to several societies which reinforced his convictions, including the Order of St. John of Jerusalem, of which he was a Knight Commander.

Bishop Campbell believed that some persons are born to lead and others to follow. He was born to lead. His utter conviction of this vocation to leadership lent him great presence and dignity, and an ability to preside graciously in any situation whatever. He was open to all sorts of persons in an aristocratic way, charming and empathetic as people are who feel in their bones that God has called them higher. His personal graciousness was accompanied by an enthusiastic acceptance of the traditional forms and values. Consequently, his tenure as Superior was a time of stability that strengthened existing commitments.

When he became Superior, Holy Cross had twenty life professed members, the same number as it had had twelve years earlier. But great changes had been made. Kent School had become independent. A new monastery had been founded on the West Coast. And the Order of St. Helena had attached itself to Holy Cross. The work in Liberia and at St. Andrew's School remained strong and demanding. So also did the work of preaching and missions, as well as the training of new men for the Order. Campbell's conservatism was right for the time. It was time to consolidate.

Two of the great men of earlier times were now seriously ill. Fr. Hughson weakened gradually from 1945 on, and died on Nov. 16, 1949. His last years were enormously productive, however. He managed to publish three books in these four years, *The Gloria Psalter* (1946), *With Christ in God* (1947) and *Spiritual Guidance* (1948). In addition, three collections of his writings were gathered together after his death: his *Spiritual Letters* (1952), a series of meditations on the *Prayer Book* collects in *Lord Hear My Prayer* (1953), and a selection of his writings on the development of the soul in *To Tell The Godly Man* (1958).

Fr. Hughson's life was by no means entirely serious. He had an uproarious sense of humor, and Fr. Tiedemann remembered how he used to structure his storytelling:[1]

> He was a great humorist and a supreme teller of stories. As he was my Novice Master for two years I have plenty to record. . . . Bp. Campbell, who was my fellow-novice, divided them into the Westminster Cycle, the Sewanee Cycle, the Squire Tate Cycle, the Fr. Sargent Cycle and others.
>
> Fr. Hughson did not hesitate to repeat his stories and Bp. Campbell and I would solemnly check up story after story in the appropriate cycle.
>
> In the Sewanee Cycle the outstanding story was about an old farmer known for his profanity. He drove into town one day and brought a sack of oats which he threw rather roughly out into the back of his cart. The bag caught on a nail, and started dribbling oats down the road as he drove away. A group of 5 or six young men started following him as his old nag ambled away. Becoming aware of the followers, the farmer pulled up, got out to see what was the trouble. He saw the dribbling line of oats, he saw the expectant group of faces, and suddenly said, "Boys, I ain't equal to it."

Fr. Sill continued on at Kent, and, although paralyzed by a stroke, gave his unique gifts to the boys of Kent as he had for so many years before. He died on July 17, 1952.

Fr. Hawkins, now 66 years old, had returned to the community in 1945 after the death of his wife, and early in 1950 he and Fr. Julien Gunn were life professed. Fr. Hawkins was restored to his place in the precedence of the community. Fr. Gunn, 37, a Virginian, was a great school administrator, and a passionate lover of Wagnerian opera.

The following year Fr. Lincoln Taylor and Fr. Lee Stevens were life professed. Taylor, 42, from Buffalo, graduated from Hobart and General Seminary, had spent the first ten years of his ministry in a multipoint ministry in rural South Carolina before he entered the Order. Fr. Stevens, 37, was from Maine, educated at Bates College, Harvard and General Seminary. Before entering the ministry he had been an actor, and throughout his ministry used acting techniques to great effect in his preaching and appeals.

Fr. Whittemore returned from Africa in 1951, and asked the Superior for permission to be enclosed at West Park. It had been a dream of his from his earliest days in the community to lead the enclosed life, and he had actually sought permission from Fr. Huntington in the 1920s, but was refused. Now, however, permission was granted, and Fr. Whittemore entered on the final stage of his extraordinary life.

He used his time as an enclosed monk in a variety of ways. Perhaps the most significant was an intensification of his ministry to those who sought spiritual guidance. By its nature such ministry is evanescent, leaving little trace behind it. But Whittemore's character shone out, and his spiritual advice was sought by more and more people.

Alan Watts, whose early writings had been published in the *Holy Cross Magazine,* came to know Whittemore when he was Superior. In his autobiography *In My Own Way,* Watts speaks of his own spiritual journey and connects it intimately with Fr. Whittemore:[2]

> I had even gone so far as attempting to use Christian forms of devotion and mental prayer in my own interior life, reciting the Divine Office from the Breviary, going to confession, and following the spiritual direction of Alan Whittemore, a saint and religious genius who was then Superior of the Order of the Holy Cross. This tall, athletic, and joyously open-hearted man was a full-blooded mystic who could not only sense the presence of God in every flicker of light and sound, but had also reached the deep state of contemplative prayer where one feels God in the very feeling of not feeling him, the state of the "divine darkness" or the "cloud of unknowing."

Watts saw what many others did in Whittemore: an utter absorption in God, to the point that his religion became entirely natural to him, and the need for religious "attitudes" dropped away almost altogether. Fr. Parsell, speaking of Whittemore's time in Africa, tells of the deep impact his teaching had on the Sisters of the Holy Name, and confirms Watts's observations about Whittemore's absorption in God:[3]

He was a man of tremendous prayer and the great thing that intrigued me and is typical of Fr. Whittemore was that about '35 or '34, he was going to give a series of theological talks to the Sisters on what we call systematic theology, dogmatic theology, you know, God the Father, God the Son, God the Holy Spirit, and all the rest going down the line. Fr. Whittemore never got off God himself. He could go on for weeks because this was his orientation. He didn't have a blind spot for liturgy, but all that comes from the Incarnation which we think's so important in the liturgy, this wasn't important, it was God himself that was.

Fr. Whittemore wrote three works that have remained unpublished, which he polished and circulated privately during his time of enclosure. The first is his private spiritual journal, *Thanks Be To God,* begun early in his time in the Order, and finished sometime before 1953. He showed this to Watts, who was very moved by it:[4]

He let me read his extraordinary spiritual journal, a manuscript which—if still extant—should be published forthwith, since it contains some of the finest mystic writing in the Christian tradition.

This journal is remarkably revealing of Whittemore's inner state, showing that he was subject to great psychological stress at several periods in his life, especially in the 1920s, and that he was not immune to the temptations to pettiness so common in the monastic life, where men of greatly differing character live close together.

The second work he wrote is one frequently quoted in this history. *O.H.C.* was written, according to an annotation in his own hand on one of its copies, "while I was marooned in Freetown early in '47; the rest, early in '49." Its first part is a series of biographical sketches, impressions of members of the community by then safely dead. These reveal many incidents of Holy Cross life which have become almost mythical for the Order, structuring the collective memory of the community. The second part is a general description of the monastic life as Holy Cross lived it at that time.

Whittemore's third work is a series of meditations he gave to the community in 1959, shortly before his death, on the Rule of Fr. Huntington. This *Retreat on the Rule* displays great sensitivity to the realities of human character in trying to live the sometimes perplexing demands of monasticism in the contemporary world.

Enclosed, Fr. Whittemore did not cease his active participation in the community. Enclosure does not mean being cut off from life, but an extra degree of stability in a single place. Novices were counseled, confessions were heard, and the community's affairs claimed their share of his time. Indeed, there is a tradition that when an outsider came to see Fr. Whittemore, a six-pack of beer was expected!

The same period which saw the emergence of Fr. Whittemore's contemplative vocation saw the publication of a remarkable novel about St. Andrew's School. James Agee, already famous for *Let Us Now Praise Famous Men,* in 1952 published the lyrical, semi-autobiographical novella *Morning Watch*. It concerns the adolescent religious consciousness of a young lad. The story centers on the early morning watch before the Blessed Sacrament during the night between Maundy Thursday and Good Friday, 1923, at St. Andrew's. Agee captures the awkwardly beautiful time of adolescence, and in this extended word picture conveys intense and poignant feelings of religious devotion and growth into manhood.

Framing the central section of the book are two descriptions, entering and leaving the Chapel, which give the flavor of Agee's writing and describe how a young boy might experience the Chapel at St. Andrew's:[5]

> The night smelled like new milk; the air which exhaled upon them when they opened the side door of the Chapel was as numb and remote as the air of a cave. Without knowing it they hesitated, subdued by the stagnant darkness and its smell of waxed pine and spent incense.
>
> They walked down the sandstone steps into an air so different from the striving candles and the expiring flowers that they were stopped flat-footed on the gravel. Morning had not yet begun but the night was nearly over. The gravel took all the light there was in the perishing darkness and shed it upward, and in the darkness among the trees below the outbuildings a blossoming dogwood flawed like winter breath.

Agee attended St. Andrew's from 1919 to 1925. His mother had a cottage on the school grounds and she ultimately married one of the teachers there, Fr. Erskine Wright. Agee formed a lasting friendship at St. Andrew's with a faculty member, Fr. James Flye. He continued to visit and write letters to Fr. Flye throughout his short, brilliant, complicated life, and the collection of letters published by his friend, *Letters to Father Flye* (1962), have themselves become classic.

Two more men were life professed during Bp. Campbell's term as Superior. Fr. Kenneth Terry, 30, from California, was a graduate of the University of California and Nashotah House. Fr. Raymond Gill, 37, from Philadelphia, was graduated from Temple University and Nashotah House, and had been a missionary at Bolahun before joining the Order.

Bishop Campbell had consistently promoted Fr. Leopold Kroll to positions of leadership, apparently grooming him to succeed him as Superior. He was Assistant Superior throughout Bp. Campbell's term as Superior, and in 1952 was made Novice Master as well. So it was not unexpected that he should be elected Superior on the first ballot in the election Chapter of August, 1954.

Fr. Kroll had spent most of his early ministry in Liberia, and Fr. Parsell has several memories of his former partner in shipwreck.[6]

> His ministry in Africa was with the Kisi people especially. That's because he began to work particularly with the hospital and that's where one learned Kisi language, and then eventually he was in charge of the Kisi patrol. By 1933 the great Depression time in America had finally hit our source of supply and money and so our budget was cut from $20,000 to $10,000, a lot of money in those days. Actually it was a lot more than $10,000 because the British had gone off the gold standard before the Americans so we were using English money and we were getting something like $13,000 for the $10,000.

Fr. Parsell remembered especially a period when he, Fr. Kroll and Fr. Whittemore were together in Bolahun in the early 1930s.[7]

> In discussions it was so interesting. Fr. Whittemore approached everything from the statistical element, Fr. Kroll from the philosophical and myself from the historical. It's like Baron von Hugel's *Elements of Origin* in the way we approached the problems, and we had a great many in those days.

His estimate of Fr. Kroll's character grows from a deep friendship.[8] "He was my best friend in the world and one I could communicate with or without speech."

> He wasn't a great preacher. . . . He was more like Fr. Allen in a way, but a very quiet and effective administrator. . . . I don't know that we have anybody that really compares with him in some ways. His father was Prussian, but his mother was of old Vermont stock; her family had been over here since the time of the Revolution. She had great courage. She had to have a colostomy and she went out to Africa even with that.

Fr. Kroll made Fr. William Turkington his Assistant Superior after his election as Superior in 1954. Bp. Campbell was appointed Novice Master, but he was out of his depth in dealing with the young men joining the Order in the mid-fifties. The novitiate soon became chaotic, the whole lot of novices was dismissed in April of 1955, and Campbell was replaced by Fr. Sydney Atkinson. This disturbance accounts for the small number of professions in the later 1950s.

Fr. Kroll sent Bp. Campbell to Bolahun in September, 1955. Bp. Campbell was not pleased with this assignment, feeling that he had been "banished," as he said in an autobiographical sketch, and admitting that "the following two years were far from happy."[9]

Between 1952 and 1960 only one man was life professed. He was Br. Michael Stonebraker, life professed in 1956, at the age of 26. Br. Michael's gifts of communication and music have made him a tireless missioner with young people and his artistic abilities placed him in charge of much of the printing and media work of the Order.

After the novitiate crisis was resolved, the Order's work proceeded normally until February of 1957. That month a situation arose in Bolahun which seemed to require the Superior's attention. The Sisters of the Holy Name had sent one of their Sisters under annual vows, Sr. Una Hill, to Bolahun. She was a physician and had set up a clinic which was soon seen to be in competition with the regular clinic operated by Fr. Dr. Joseph Smyth, a former member of Holy Cross. This perceived opposition was so severe that the Superior was asked to travel to Bolahun to resolve the problem.

He was visiting Mount Calvary when the message reached him. He decided to take advantage of the new airplane routes across the Atlantic, and left for Africa on Feb. 11. After Fr. Kroll investigated the situation, Sr. Dr. Una was asked to return to her Mother House in Malvern Link. She became ill, and Fr. Kroll's concern for her health led him to spend time with her, in hopes of speeding her recovery. They fell in love, and on May 6 they both left for England. On May 20 the first of several letters to the heads of the Order's houses in the United States was received, in which Fr. Kroll declared his intention to abandon his vows and the community and to marry Sr. Una.

In his letter to Fr. Turkington dated May 17, Fr. Kroll gave a series of reasons for his decision to leave:[10]

Please say some prayers while you read this as it will come as a great shock to you. For reasons of conscience which have been increasingly troubling me for some time I have decided that I must give up the Religious Life and return to the secular priesthood.

What has been bothering me is that our financial security and prestige in the Church combine to make it impossible to be fully identified with the poor of the world and to share their burdens, their insecurities and the difficulties of the ordinary stresses of life. If I were to continue feeling as I do, it could only result in deadening my conscience and living falsely as a Religious. I know this decision will bring much sorrow to you and my brethren whom I deeply love. I beg your mercy and forgiveness and continued prayers.

While ministering spiritually to Sr. Una CHN in Africa we realized we both felt much the same way. She had already asked for release on conscientious grounds over a year ago. We also discovered a deep spiritual and mental affinity, which led us to a mutual love and the decision to marry each other and to continue our consecration to God in marriage and by complete identification with ordinary people.

The blow fell very hard on the Order. Bp. Campbell's reaction is especially interesting, as he was stationed at the mission during this period.[11]

Fr. K's defection hurts me especially, for I have always admired him and all his family. In the spring of '28 I ordained him to the priesthood in St. George's, Newburgh. In Febr. '36 I was one of his father's consecrators as Bp. of Liberia; and in March '45 conducted his funeral in Salisbury, N.C. The whole time I was Superior I kept Fr. Kroll as my Asst., and gave him personal and special training to succeed me; and of course felt highly gratified when the brethren elected him in August of '54. Frankly, I was not a little annoyed when he determined to send me out here again, especially when it came to light that one of the brethren had talked him into it. However, as you know, I made no fuss, for I know that it is good policy to ship an ex-sup. off for a good change of scenery after he goes out of office. But under it all, and in spite of recent happenings, I still pray with earnestness for him.

Bishop Campbell blamed Sr. Una entirely for the affair, holding that she had seduced Fr. Kroll. He could not bring himself to believe that the Superior of the Order of the Holy Cross could freely decide to leave the community for marriage and a totally uncertain future.

The mission at Bolahun was strongly staffed, however, and the work there proceeded without any discernible damage. Bishop Campbell had been working on a history of the Bolahun Mission, *Within the Green Wall,* which he finished that year. The work at Bolahun had always depended on a large staff of secular doctors, nurses, teachers and priests, as well as the Holy Cross Fathers and Brothers. Fr. Parsell, Prior since 1947, had on his staff Bp. Campbell and Frs. Taylor and Gill, the CHN community, and also a staff of seven secular helpers, including Fr. Dr. Smyth, Mary Juchter (later Sr. Ruth OSH), Mr. and Mrs. Sterling Sorenson, Nancy Morris, Lucienne Sanchez, and two young priests who had come out to Bolahun immediately after graduating from the Church Divinity School of the Pacific, Fr. Connor Lynn and Fr. Robert Worster. Both eventually joined the novitiate, Fr. Lynn ultimately becoming Superior, and Fr. Worster a parish priest and strong Associate and friend of the Order at St. Mary's Church, Palms, in Los Angeles.

Fr. Parsell was dispatched to England on May 22. According to a statement of the Council he was "with the help of priests and Sisters to dissuade him from his plans." This attempt failed. Sr. Una had been released from her temporary vows. "The latter [Fr. Kroll] did nothing more than restate his position. On June 1st, the doctor and Father Kroll were married in a registry office in Birmingham, England."[12]

The Order now had two crises to deal with. The first was the question of its internal leadership. Fr. Turkington, now the Acting Superior, called a special Chapter for July 22. Fr. Kroll was deposed as Superior and expelled from the Order. At the annual Chapter on August 2, Fr. Turkington was elected Superior, though not without opposition. The conservatives in the community had coalesced around Fr. Baldwin, who made a strong showing.

The second crisis was not so simple of solution. Fr. Kroll had left the Order, had abandoned his vows, and had been expelled. But now that he was expelled from the community, what became of his vows? The fact that he had broken them did not mean that they were no longer in effect. Holy Cross, by expelling him, had relinquished jurisdiction over his vows, but they still bound him before God. There was, furthermore, no clear canon law on this subject in the Episcopal Church. The Church of England granted to the Archbishop of Canterbury final authority in such matters, but he held (and holds) no canonical jurisdiction in the American Church.

This quandary continued for years. Fr. Kroll was at first inhibited from exercising his priesthood by Bishop Horace W. B. Donegan, the Bishop of New York. Bishop Donegan was also the Visitor to the Order, and he was very supportive of the community throughout this crisis. But he finally could not understand the community's inability and unwillingness to dispense Fr. Kroll from his vows. That the Order did not possess the canonical authority to do so escaped him, for it seemed to have the moral authority.

Fr. Kroll was eventually allowed to act as a priest in England. It was not until 1976 that the Constitution of the Order was finally amended to allow him to be dispensed from his vows by virtue of his expulsion.

The crisis over Fr. Kroll pointed up other, deeper concerns than the particular set of events and circumstances surrounding his decision to leave the community. The first and most immediate concerned the status of monastic vows in the Episcopal Church. Were they recognized by the Church as binding? Would they be an impediment to a lawful marriage? Would the Church officially uphold them once taken and insist that the person making them take them seriously? Or were monastic vows in the Episcopal Church simply private devotional covenants, edifying to the faithful but not binding in the eyes of the Church outside the context in which they were taken? This issue is still unresolved, though the Church now defines what such vows are while still leaving the question of their binding character in canon law unanswered.

The canonical status of vows is central to the position of monastic and religious communities in the Church. From an initially hostile stance in the 1880s and the decades following, monastic and religious communities had been gradually accepted as part of the ministry of the Church, if still regarded as exotic by most and unknown by many. But unless the Church recognizes the vows monastics make as having the force which those vows intend in their formulations, they still remain essentially private and personal moral covenants, and the communities in which they are taken remain essentially private devotional societies, and not yet fully recognized parts of the ministry of the Church.

The second question Fr. Kroll's leaving raised is the issue of the involvement of the monk as a Christian with the world. Fr. Kroll saw as early as the 1950s that it was not entirely legitimate for a monastic community to insulate itself from the world in which it lived. His question was prophetic and would not go away. Much of the upheaval of the following decades in the monastic life all around the world revolves around issues of legitimate involvement and disengagement. To what extent is it legitimate to maintain a community isolated from the real concerns of the world? The attempt to build a truly contemporary monasticism would begin in Holy Cross in the mid-1960s and would change the Order dramatically.

For the moment, however, Fr. Turkington had to shore up the institutional fabric of the Order. He was the ideal man to step into the leadership of the community at this time. A gentle and kind person, Fr. Turkington's irenic approach and trusting demeanor helped the wounds to heal quickly, and under his leadership the Order soon put this trauma behind it. Fr. Taylor had this estimate of Fr. Turkington's character:[13]

[Fr. Turkington] is one of the most wonderful pastors that I know of. He has a tremendous interest in persons as individuals and in their ideas and he is a good teacher, obviously. And also an unsatisfied thirst for travel and historic information. He never has exhausted that. He never went on a trip before having thought of 62 things that he wanted to do when he got there.

For the first year he retained Fr. Atkinson as Assistant Superior and Novice Master, but in July, 1958 appointed Fr. Lincoln Taylor to both of those posts. Fr. Taylor had been stationed at the mission at Bolahun, and now Fr. Atkinson was sent there to replace him. The novitiate had begun to grow again under Fr. Atkinson's direction, and under Fr. Taylor more novices began persevering to profession, setting the scene for the great expansion in professed members and work which the Order would shortly experience.

Fr. Kroll's leaving had affected the Order of St. Helena quite as much as it had Holy Cross, since he was their Superior as well, though they had no voice in his selection. Fr. Turkington decided that the time had come for the Sisters to have their own leadership. Sr. Josephine Remley remembered this decision in her short history of OSH, connecting it with the beginnings of independence for the Sisters:[14]

> In 1958, while he was Superior he [Fr. Turkington] told us he thought that, instead of a member of the Order of the Holy Cross, we should have a Sister as Assistant Superior [of OSH] in order to give greater unity to the Order. He appointed me to this position (I was then prioress of the Mother House and Novice Mistress) and though we accepted his decision with some qualms at the time we soon became accustomed to the idea and our progress towards independence was begun.

It is to be noted that the Sisters were not yet thought capable of making their own decisions in such matters.

Three members of the Order died during Fr. Turkington's term as Superior. Fr. Francis Parker, died on Sept. 2, 1958, at the age of 69. Fr. Taylor remembered Fr. Parker:[15]

> Fr. Parker as an Englishman took great joy in the Holy Cross vocation, the life, the monastery, what we did, everything. He was always busy. He could hardly read his own writing, and when he gave a sermon or a retreat address it would start off inte-grated and clear and so on but in two paragraphs it was so jumbled up you couldn't find out where he was located or what he was

trying to get at at that point. It was just that so many ideas came into his mind.

Fr. McVeigh Harrison, 80, died the following Jan. 27. He had been senile for many years, although he continued to write a massive tirade against modern biblical criticism, which he made the Superior promise to publish, called *First Century Christianity*. Br. Dominic Taylor died on March 22, 1960, one day short of his 76th birthday. He was much loved at St. Andrew's School for his gentle and witty character and his unfailing kindness.

The election for Superior at the Chapter of 1960 was between Fr. Turkington and Fr. Taylor. After two ballots, Fr. Taylor was chosen. This election was interesting in that there was no progressive-conservative orientation to the two candidates. Both would fairly be described as progressive.

Fr. Spencer was ecstatic over the new Superior and his policies and appointments:[16]

> Fr. Superior has taken hold wonderfully. He has demonstrated he is not afraid to tackle problems, and to try daring solutions. I honestly believe more has happened in the last four days than under the last three Superiors put together. Yet all has been done so lovingly and gently that I have not seen a ruffled feeling around the place. It was a sheer joy to watch the tenderness with which he handled Fr. Hawkins, and Fr. Whitall (who spoke interminably on things which had nothing to do with the question at hand).

Fr. Taylor was a truly contemplative man. His character was a unique blend of a deep love of silence, nature and prayer, and a willingness to move, to risk, to trust others, that the Order had not seen perhaps since Fr. Huntington's time. Though their outward appearance and their background were quite different, Fr. Taylor was very like Fr. Huntington in his trust of the future and his willingness to enable others to carry on the work of the Order, even to determine its policies. Fr. Taylor's actions in his first days foreshadowed a generation of change and dynamic growth for the Order, with many attendant problems, but in the end leaving it larger, stronger and more influential than ever before.

Shortly before his death in 1984, Fr. Taylor looked back at his work as Superior, and indicated that for many years before he had become Superior, he knew that change needed to come to Holy Cross:[17]

> I asked myself whether I should tell you this experience that I had.
> I think it was Fr. Anthony Gerald [Fr. Stevens] and Fr. Terry and

myself. I had just had a session with Fr. Kroll a couple of days before and he told me the condition as it was in the Order, and it wasn't pretty, and it was very distressing. . . . There was a lot of tension within the Order. So when Fr. Kroll told me this I was really distressed. I didn't know whether I was going in the wrong direction myself. Well, Fr. A. G. (not at that time, just Fr. Lee Stevens) and Terry and I, the three of us went to Kingston to get an ice cream or something. We stopped outside of an ice cream shop and we started talking, we must have talked for three hours. And it really was, to me, it really was at that—that evening that we had two options, either we would also surrender, say, well this is really going to be hopeless, or we say it's hopeless but it isn't hopeless if someone wants to pick it up and go. And those two men and myself, we said, no, we're going to go back to that monastery and we're gonna work, and try and see if we can't get the thing restored, rebuild it again.

The three were not agreed on what needed to be done. Fr. Stevens thought that the Order was not ascetic enough. Fr. Terry was, as Fr. Taylor said, "never a very subvertive person." Fr. Taylor held his counsel. But when the responsibility of leadership was given to him, he acted.

Fr. Taylor immediately changed most of the leadership of the Order. He brought Fr. Tiedemann back from Mount Calvary to be Assistant Superior, to free Mount Calvary to become more a community house and less an extension of Fr. Tiedemann's remarkable character. Fr. Baldwin was relieved as Prior of Mount Calvary to handle the outside preaching at St. Andrew's, and Fr. Packard was made Prior in his place. Fr. Bessom, who had been Assistant Novice Master under Fr. Taylor, was sent back to Bolahun, and Fr. Atkinson, Prior there since June, was confirmed in that post. Fr. Terry was made Novice Master with Fr. Turkington as his Assistant. In a few short days Fr. Taylor had changed the face of the community, signaling his desire for fresh approaches.

In 1960 and 1961 the first additions to the life professed community in more than four years were made. In October Fr. Dr. Joseph Smyth, 70, who had been petitioning the Order for years to return to vows, was restored to the Order and to profession. He had left the community in 1925, and had spent the previous seven years running the clinic at Bolahun. In November, Br. Charles Smythe was life professed. He did not remain in the community long, however, being dispensed from his vows in December, 1963. In April, 1961, Fr. Allan Smith, 38, was life professed. He was immediately sent to Bolahun, where he spent the next ten years.

On Sept. 24, 1960, Fr. Whittemore died at the age of 70. His impact on Holy Cross is incalculable. Not a founder or a great initiator, he established the principle that the Order should control its own works, and that its internal life should be open to change. His spiritual life extended far beyond himself, and drew many to seek God. His writings on the Order established the basic pattern by which institutional memory was maintained for a generation. Most of all, he combined in his person the gentleness of the genuinely praying man with that iron in the soul which makes lifelong dedication and genuine accomplishment possible. Some of his remarkable gift for spiritual direction and his own personal sanctity are displayed in a collection of his letters and miscellaneous writings published in 1964, *Joy in Holiness.*

Fr. Taylor's first leadership team continued intact for two years. In April, 1962, Fr. Turkington replaced Fr. Packard as Prior of Mount Calvary, and that August Fr. Adams replaced Fr. Tiedemann as Assistant Superior. Fr. Taylor was attempting to bring Fr. Adams into a more prominent leadership position in the community, but Fr. Adams died on Jan. 4, 1963, at the early age of 58. Fr. Terry was named to replace him in March, 1963, and in August Fr. Spencer became Novice Master replacing Fr. Terry. Fr. Taylor was already displaying that security as a leader which allowed a remarkable degree of fluidity in the leadership of the community.

Fr. Connor Lynn, 29, and Fr. Murray Belway, 36, were life professed in 1963. Lynn was reassigned to Bolahun, and Belway to St. Andrew's School.

The following year three more men took life vows, bringing the strength of the life professed community to a historical high of twenty-six. Fr. Thomas Schultz, 30, and Fr. John Ryan, 32, were life professed together in February, 1964. Fr. Robert Sullivan, 39, was sent to Bolahun, where he remained until he left the Order and was dispensed in 1970.

The community grew in the 1960s. It was not so much that novitiate classes were larger (1958 had had seven; 1959, four; 1960, five; 1961, six; 1962, eight; 1963, six; 1964, eight). But more of the men entering the community were staying to profession. The postulant classes were growing as well, and although not all these men stayed to be clothed as novices, the monastery was bursting at the seams.

Three men were life professed in the remainder of Fr. Taylor's first term. Fr. George Swayne, 31, and Br. Kevin Dunn, 33, were both life professed in March, 1965. Br. Boniface Challinor, 26, was life professed the following year, in March, 1966. He was the first black man to be life professed in Holy Cross.

Fr. Joseph Bessom died on Aug. 25, 1965. He had spent almost all of his ministry in Liberia, and was revered by the Liberians almost as a saint. Stephen Palima, who had been with the Mission since its earliest days, when asked in 1983 which of the Fathers and Brothers he remembered most vividly, immediately named Fr. Allen and "Fr. Bessie." Fr. Taylor thought Fr. Bessom a very holy man:[18]

> Fr. Parsell thinks that Bessom was, and I do too, the closest thing to a saint you'd ever imagine, and his name doesn't stand out that way at all. But the spirit within him, the way he spent himself in Liberia, really add up to something dreadfully significant.
>
> He wanted to move out from the security of a monastic family and spend himself as a missionary. He was one of the greatest missionaries, a tireless missionary. His veins, you know, he had to have them stripped, just from walking when he shouldn't have been walking. [He was concerned] not just about their religion in the technical sense, but how to help them to build.
>
> For example, he, against a man's will, convinced him to plant some coffee trees, and he really almost had to hit the man over the head to make him do it. Five years later the man comes back and said, "You know, Fr. Beeson, I'll thank you for the rest of my days for what you did for me." Now Bessom could see the movement which he couldn't see and he knew what was possible for the guy and he kept after him. He tried to find a way of taking latex from rubber trees and making roofs for our WC's. He tried to learn Arabic so that he could teach Arabic reading to uninformed Malis so they could read Christian literature. . . . He was constantly self-spending, he never held back his own energies, his own hours, his own times, his own privacy, never! He was always giving, giving, giving, giving, giving. . . . He took care of the sick and visited them. . . . He was a great one for visiting the hospital too when he was there, and visiting the sick in the outstations. He just walked and walked and walked. That was his life.

It was soon obvious that a new building must be built at West Park to accommodate the growing community. Fr. Taylor had seen the new monastery built for the Benedictine monastery of Mount Savior in Elmira, NY and admired it. He contacted its architects, Hirsch and Cassetti, of Elmira, and had them draw up plans early in his term. A fund-raiser was engaged, and a large capital campaign started to raise the large sums needed for the new buildings. As time went on, it became clear that the funds for the building would not all be forthcoming from gifts. So Fr. Taylor convinced the community to venture its future in building the new monastery by committing much of its modest endowment and undertaking, for the first time in its history, a substantial mortgage.

The building plan by Hirsch and Cassetti was designed to express the spirituality of the Order. Both the new monastery and the new refectory were to be octagonal, representing the number eight, which signifies perfection in Christian mystical tradition, and stands for contemplation. The structure was to be open to light and to nature, and its circular forms emphasize the gatheredness of the community. The refectory was to be a remarkable room, with enormous arched windows open onto the Hudson River. Ronald Cassetti expressed his vision this way:[19]

> The architecture of Holy Cross Monastery is based on that special quality with which the Rule charges its faithful: that is, the balance between contemplation and an active ministry in the world. When a man leaves the world to become a monk, he reflects to the world a radiance; a radiance of good works and a life of prayer. It is precisely this quality which has drawn our society in closer contact with monasteries and precisely this radiance on which the new architecture of Holy Cross draws its vitality.
>
> The design of the monastery also is concerned with light and the spiritual interaction with nature. The towers reach up to capture it; the skywells in the courtyards transmit it below, even into the recesses of the library stacks below ground. Corridors which usually are treated as joyless tunnels in so many buildings, are punctured to admit sunlight and view, and to make visible from the inside the radial groups of cells extending outward.

Ground for the new monastery was broken on May 19, 1964, by Bishop Charles Boynton, the Suffragan Bishop of New York. Work began almost immediately, and for more than eighteen months the Turner Construction Co. shared the monastery grounds with the Brethren. The building was substantially complete by the end of 1965. On December 14, Bishop Albert Stuart of Georgia blessed the cornerstone of the new monastery, which had originally been set in the monastery at Westminster, MD. The Brethren moved into the monastery on Christmas Day, 1965. The monastery itself was blessed on January 8, 1966, by the Bishop of New York and Visitor of the Order, Horace W. B. Donegan. Bishop Chandler Sterling of Montana preached the sermon.

The new building was furnished simply, in spare contemporary style. The windows along the ambulatory leading from the monastery to the chapel are perhaps the most outstanding decorative feature of the buildings, representing the seven days of creation. Symbolic contemporary painted representations of the days on irregular, mottled translucent glass carry one from chaos, at the entrance to the ambulatory, to the final day of creation as one approaches the monastery, carrying out the symbolic meaning of the number eight as one reenters the chapel or goes forward into the monastery.

Fr. Taylor made his third major shift of leadership in 1965. In May he replaced Fr. Gunn, who had been Prior of St. Andrew's for ten years, with Fr. Murray Belway. In June he brought Fr. Lynn back from Africa, leaving Fr. Allan Smith in charge of the mission. In September he made Fr. Lynn Assistant Superior and in November, Novice Master. The shift put the leadership of the community more firmly in the hands of the progressives, and set the stage for their ascendancy during his second term.

The changes which the Second Vatican Council was working on the Roman Catholic Church took some time to reach Holy Cross. There had always been a contingent of Anglo-Catholics in the Order who looked to Rome for inspiration, particularly in liturgical matters. But the reforms which were being adopted by the Council for the Roman Church did not make themselves felt in practical ways until a few years afterwards.

Fr. Bonnell Spencer had been working for some years, however, on the history of the *Book of Common Prayer*. While Prior of Mount Calvary from 1955 to 1959, he found that he had time on his hands:[20]

> Fr. Tiedemann was there [at Mount Calvary] all the years that I was, and I saw at once that the obvious thing to do was to leave him in charge of the house, because that was his forte, and therefore I took care of Missions throughout the West. But that didn't fully occupy me and I decided to work on something in the form of liturgies. My original idea was that I wanted to see a new form of missal put out for the American Church that would utilize the liturgical material in terms of lessons and in terms of lesser feasts and all the rest of it that was surfacing in various prayer books of the Anglican Communion.

He enrolled as a reader at the Huntington Library in San Marino, which has a fine collection of *Prayer Books,* and soon discovered that his real interest lay in the eucharist. He prepared a collection of all the variants of the Anglican Communion service, and was soon in touch with Massey Shepherd, the great liturgical scholar at the Church Divinity School of the Pacific in Berkeley. In October, 1957 he delivered his first liturgical paper before the Los Angeles branch of the American Church Union called "Thomas Cranmer and the Eucharist." In 1959 Fr. Turkington sent Spencer to a meeting of Associated Parishes in Austin, Texas, to offer the pages of the *Holy Cross Magazine* to that liturgical spearhead group. He was instantly accepted and made a part of the Council of that organization. In 1961 he published an article called "A Functional Liturgy," which was a proposed new communion liturgy. All this attracted sufficient attention that after the General Convention of 1964 he was made a member of the Standing Liturgical Commission of the Episcopal Church, at just the same time that the commission was asked to draw up plans for a revision of the *Book of Common Prayer.* So from the beginning of the movement for liturgical revision, a member of the Order was present, and this directly affected the liturgical life of Holy Cross, first in the eucharist and then in the Divine Office.

Until the early 1960s, the liturgical life of the Order had remained static for more than a generation. Every priest was expected to say mass every morning, and the monastic life was organized to make that possible. Community eucharists were for the most part non-communicating. When there were not enough laymen in the community or among the guests to serve each mass, the priests would serve each other. It is said that Fr. Parsell had the record for the fastest private mass in the community: 14 minutes, amice-to-amice. Fr. Spencer was Novice Master from 1963 to 1965, and this gave him a base from which to experiment with the liturgy. The men joining the community from CDSP, who had learned liturgics from Massey Shepherd, assisted Fr. Spencer in this effort: "These people came in absolutely determined to do something about the business of every priest dashing off and saying a private mass in the morning."[21]

Fr. Spencer and members of the community supporting him worked out a new ceremonial for the eucharist which incorporated the new ideas. When they proposed it to the community, however, it was rejected. In the meanwhile, the new monastery had been built, and it contained a chapel. Fr. Taylor was supportive of Fr. Spencer's work, and so a novitiate mass was begun:[22]

The novices and novice master crew started a communal mass over in the Holy Spirit Chapel. They gathered around that and had a mass with guitars and talk and all the rest of it, while the rest of the House had their private masses over in the various chapels in and around the old chapel. . . . What happened was that gradually more and more professed as they saw the light shifted to that and so finally we got down to 3 or 4 people having private masses and then what happened was the laymen put their foot down and said, "We will not serve private masses." So then that meant that there was nobody to serve the private masses very much and so those that wanted them served each other and that was it. And meanwhile everybody else shifted to a community mass at the high altar.

The first communicating high mass at Holy Cross was on Christmas Day, 1965, and that is a good day from which to date the victory of the new liturgical movement in Holy Cross. Reform of the Divine Office took longer to accomplish.

Fr. Spencer connects the general movement of change within Holy Cross, which was beginning in the early 1960s, to the liturgical movement. It was certainly the most visible and symbolic change for a community whose principal function was prayer and worship; the substitution of community for private communion had the most powerful social and psychological effect on the Order. The practice of private mass and communion reinforced the idea that the Order was fundamentally a group of associated individuals with individual goals and lives united spiritually but in only the most formal ways to each other. A communal eucharist promoted the idea of community itself, and from this point on the idea of community came to dominate the Order's discussions and self-image.

In his first term as Superior, Fr. Taylor had accomplished a great deal. His dream of rebuilding the Order had begun to bear fruit in liturgical reform, and in a greater sense of energy and spirit among the leadership. A new type of man was being drawn to the community, far more willing to question venerable assumptions and devoted to making monasticism a living force rather than a museum piece. There had been to this point no visible rupture in the community's structure. Not one person had thus far left the community over the changes. But it was too much to expect that opposition would not surface. And indeed, it did.

Reform (1966-1972)

Fr. Taylor was vigorously opposed for reelection in 1966. Fr. Gunn, who had been removed as Prior of St. Andrew's School the previous year, was the person around whom the conservative elements of the community coalesced. It was clear that many in the community opposed Fr. Taylor's attempts to restructure and reform the Order, that they were determined to be heard and, if possible, to prevail. Fr. Taylor was reelected by only a single vote and he was somewhat shaken by this division in the community. For the next six years the Order would be in the throes of major change, some of it traumatic. At the end of Fr. Taylor's second term as Superior the Order of the Holy Cross would be a very different institution than he had found it in 1960.

In the self-understanding of the Order since its founding, there was to be no campaigning for office. This was observed largely in intention rather than in fact, but there was still a sense of impropriety in direct discussion of the election of a Superior. The election for Superior was, in those days, preceded by the annual silent ten-day community Long Retreat, and in 1966 that retreat was filled with conversation. Fr. Taylor remembered that election, in which he was strongly supported by the younger members of the community, especially Fr. Lynn:[1]

> I was so tender even in those years. I may not be so tender now, but I was so tender in those years that I didn't like politics at all, and yet somehow or other Connor Lynn took up the banner to get me elected and not Fr. Gunn. . . . I think there was a lot of politics going on. . . . In my experience they [the retreats] go to pieces because people would be writing notes to one another, getting behind doors and talking to one another about the election, and I didn't really know what was going to happen. I was astounded in the way that it came out. It was kind of hard for me to tell the Chapter. I said,

"I recognize that I've been elected by one vote and that's very difficult for some of you."

Fr. Taylor relied on the younger men in the Order for support, but his vision for the community was his own. To his understanding the Order needed to move away from a somewhat lifeless, museum-like atmosphere and recapture the dedication and excitement of its earlier days. He believed that the attachment of the Order to the Anglo-Catholic cause inevitably led to perpetuation of the institution the earlier men had built, but lacked their fire and life. And he theorized about the earlier members, especially Fr. Hughson:[2]

> They were producing things from the church of life. They were beginning to share with the Church and the laity within it the riches of the Catholic religion, and they just fed it out. And monasticism to my mind is a necessary ingredient in the Catholic community, and I think that people found a monastery. [It] looked like a monastery and they saw men that looked like monks and heard Office going on and found it authentic, and I think that was such a strong draft of wine, that when that began to wear off, and the men began to die off or move on, the ones that were left would work their pants off, but they didn't, they couldn't, keep it. They couldn't keep the same things going.

Was the monastic life at Holy Cross to become more and more a derivative of the past, a reconstructed fantasy of imagined historic practice and ever more dimly remembered Holy Cross tradition? Or would the community challenge itself to burn anew with the original catholic energy and drive—not to maintain a museum but to construct a living, contemporary monasticism? To choose the first would assure the approval of the aging Anglo-Catholic constituency of the Order, and in the short run cost less in community energy and anxiety. But would it be faithful to its founders' vision of a fully contemporary monasticism growing from American culture? To choose the second path would ensure turmoil within the Order and disaffection among old friends. But it would set the community on a new path, rather than constricting the members of the Order to the well-worn paths of the past, invigorating when they were first blazed but now constricting in their familiarity. And, most importantly, it would provide room for a new generation of monks.

The past to Fr. Taylor was glorious, but an inspiration rather than a pattern for all time. He wanted the Order to recapture some of the dangerous creative energy of the earlier days, and that would take risk:[3]

One of the greatest things that happened was that the Order was hand in hand with the Catholic movement and all that that meant, all the glory of the Catholic congresses and all the rest of it. They were all part and parcel of that, and they were substantiating, giving that a living, day by day stability. When that began to change, the Order, instead of letting itself get out of date and fight for the old cause, confessions, holy water, rosaries and all that kind of business, said "No." The men in the Order had enough sense to know that there really was going to be a renewal or a liturgical revival. And they got on board. And so they went through a period then of shocking rather than helping their clientele.

But the important point to Fr. Taylor, and the reason he encouraged, even initiated the process of reform, was that it was the really catholic movement of the time:[4]

The Order went ahead and picked up a new, clearer vision of Catholicism than it had been sharing before. And this made a tremendous difference in the exterior appearance and behavior of the Order itself. The men were different. The authority of the Superior, or the unquestioning obedience, of the matter of discipline and prayer and meditation and study, those things began to fade a bit, to lose their grasp. They were no longer the substantial things that held the life in its place. Instead of that, it seems to me, what they had was a [new] vision of the Church . . . and they were for that 100%.

The whole Christian Church and much of American society was undergoing change at the same time. Holy Cross was far from immune from the changes of the day. In fact, as an institution, it was relatively quick to respond to those changes. The Episcopal Church was producing a new *Book of Common Prayer,* a process which lasted from 1965 to 1979 in public worship, and longer than that in preparation. Whole areas of the Church's life were opening up as never before, including the full participation of the laity in the work and ministry of the Church, the beginning of the movement towards the ordination of women, and a reawakening of interest in the spiritual life among masses of people. Community became a focus of concern far beyond the walls of convents and monasteries. The new psychological understandings of personality opened up questions about the life under vows and its goals, indeed, about how God was perceived by the self at all. And a growing attention to issues of poverty and justice put into a new perspective the monastic commitment to poverty and its sometimes less than destitute reality. Between 1960 and 1970, it is fair to say, the American Christian world was changed utterly, a change that went far beyond its origins in the Second Vatican Council to include virtually all Christians, including fundamentalists, conservatives and charismatics, whose enthusiasm also touched the monasteries. Holy Cross was affected by all these movements. Indeed, it could hardly avoid them if it was to be true to its vocation to be alive to the Spirit.

But Holy Cross also faced a new situation within its own self-understanding. What had happened, in fact, was a massive shift in the perception of the source of legitimacy for its monastic life. To the original members, and indeed to the vast number of founders and refounders of the religious and monastic life in the nineteenth century, there was a way to be recaptured, an ideal to be approximated. But after eighty years and more of living after that ideal, the monastic communities in fact existed, had histories, traditions, living memories of experience and practice of their own. The legitimacy of the monastic life had shifted from theoretical to experiential ground. It was possible to change, to experiment, to vary traditional patterns, because the psychic security necessary to lead the monastic life no longer needed to be derived from reconstructions of the past. The living community, the dozens of holy lives lived within living memory, all gave the Order its own legitimacy. It was now free, thanks to its past lived in faithfulness to a reconstructed, theoretical idea, to step out into the world of risking experience.

The newer members of the Order did not perceive it as fragile and beleaguered, a beacon of Anglo-Catholicism in a hostile Protestant world. Rather, they saw a confident and strong community which had capital to expend for the rest of the Church and society. There was energy waiting to be unleashed in the monastic life, and Fr. Taylor sensed this:[5]

> Our life generates energy. You cannot love God the way we love God and pray to God so much without having to find some outlet to express this. So we generate energy that has to be expressed, and it seems to me that it's so strong a thing . . . [that Holy Cross is] not an Order supporting studies, not an Order supporting social work, but an Order doing all these different things. But if it's kept integrated, that energy is bound to be stronger than the influence of some outsider who has only a weekly or a monthly or an annual effect upon us. And that rides roughshod over some people who think we should do such and such a thing. They don't like it. But that's the way the Order is. You cannot, you cannot defeat it.

To Fr. Taylor the idea that the Order should live for other people's expectations and understandings of the monastic life denied the mystical energy of the community, and was close to blasphemy. The monastic life must be derived from the living prayer and intention of its faithful members. If it was, it would have the strength of the Spirit.

After his reelection Fr. Taylor appointed Fr. Lynn Novice Master and Fr. George Swayne the Assistant Novice Master. Fr. Swayne became Novice Master in April, 1968, and led the novitiate through a period of enormous expansion as a dozen or more each year arrived to try their vocations. As if to smooth troubled waters, Fr. Turkington was appointed Assistant Superior. Fr. Belway, who had replaced Fr. Gunn as Prior of St. Andrew's, remained. Fr. Allan Smith remained Prior at Bolahun, and Fr. Parsell was appointed Prior of Mount Calvary.

The first new house of the Order to be started in twenty years was begun in 1967. Fr. Spencer had been spending an increasing amount of time preaching and giving missions in Texas, and the Order received an invitation from Bishop Charles Avery Mason of the Diocese of Dallas to open a house of the Order there. He offered space at the Bishop Mason Conference Center to the Order, and Fr. Spencer arrived in the diocese early in the spring to continue his mission work and make the necessary arrangements. He was joined in June by Br. Nicholas Jamieson and in July by Fr. Sydney Atkinson. Together the three of them began the ministry of Whitby House, as it was known until 1976, when its name was changed to James Huntington Priory.

The ministry of Whitby House soon extended itself throughout the rapidly growing Episcopal Church in Texas and through the Southwest. Br. Nicholas became involved in youth work at Camp Crucis and as an assistant at the Church of the Redeemer, Irving, TX, and attended the University of Dallas. Fr. Atkinson supervised the retreat center and gave many clergy and parish retreats. Fr. Spencer continued his itinerant preaching and mission-giving. The relation with the University of Dallas grew, and Fr. Atkinson was appointed chaplain to the Episcopal students there. Whitby House rapidly established itself in a solid ministry.

It did not take long for further changes in the Order's worship and life to begin. In September, 1967, the community instituted Recreation for novices apart from the professed. Recreation is a formal exercise in monastic communities, and as it had been practiced in Holy Cross, was an hour spent sitting in strict precedence, with the senior Father beginning the conversation and determining its content. The novitiate soon broke that pattern when no longer together with the professed, and started a much more informal community time.

The following month, October, 1967, it was decided to allow women to receive Holy Communion at the normal place in the chapel at West Park, rather than having it carried back to them in the women's gallery. Up to this time women had only been allowed in the chapel and in the rest of the monastery in separate specified areas. Similar restrictions were in force at St. Andrew's, Bolahun and Mount Calvary. As a special privilege the mother and other women relatives of a man being life professed were allowed to have dinner with him in a small room near the entrance of the monastery, but could not join the community in the refectory. Sr. Catherine Josephine, OSH, remembered how the Sisters were received in those days at the monastery:[6]

> In those days there were very few areas into which women were permitted to enter, so we sat in the "Women's Gallery" at the back of the Chapel, and did not go to the altar even for communion. It was brought to us. Once or twice we were taken down to the crypt to visit the Fr. Founder's tomb; if we were there for a meal (which seldom happened) we were served separately in a little room near the refectory (the present "coffee shop"). We talked with whoever we had come to see in a small reception room in the Middle House, and that was that.

The following April, in 1968, women were finally allowed to sit in chapel and eat in the refectory, although some of the older Brethren, notably Fr. Hawkins, were never completely reconciled to this change. Fr. Hawkins would mutter audibly his complaints about women in chapel and refectory whenever he saw them there.

The liturgical changes continued as well. Fr. Spencer had begun a revision of the Breviary for the Divine Office shortly after he joined the Liturgical Commission of the Church, and the Order was asked by the commission to try the Psalter from the Revised Standard Version, to see how it would do for common recitation, as it was one option for the Psalter in the new *Book of Common Prayer*. For some years he worked on the Breviary, consulting many liturgical experts and current movements in monastic liturgy. In place of the complicated traditional eight hours, which had for years been grouped together to reduce the number of times the Brethren came to chapel, he settled on a four-office structure. In his introduction the new Breviary, Fr. Spencer explained the reasons for this change:[7]

> One purpose of the Divine Office is the sanctification of time. Formerly, when monasteries were predominantly rural establishments,

the day was regulated by the sun. It therefore was fitting that the monks should anticipate the dawn with Matins and greet it with Lauds. Prime celebrated sunrise; and the three divisions of the day, the third, sixth, and ninth hours, were hallowed by Terce, Sext and None. Vespers was recited at sunset and Compline at nightfall. Thus the eightfold office was appropriate to life as actually lived.

It is so no longer. Our days are regulated not by the sun but by clocks. When Matins and Lauds are scheduled at a particular hour, they are sometimes recited long before dawn and at other times after sunrise. The same disassociation from meaningful time divisions befalls the other Offices. Then the temptation to bunch them together becomes irresistible. Few are the monastic communities that go to chapel seven or eight separate times a day for the recitation of the Offices. They are more likely to combine them so as to visit the Chapel four times.

A fourfold Office is relevant to our natural time divisions. This breviary seeks to provide one. Matins starts the day with praise and prayer. The noontide pause is the occasion for Diurnum. Vespers ends the working day and Compline terminates the evening.

The Office structure in the 1979 *Book of Common Prayer* now follows this form as well. The traditional monastic hymns were retranslated and distributed according to the new system. Antiphons, collects and other necessary parts of the Office were retranslated or written new. The new lectionary for the Episcopal Church was incorporated. *A Four Office Breviary* was finished in the winter of 1967-68, and it was printed in March, 1968. The Order began using it immediately, replacing the *Monastic Diurnal* of 1932 which, with modifications and additions, had been the Order's Breviary for thirty-six years.

The second major liturgical change was the adoption of the new trial liturgy for the eucharist. The General Convention in the fall of 1967 had authorized its use throughout the Episcopal Church. It was used for the first time as normative for the community on the First Sunday in Advent, 1968. From that time on, although there continued to be private masses by the more traditional Brethren, the community eucharist assumed its new character: the "new liturgy" and full participation of those present in a liturgy fully expressive of the communitarian ideal of the liturgical reform. The Order has adhered to those liturgical ideals firmly ever since.

Three men were life professed early in Fr. Taylor's second term: Br. Laurence Harms, 37, in September, 1966; Br. Nicholas Jamieson, 25, in March, 1967; and Fr. John Walsted, 36, in April, 1968.

On Aug. 19, 1968, a special Chapter was called to vote on two more men for Life Profession. Under the formularies of the Order for generations, election to Life Profession was by a majority vote of all life professed eligible to vote in Chapter. Men had been turned down for profession infrequently but it was not unknown. Usually there was some clear reason why the person was not elected to profession. In this election Br. James (later Samuel) DeMerell was elected but Fr. Andrew Mepham was not. Br. James, 37, made his Life Profession in September, 1968. But the reform element of the community was outraged by the refusal to elect Fr. Mepham, 44, a priest-psychiatrist. Fr. Mepham was identified with the reform group of the Order, and would clearly have been a strong force in the community. He was denied election by one vote.

Had Fr. Mepham been elected to Life Profession it is probable that the radical reorganization of the Order's constitutional life which followed would have occurred more gradually. But as it happened, the non-election of Fr. Mepham set in motion a series of events which changed the community's formularies more than they had been changed since the founding of the Order.

One of those voting by proxy against Fr. Mepham died just two days later, on August 21, 1968. Fr. Karl Tiedemann, 78, had had a remarkable ministry, leading the Order's work at Ripon and Nixon and founding Mount Calvary. In the 1950s and early 1960s he had developed a strong ministry at Berkeley to the seminarians at the Church Divinity School of the Pacific. For some of those years he was not permitted on the campus of the seminary, and so he saw seminarians elsewhere. It is largely due to this ministry that so many men from CDSP joined the Order in those days. The reform movement in the Order is itself an ironic tribute to Fr. Tiedemann, conservative that he was, as so many of its leaders came from CDSP or were influenced by its liturgical and theological teaching. From 1960-68 he had produced the *Holy Cross Magazine*. On Dec. 21, 1967, at Mount Calvary, he and Bp. Campbell had celebrated the fiftieth anniversary of their joint Life Profession in 1917. Fr. Tiedemann's genial hospitality and devotion to the retreat ministry set the permanent tone for Mount Calvary.

Fr. Tiedemann left a little story about his novitiate days which tells a great deal about his own character, as well as about his Novice Master, Fr. Hughson:[8]

Fr. Hughson was accustomed to take us novices on long walks daily. If there was a path that was a reason for *not* taking it. On one hot summer afternoon we came to Black Creek. I fondly thought that if

I could fall in he would let me go home without finishing the walk to get into some dry clothes. So after the others had nimbly jumped the creek, I fell in! It was deeper than I thought and I was thoroughly soaked—and in a habit too. He was not deceived but just smiled and said, "Just walk a little faster, father, and you will soon dry off!"

Father Hughson was the soul of kindness. One day he was absent and not expected home until Vespers. Bp. Campbell and I decided it was too hot to work in the garden (and in those days we worked in black tunics!). We decided to spend the afternoon reading in the library which overlooked the garden. In the middle of the afternoon, Bp. Campbell beckoned me to the window and pointed out. There was our Novice Master working all by himself. We got out there in a hurry to join him. But he never said a word about being late.

Fr. Tiedemann took enormous pride in building Mount Calvary, both in the physical work and in establishing its retreat ministry. He let it be known that he wished Mount Calvary to be his memorial, and his epitaph, "And the beggar died." His ashes are buried there in the succulent garden.

In the year remaining before the next annual Chapter in 1969, much time and energy was spent by the reform party in the Order trying to devise new formularies which would allow the Order to continue on its reforming path. Equal energy was spent by the traditionalist party in garnering support to defeat those proposals. The Order was pretty evenly divided between the two camps, and as the year wore on tensions rose. As the date of Chapter in August drew closer, there was talk of splitting the Order into two parts, or forming a new community altogether, using Whitby House as its base.

Fr. Edwin Clark Whitall, 91, died on March 11, 1969. He had been a powerful man in the community in the 1930s and 1940s, and had since become more and more ascetic. Fr. Taylor remembered his character:[9]

Fr. Whitall was a very, very stubborn man. Stubborn like you couldn't believe. You had to blast him with dynamite and then you probably couldn't, wouldn't move him. And he was very hard on his physical self. He would not sleep in the beds which the monastery provided. He insisted on having a chair, opening the window of his cell and having the chair back, and he had a cot, a folded-up cot stretched from the window ledge to the back of this chair. That's where he slept, so his head was almost outdoors, and I don't mean just in good weather, I mean that's where he slept all the time. . . . I can remember when his sight was getting very poor, he asked me one time to read a point that he wanted to make, and [when] I'd read it, then he would talk to it. This was a Sunday sermon at the Mass. I could hear him typing his meditations in his cell without the ribbon recording almost anything because it was all worn out. He was a touch typist and he used to type like that. But I would put him down as the most ascetically disciplined person in the Holy Cross that I've known. I think his stubbornness was almost beyond the ability of the community to handle. . . . I thought he was a fairly holy man. I guess I didn't know enough about Jerome to know that you can have a, well, he didn't have a temper, he was just stubborn. But I didn't know how far his stubbornness would cast him off Peter's list, but a very saintly person, in my mind, and a very hard person to deal with. When he had a standard that he identified and believed in then you couldn't do anything about it. There was no way in the world.

Fr. Whitall was a vegetarian, and was given meat one day by mistake. Unable to see it, he choked on the meat and died instantly.

In the spring of 1969 it was thought prudent to remove some of the younger men from the tension before Chapter, for which they bore some responsibility as well. At Easter, 1969, a project was begun in Savannah, GA, working in a slum area on community redevelopment, which lasted until the following September. Fr. Lynn and two of the most recent class of annually professed, Fr. Clark Trafton and Br. Rafael Campbell-Dixon, were joined by Srs. Josephine and Columba from the Order of St. Helena. In September the three Holy Cross men began a four-month West Indian mission tour, centered in Georgetown, Guyana. A second tour was organized in Jamaica from January until June 1970 with the addition of Fr. Thomas (later Bede) Mudge and Br. Dunstan (later Fr. Roy Waywell). This was followed by a nine-month West Indian mission tour with Frs. Trafton and Mudge and Br. Simon Garraway, himself from Guyana, in Grenada and Trinidad. Two objectives were served by these tours. First, Holy Cross was made known in the West Indies, with results for the future in vocations and invitations to work. Secondly, some of the pressure building at West Park for change in the Order was released in the energy of work.

The Chapter of 1969 was the most important since that of 1939 in restructuring the Order. It is probably no accident that a generation had elapsed since the last substantive change in the Order's structure. At the 1969 Chapter a new procedure for election to profession was passed, giving that authority to the Council and Superior after the community was canvassed concerning the readiness of men for profession. As the new method could not be implemented until it was passed a second time in 1970, several men in annual vows chose to delay asking for Life Profession until the new legislation was in effect. This change opened up the community to a far larger number of professions than it had experienced before. In its entire history to 1969 the Order had life professed fifty-seven men. In the following sixteen years, another fifty would take the monastic vows for life, a phenomenal increase. It also opened the community to a far wider range of social, racial and national origins than ever before, making the Order of the Holy Cross an international, multicultural and multi-professional community, and the largest monastic community for men in the Episcopal Church.

The second change made by the Chapter was to allow significant experimentation with the monastic life by the various houses in the Order. The pressure building for some years was not only to life profess a greater variety of men and to modernize the liturgy, but to make monasticism in Holy Cross truly contemporary. Community discussions through the year and then at Chapter led the Chapter to authorize significant experimentation. The Rule, Custumal and Constitution were not formally suspended, but wide latitude for experimentation, within certain requisites, was allowed. Planning was to be done carefully beforehand, with all the available Brethren taking part. Each experiment was to be evaluated and reported to Chapter. Not too many experiments were to be run at any given time. Those who wished to keep the traditional observance were allowed to do so, "but without thereby nullifying the Community's right to experiment." No experiment was to jeopardize the basic essentials of the monastic life in Holy Cross, which were defined as:

1. The Four Offices
2. Daily Eucharist
3. One hour of personal prayer
4. Community intercession
5. One meal in common
6. Community recreation, discussions, common ministry and retreats were still to be held

There was no attempt to change the vowed commitments of poverty, chastity and obedience. Rather, the purpose was to allow the lifestyle of each house to be restructured.[10]

Two men were ready for Life Profession in the fall of 1969, and went through the traditional process of election. William Fields (Br. Cyprian), 45, and Robert Brown (Br. Augustine), 25, were elected on Holy Cross Day, Sept. 14, 1969. Both black, they brought to three the number of black life professed members of the Order.

The 1970 Chapter was the first to be held in June rather than August. At that Chapter the new legislation for election to profession was passed, together with a new section in the Constitution on the houses of the Order. They were allowed to determine their own lifestyle, within the limits of the Rule, Constitution and Custumal and decisions of Chapter, thus enshrining experimentation as an ongoing process. The men who had been waiting for the new election legislation to be confirmed were then elected. It was the largest group of men ever life professed in Holy Cross: Fr. Clark Trafton, 35; Robert Campbell-Dixon (Br. Rafael), 35; Eric Smith (Br. Martin), 26; Donald Wortman (Br. Joseph of Bethlehem), also 26; and John Brice (Br. Ambrose), 34. Six men were also elected to annual profession. In one stroke the reform party in the Order had completely shifted the balance of political power. In the future the question would not be tradition or reform, but, what kind of reform.

The 1970 Chapter also adopted a paper on the meaning of the three vows of poverty, chastity and obedience by Fr. Spencer. In it Fr. Spencer tried to express the positive meanings of the vows in contemporary terms, and the Order adopted his definitions as official understandings of the vows. The key concept for understanding the vows in this interpretation is integrity.[11] "Poverty is reverence for the integrity of creation." That is, an acceptance of creation for its own meaning, and a refusal to exploit it selfishly. "Chastity is a reverence for the integrity of persons." It refuses to exploit others, and in celibacy seeks not genital relationships, but loving relationships "with as many people as possible, not just with those for whom he feels a physical, emotional, intellectual or spiritual attraction." "Obedience is reverence for the integrity of oneself." Man is called to offer praise to the Creator, and to co-create with Him a society of love. Obedience is not passive, but means contributing initiative as well as ability to the community project. The community has a large place in the scheme of God's project. It is to be a "school of love" (echoing St. Benedict's definition of the monastery as a "school for the Lord's service"):

in which the individual may learn the art of self-surrender and service. It is a society of love which should reflect in microcosm what God intends for all mankind. It is a fellowship of love which guides and supports its members as they go forth, singly or in groups, to share in Christ's ministry of reconciliation to the world. Insofar as these purposes and ideals are accomplished and embodied in the Community, it reflects and manifests, corporately and individually, the image of God in which man is created, the fecundity of the self-giving love of the Holy and Eternal Trinity.[12]

There is probably no better summation of the community ideal which was now Holy Cross's official self-understanding. Fr. Spencer had combined elements of the active ministry, which had been so much of Holy Cross's tradition, with a Benedictine emphasis on the community as a school for holiness, with its own mystical energies and existing not for its work alone but in its own right as a worthy project of God. To this he grafted a contemporary understanding of personality and ecology, to produce this remarkable, brief theology of the monastic life.

The Chapter of 1970 also decided to divest itself of ownership and control of St. Andrew's School, and as a first step to allow the Board of Directors to have members who were not members of Holy Cross.

Unlike the situation at Kent, at St. Andrew's there had always been a Prior for the monastic community. He was responsible for the entire operation of St. Andrew's, which included the monastery and mission work in the South as well as the school, and the headmaster of the school was responsible to him. Frequently the headmaster had himself been a Holy Cross man. Fr. Gunn was Prior from 1955 to 1965. He was a strong administrator and fully capable of holding the various elements of St. Andrew's together under united leadership. In 1960 Fr. Franklin Martin was appointed headmaster. He was quite as strong and determined as Fr. Gunn. This combination worked well, particularly as the requirements for operating a school increased. Gone were the days when well-intentioned clergymen and their friends could operate a school according to their own principles without outside expectations. Over the years the standards for teachers, buildings, staff and curriculum were mandated more and more by the state, and more and more it was clear that Holy Cross could not supply the needs of the school solely from its own resources.

Fr. Taylor replaced Fr. Gunn as Prior with Fr. Murray Belway in 1965. He may have reasoned that Fr. Gunn would duplicate Fr. Sill's career, making a fiefdom of St. Andrew's. For whatever reason, Fr. Belway was very different. A warm and effective teacher, Fr. Belway did not possess Fr. Gunn's administrative gifts. The school gradually passed under the effective control of Fr. Martin. Fr. Belway was replaced as Prior in 1968 by Fr. Lee Stevens, whose great personal asceticism contrasted strongly with the reforming energy of some of the men stationed with him at St. Andrew's, Brs. William Sibley, Ambrose Brice and James DeMerrell among them. In their attempts to bring the reforming currents of the Order to St. Andrew's, they found that Fr. Martin, not the Prior, was firmly in control, and were soon in conflict with him. By 1970 it was clear that a new relationship had to be worked out.

The Chapter's intention at first was to retain the Order's connection with St. Andrew's, while recognizing that the objective needs of the school required that another agency than the Order own and operate the school. The decision of Chapter urged that a new relationship be negotiated. Fr. Atkinson was made Prior and a two-year period of adjustment and uncertainty ensued. By 1972 it was clear that this process was not satisfactory, and the Order withdrew all its men from St. Andrew's, turning St. Andrew's into a completely independent school.

Leaving St. Andrew's was not nearly as traumatic for the Order as leaving Kent had been. But it was far more difficult for the staff and faculty at St. Andrew's than had been the case at Kent. The sixty-five years of continuous operation of the school, and the close association of such people as the family of Fr. Harvey Simmonds, who had built the monastery at Bolahun in the late 1920s, were an important part of the ethos of St. Andrew's. (In the early 1980s the old St. Michael's Monastery, a small copy of the original monastery at West Park, burned to the ground, and St. Andrew's merged with the Sewanee Military Academy to become St. Andrew's-Sewanee School.)

Not everyone in the community was able to adjust to the changes the reform brought. During Fr. Taylor's second term five men left the Order. At the Chapter of August, 1969, Frs. Herbert Bicknell and Murray Belway, who had both been at St. Andrew's, were dispensed, and Wallace Look (Br. Gregory) was dismissed. The following June, Fr. Robert Sullivan, who had been stationed at Bolahun, was dispensed. And in June of 1971 Fr. Terry, who had been part of the original movement for reform, was dispensed from his vows as well.

On Nov. 29, 1970, Fr. Edward Harris, despondent over some private sorrow and confused about the changes in the Order, committed suicide at St. Andrew's. He had been under medication for some time for a heart ailment, and seems to have been chemically depressed. Fr. Harris took religion seriously, and tried to identify his daily life with various acts of prayer. Fr. Taylor vividly remembered a walk with Fr. Harris when Taylor was a novice:[13]

The professed were allowed to invite the novices to go for the Sunday walks sometimes, and he took me for a walk, and as we started up the hill, this was the winter time, when we started up the hill he kept silence from the front door until he got up the hill and he said, "This walk, I'm taking this walk in intention for so and so," he told me, who was a cripple and can't walk at all. Well, you can imagine what that did to me. The whole walk was something different from just a Sunday afternoon walk.

Fr. Taylor believed that Fr. Harris was out of touch with what was going on in. the Order, and had become increasingly isolated:[14]

I think that he felt that the Order was moving away from where it had been and it was disquieting to him. He was a quiet sufferer that felt as though the Order was losing its direction. I think I worried him a great deal myself, although I was good friends with him. I think that he worried about things that I did myself and this ate away at him.

Fr. Taylor's sensitivity to the effect of his actions on Fr. Harris, without thereby regretting his policy for the Order, is a measure of his greatness as a leader.

Five more men were life professed in the Order during Fr. Taylor's second term, bringing the total number of life professed in the community at the end of his time as Superior to thirty-five: Br. Simon Garraway, 43; Br. William Sibley, 37; Fr. Thomas (later Bede) Mudge, 34; Br. (later Fr.) Brian McHugh, 25; and Br. Robert Kendrick, 27.

In Fr. Taylor's final year as Superior two new works were established, in St. Louis, MO, and Gales Ferry, CT. The Order had received an invitation from Trinity Parish in St. Louis to establish a house there to do some inner city and parish work. In June, 1971 Br. Cyprian opened the house there, which lasted just over a year, closing in September, 1972. At the same time Fr. Trafton opened the Connecticut house at Gales Ferry, closely connected with, but independent of, St. David's Parish. This house had an active ministry to young people and lasted two years, until June, 1973.

In December, 1971, the Council, at the Superior's request, acted to change the status of the mission and monastery at Bolahun. In response to the growing movement toward self-determination in Liberia, as in other third world countries, and on the advice of the Prior of Bolahun, Fr. Lynn, the Council voted to recognize the jurisdiction of the Bishop of Liberia over the work in Bolahun and to entrust to the diocese all the properties owned by the Order there. The name of the monastery there was changed from St. Anthanasius Monastery to the Holy Cross Community in Liberia, and it was relinquished, after almost exactly fifty years, as a house of the Order.

On Jan. 17, 1972, Fr. Alpheus Appleton Packard, 67, died. He had been in a coma for some weeks after collapsing with a heart attack. In his later life "Tony" Packard had become obsessed with publishing his poetry and sermons. At one point he asked if he could have his poetry published, and the Superior assented, thinking that Fr. Packard would submit it to a reputable commercial publisher, who would probably reject it. Instead, Fr. Packard literally had it published, presenting the bill to the Superior. He was known to offer to autograph a copy of one of his books for the rector of a parish where he was preaching, and then tell him the price, once it had been personally inscribed. He scrupulously saved his papers and memorabilia. As archivist he preserved much of what remains from Holy Cross history, and this history owes much to his work preserving what was left from the past.

Fr. Taylor's second term was absolutely revolutionary for the Order of the Holy Cross. In six short years the polity, spirituality, community life and self-understanding of the Order had been completely changed. Fr. Taylor's own placid manner and patience healed many, though not all, wounds. Only five men had chosen to leave the community to this point. Under Fr. Swayne's charismatic leadership the novitiate was bursting the seams of the new monastery. The community had resolved most of its issues of reform, and now the question was, what would it do with its new-found freedom?

Expansion and the Benedictine Decision (1972-1985)

In June, 1972, Fr. Connor Lynn was elected Superior. The other strong candidate was Fr. George Swayne, an indication of the success of the reform party. Fr. Lynn had spent most of his life in the Order either in Bolahun or working with the novitiate. Forty years old, a graduate of Stanford and the Church Divinity School of the Pacific, he brought a restless energy to the office of Superior. A tireless traveler and innovator, his nine years as Superior were characterized by constant movement, growth, change and challenge to the community.

Fr. Lynn did not initiate new reforms in the community, but worked within the new consensus achieved under Fr. Taylor to inject two significant new agendas into Holy Cross: internationalization and ecumenism. His experience in Africa led him to see the Church as wider than the American, Episcopalian, Anglo-Catholic stance the Order had largely adhered to in the past. Caught up in the excitement of awakening aspirations among third-world people, with whom he strongly identified, Fr. Lynn wanted to align the community with the Church in Africa, the Caribbean and Latin America. Much of the expansion of the Order during his terms as Superior emerges from this desire. He was also convinced of the necessity for ecumenical action, particularly with the Roman Catholic Church, and this gave much of the impetus to the Order's decision to adopt the Benedictine Rule.

His first leadership team confirmed these priorities. Br. Cyprian Fields was made Assistant Superior, the first layman to hold that post, and the first black man to hold leadership in the community. Fr. Trafton was made Novice Master, bringing to prominence another man trained at the Church Divinity School of the Pacific, with its emphasis on contemporary theology and liturgics. Fr. John Ryan was made Prior of West Park, a position created in 1967. (Before that time the Superior was formally the head of the house at West Park, with actual authority devolving on the Fathers in order of precedence.) Fr. Ryan was not in that position long, however, as he left for Rome in the fall to study at the Anselmianum. He was replaced by Fr. John Walsted, another CDSP man. Fr. Allan Smith remained as Prior of the Holy Cross Community in Liberia until Br. Rafael could arrive there in 1973. Fr. Swayne was made Prior of Mount Calvary, in an attempt to bring that usually traditional house into the mainstream of the reformed community.

Immediately after his election as Superior, Fr. Lynn closed the one-year-old house at St. Louis and withdrew the Brethren from St. Andrew's pending a reevaluation of the Holy Cross presence there. At the same time he moved to open three new houses of the Order, in Toronto, Berkeley, CA, and New York City.

The Order had long dreamed of a house in Canada, and in 1972 had four Canadian members. Several invitations to establish the Order there had been received and deferred over the years. Bishop Hugh Stiff of Keewaitin (later the Dean of St. James Cathedral in Toronto) had become close to the community, and he was named Chaplain of Holy Cross in Canada. In the summer of 1972 Fr. Harold Payne and Br. David Khan both went to Toronto to establish the new house, awaiting the arrival of Fr. Taylor, who after a long vacation was to be the first Prior. After renting for some months, a suitable house was purchased at 3 Humewood Drive, off St. Clair Avenue. There, under the leadership first of Fr. Taylor, then Fr. Brian McHugh and Br. Jay Launt, the ministry of the Toronto Priory grew to encompass two parishes, involvement with the cathedral, various kinds of counseling and social work, and wide involvement with the Canadian Church.

In 1972 Frederick Houk Borsch became Dean of the Church Divinity School of the Pacific. A strong Associate of Holy Cross, he envisioned a monastic community on the campus of CDSP to provide spiritual direction, a sense of community, and connection with a wider aspect of the Church for the seminary community. He had been in touch with Br. William Sibley, then at Mount Calvary, and invited him to begin a house at CDSP. Br. William, together with Fr. Baldwin and Br. Paul Hayes, moved into an unused portion of the Dean's House (now the Dominican School of Philosophy and Theology) and began to live the monastic life at the seminary. Br. William was followed as Prior by Br. Paul Hayes and then in 1976 by Fr. Roy Parker. Several members of the Order were trained for the priesthood there, including Frs. Dominic Wilson, John Kpoto, Adam McCoy and Paul Lauer. The house was known initially as Holy Cross Priory, then as St. Dominic's, and finally, with the addition of the Camaldolese in 1979, as Incarnation Priory.

The new work in New York City was authorized at the same time as Toronto and Berkeley, but it took longer to start. There were negotiations at first with the Church of the Holy Communion, Dr. Muhlenberg's historic parish, which might have led to a Holy Cross presence there, but they were inconclusive. The Order was then invited by the Manhattan North Inter-Parish Council to establish a house in Harlem to work among the various Episcopal parishes there. On Dec. 6, 1973, the community took up residence at the Chapel (now the Church) of the Intercession at 155th St. and Broadway. Br. Augustine Brown was the first Prior of Holy Cross House, later named Absalom Jones Priory, after the first black priest of the Episcopal Church. The Brethren soon began to find pastoral work among the various parishes in the area, and several attended the Cathedral School of Theology. In September, 1974, Br. Peter Patrick replaced Br. Augustine as Prior until February, 1977, when Augustine stepped in again. In the fall of 1977 a house was purchased (with a timely loan from the Bishop of New York, Paul Moore) at 455 West 148th St., near Convent Avenue in the Sugar Hill district, north of City College, and the settled life of the community in New York really began.

During Fr. Lynn's first two years as Superior three men were life professed. Br. (later Fr.) Roy Waywell, 28, Br. Ronald Haynes, 33, and Br. Paul Hayes, 67.

After failing to be elected Superior in 1966 Fr. Julien Gunn remained at West Park, giving missions and retreats and acting as the Eastern Provincial Chaplain for the Community of St. Mary. In 1969 he took a leave of absence from the community and was elected Rector of St. James Episcopal Church, Memphis, TN, a post he held for two years. In 1971 he was named headmaster of St. Mary's School, Peekskill, NY, operated by the Community of St. Mary, where he remained until 1974. He had gradually grown away from the Order in those five years out of community, and in May, 1974, asked to be dispensed from his vows, after twenty-four years in the community. On the same day Br. Martin (Eric Smith) was also dispensed. He had been professed less than four years.

In 1974 four men were life professed: Br. Gerald Stading, 39; Br. Brian Youngward, 30; Br. Roy Jude Arnold, 37; and Br. (later Fr.) Damian Williams, 28.

The three years after the election of Fr. Lynn were characterized by large novitiates at West Park. Classes of as many as ten men entering as postulants both in September and February were not unusual. Fr. Trafton, assisted by Fr. Turkington, Fr. Schultz and Br. Rafael, pursued a policy of training which strongly emphasized community life without diminishing training in prayer and the community's work. At times West Park was so full of novices that it seemed almost as though the community's entire purpose was to train novices, and in the early 1970s the community was very large indeed. The choir was full most of the time, and the singing of the Divine Office glorious, with as many as thirty or forty voices present at any given time.

A characteristic feature of novitiate life at this period was the novitiate vacation. Fr. and Mrs. Karl Lutge, friends of the Order, had given the Order a summer house in New London, NH, near Little Lake Sunapee. Every summer the novitiate was divided in half, and the novitiate trooped off to New Hampshire for two weeks of rustication, visits to the nearby Shaker Village and to the shrine of Our Lady of La Sallette in the northern part of the state. These vacations were really exercises in the ascetical discipline of community living, and opportunities for further varieties of monkly behavior to manifest themselves in those new to the community. Even on vacation the incipient monks were tested in the arts of tolerance and inner strength.

There is a choice to be made in the monastic life between adherence to a predetermined, somewhat stereotypical, and largely imaginary role model of the monk and the monastery, and openness to one's own experience as the path to becoming *monos,* the one who is whole before God. Many who desire to enter the monastic life are possessed by romantic fantasy, from Hollywood images and monastery or convent novels, from half-informed ideas of medieval culture, or from admiration for a figure like Thomas Merton. Such fantasy can provide much of the psychic energy necessary to undertake such an arduous journey. But the way in which the community decides to move from illusion to reality helps to form the monastic character which emerges from novitiate training.

The traditional Holy Cross style was to display the monastic life in all its harsh rigor and seemingly arbitrary discipline. For many years this worked, producing men of great inner strength and discipline. But it also produced the defect of its quality, men who found in the discipline and rigor of the monastic life itself the reason for being a monastic, rather than a path to God. By the 1960s, however, the psychological and social climate of Christian theology called into question the fitness of such a path. Such a program might well stifle the personality. The goal of the community had always been to produce men of strength and determination who would will to persevere in the face of uncertainty about their vocation. The same goal still existed. But the community's decision was to throw the new men into as complex and interactive a situation as possible, to force them to make their own decisions about vocation so that when the moments of trial and demand arrived, they had their own conviction, assisted by tested grace, to sustain them. This, too, carried the defect of its quality, for it meant that men newly arrived to the monastic life must discover the path primarily in their own experience, not unaided by the community's tradition, but also not forced into rigid conformity. If there was a "wild and woolly" side to Holy Cross in the late 1960s and 1970s, this is its origin and base. It was unavoidable. But in the end it produced a community strong and oriented to the contemporary world and to the future, instead of a self-enclosed society of traditional observance.

The professed community's energies in the first three years of Fr. Lynn's term were spent largely in adjusting to the establishment of three new communities and the reorientation of the work in Bolahun. As Assistant Superior Br. Cyprian visited Bolahun in March and April of 1973. He reported that there was some ambiguity in the implementation of the program of "Liberianization":[1]

> The Central Mission Committee . . . is the administrative, "expediting" and policy making body of the town. It was formed while Holy Cross was still in total control. However, it now has a far larger role thrust upon it much sooner than it anticipated. This came about last year when total Holy Cross control, after fifty years, came to an abrupt end. "Independence" from OHC for the younger and civic aware people in Bolahun seems to be welcomed along with the pain and perhaps temporary chaos. I do not believe CMC, representing the townspeople, fully understand the implications, let alone the details of the OHC transfer of ownership to the Diocese of Liberia. Their "expediting" role seems to at least for a short while, have consisted of "taking it to Fr. Parsell." In many ways, especially in matters relating Bolahun to the larger Lofa County area, the CMC does not have the requisite experience and contacts. The 40 years Fr. Parsell has spent in Lofa County and northwest Liberia are no match for the CMC—or the entire Diocese of Liberia for that matter. But the CMC is aware that Fr. Parsell probably will not be available to them in a few months and seem to be preparing to the best of their ability for this time.

In fact, in order for the town of Bolahun to begin to express its own independence it would be necessary for the Holy Cross Community to move out of the monastery. In 1974 it did precisely that, taking a large house in Kolahun, some miles away, and pursued the monastic life there, more or less divorced from day-to-day contact with life in Bolahun. Eventually the community moved back into the monastery, but the old ties had changed enough that the Brethren did not automatically rule Bolahun by their presence.

On March 15, 1975, Fr. Sydney Atkinson, who had spent the last few years of his life assisting at the Church of St. Mary the Virgin in New York City, died at St. Luke's Hospital after a long bout with cancer. He was only 59. His last administrative assignment had been as the final Prior of St. Andrew's, a work he had carried out with grace and humor under much pressure.

The next day Br. Peter Patrick, 30, was life professed. He had been Prior of the new house in New York City since the previous September, an unusual assignment for a man only in annual vows. In April, 1975, two more men were life professed. Fr. Nicholas Radelmiller, 35, and Br. Jay Launt, 27. That June at the annual Chapter Br. Robert Kendrick, who had been in vows for only three years, was dispensed.

At its annual Chapter in 1975 the Order of St. Helena made the final decision to become a completely self-governing community. The Superiors of Holy Cross, who were also the Superiors of St. Helena, had gradually delegated more and more responsibility to the Assistant Superiors of the Order of St. Helena, and the time had finally come for the Sisters to become autonomous. Sr. Catherine Josephine Remley had been Assistant Superior from 1958 to 1962, and Sister Alice Stebbins succeeded her. In 1975 Sr. Andrea Walker was elected the first Superior of the Order from within OSH.

The Sisters had started a second permanent house in Augusta, GA, in the spring of 1961, and that same autumn had joined the Holy Cross Mission in Liberia, withdrawing only when the decision was made in 1971 to Africanize the mission. They withdrew from Margaret Hall in 1971 because of an inability to provide sufficient staff for the school, which itself closed in 1980. The same year that the Brethren opened the new Holy Cross house in Harlem, the Sisters opened their New York City work at Calvary Church on Gramercy Park. After two more moves a permanent house was purchased for a convent at 134 East 28th Street.

At the time of claiming their autonomy from Holy Cross, the Sisters made it clear that they wished the close ties which had bound the two communities together for thirty years to continue, and since that time Holy Cross and St. Helena have shared work and worship as closely as possible.

Ever since the first mission trip to the West Indies in 1969, which had brought the first of many men to Holy Cross from the West Indies to try their vocations, the idea of a house of the Order in that area was seriously considered. In the fall of 1974 Br. Cyprian resigned as Assistant Superior to begin seminary at the United Theological College of the West Indies in Jamaica, where he studied for the next two years, earned a Lic. Theol. degree in 1976 and was ordained priest by the Bishop of Jamaica the same year. The Bishop of Nassau and the Bahamas, Michael Eldon, proposed that the Order establish a house in Nassau both as a center for mission and work and as a novitiate for the West Indies.

In 1975 the Order accepted Bishop Eldon's offer. The Order of St. Helena opened a Bahamian House as well, with Sr. Cornelia in charge. In the spring Br. Laurence Harms arrived to begin teaching mathematics and science in the parochial schools. He was followed in August by Br. Brian Youngward, the first Prior of the new work, and Br. David Bryan Hoopes, recently annually professed, who was given a job teaching Latin in the parochial schools. After setting up the new house, Br. Brian was replaced in May, 1976, by Fr. Hoopes, who had just been ordained. When he joined the Order Fr. Hoopes already possessed a theological degree from Andover Newton Theological School and was ordained a deacon by Bp. Eldon in November, 1975, and a priest the following May. He immediately undertook a heavy round of pastoral responsibilities at the Cathedral and in various parishes, in addition to his teaching and administration of Holy Redeemer Priory, as the new work was called.

In fall of 1975 yet another new house of the Order was established. Mrs. Frank Marion, a widow of many years and a former parishioner of Fr. Taylor in Pineville, SC, offered her plantation, Tower Hill, to the Order. Tower Hill is a historic site, the ancestral home of the Marion family; its most famous resident was the Revolutionary War General Francis Marion, the Swamp Fox. Tower Hill is situated on gently rolling terrain covered with piney woods an hour northwest of Charleston. The main house is modern, but built in gracious plantation style, an avenue of tall trees leading up to its pillared porch.

Fr. Taylor had for a long time dreamed of a rural monastery for the Order, where there could be a greater degree of seclusion and contemplative silence close to nature. Tower Hill offered that combination, and in the fall of 1975 he and Frs. Parsell and Stevens arrived to begin the work of establishing the monastic presence there. Before long it was decided to build small, independent houses, 16' x 16', to house the community. This semi-eremitical style of living has given a unique character to Holy Saviour Priory, as it was named. It was at Tower Hill that Fr. Anthony-Gerald Stevens decided to pursue a calling to the hermit life. He approached the Superior in 1978, and by spring of 1979 had received the Community's permission to try for a one year probationary period. On April 9, 1980, Fr. Stevens made his vow to Bishop Reeves of Georgia as a hermit at his hermitage at Pinelands, a few miles from the monastery at Tower Hill. In September, 1982 he interrupted his eremitical life to return to Liberia and work at the Bolahun Mission. But he returned to Tower Hill in 1984,

and on Fr. Huntington's feast day, Nov. 25, 1984, renewed his commitment as a hermit to Bp. Dickson of West Tennessee. Fr. Stevens may be
the first priest in the Episcopal Church to become a hermit. He certainly
was the first to receive official recognition as such from the Episcopal
Church: Presiding Bishop John Allin gave Fr. Stevens permission early
on to say the eucharist alone in his hermitage.

With the establishment of Holy Saviour Priory, Holy Cross now had
the full range of monastic living situations. In West Park it possessed a
monastery of the classic type: large buildings, great chapel, scenic setting,
filled with monks who divided their time between the choral Divine Office,
work, study and private prayer. Mount Calvary's ministry was focused
on the retreat ministry in a more intimate setting, where the small monastic
community could make a direct impact on the retreatants. The monastic
missionary work of primary evangelization continued strong in Liberia.
Two urban monasteries, in Toronto and New York City, had been planted,
opening the community once again to its original apostolate, city work.
A community had been started in a seminary, locating the Order for the
first time in an intellectual environment. And in South Carolina the rural,
agricultural and contemplative life was now a possibility. In a few short
years the Order had established a constellation of monastic lifestyles rich
enough in variety to satisfy almost every possible vocational type. And,
more important, it gave the promise of multiple vocation to the members
of the Order already professed. One might now envision a life spent for
some years in active ministry, then a period in a more contemplative or
enclosed life, as the normal stages of personal and vocational development
might suggest.

Seven men were life professed in 1976, more than in any other year in
the history of Holy Cross: Fr. Roy Parker, 42; Br. (later Fr.) Dominic
Wilson, 30; Br. Benedict Robins, 27; Br. Philip Mantle; Br. Richard (later
Adrian) Gill, 28; Br. Stephen-Christopher Harrell, 35; and Br. (later Fr.)
John Kpoto, 30, the first African to be life professed in the Order. Son
of one of the most effective Holy Cross Bandi evangelists, Zacharias
Kpoto, Kpoto grew up at Bolahun.

Fr. Spencer had begun work on a revision of the *Four Office Breviary*
almost immediately after its publication in 1968. As the Episcopal Church's
proposed new *Book of Common Prayer* took definite shape, the Order
desired to conform the Divine Office to it as much as possible. In 1976
A Monastic Breviary was published and adopted by the community. It
utilized the new *Prayer Book* Psalter, and conformed to the lectionary
and calendar of the Church.

The largest number of dispensations in the history of the community occurred in 1976 as five men decided to leave the community. A new constitutional provision made it possible to dismiss a member, his vows being *ipso facto* dispensed. Upon final passage of this provision at the annual Chapter of 1976, Fr. Kroll's vows were formally declared dispensed. His dear friend Fr. Parsell was so relieved to have the matter finally settled that he wept openly.

Fr. Kevin Dunn had graduated from Trinity College, Toronto and was ordained in June of 1974. He was assigned to Mount Calvary, where from 1970-72 he had been the first layman to be a prior in Holy Cross. A year later he asked the Chapter to dispense his vows, but was refused in the hope that he might reconsider. He did not, and so in 1976 was dispensed. At the same Chapter Br. Boniface Challinor was dispensed. Br. Simon Garraway was also dispensed, and returned to Guyana.

In November, 1976, a special Chapter was held to dispense Brs. Gerald Stading and Ambrose Brice. Br. Gerry had abandoned the community in Berkeley without notice. Br. Ambrose had grown further and further from the normative observance and spiritual discipline of the Order.

On Nov. 5, 1976, Fr. Dr. Joseph Smyth, 86, died in Santa Barbara. For many years he and Bp. Campbell had been the presiding presences at Mount Calvary, providing stability to the house as Brethren came and went and the changes of the years washed over the community. "Father Doctor" was invariably kind and naturally drew guests to himself. Tea at Mount Calvary almost every afternoon was provided by the two of them and a small circle of regular friends gathered frequently on the south loggia overlooking the Santa Barbara Channel. Fr. Smyth was the first divorced man to be professed in the Order, having been married after he left the community in 1925; he had two daughters, both Roman Catholic Sisters.

In the spring of 1976 the Council urged the creation of two new novitiates for the Order, one in Africa and the other in Nassau. The Nassau novitiate attracted only one postulant while it operated. But the novitiate in Bolahun, begun in the winter of 1976, soon began to grow and became the basis of the next move by the Order, in the direction of a truly international community.

The change in the focus of the ministry of the Order in Africa required a major shift in personnel. Fr. Swayne, who had succeeded Br. Cyprian as Assistant Superior and was also Prior of Mount Calvary, was chosen by Fr. Lynn to lead the new African novitiate. He was replaced at Santa Barbara by Fr. Brian McHugh. Br. Jay Launt succeeded McHugh as Prior of Toronto.

Fr. McHugh proved fragile in his new position. After a year at Mount Calvary, he was unable to continue as Prior, and the Superior faced a difficult choice to provide the necessary leadership for all the houses of the Order, as well as two new novitiates. In the winter of 1977 it was decided to close the house in Texas, now known as James Huntington Priory, so that Fr. Radelmiller, the Prior there, could become the Prior of Mount Calvary. This meant leaving behind ten years of solid and successful ministry in Texas, and was a difficult move to make, but one consistent with Fr. Lynn's priorities. The other alternative was to close Holy Redeemer Priory in Nassau, but Fr. Lynn's determination to move Holy Cross into the mainstream of the growth of the Church in the third world was the prevailing value.

One further policy decision had yet to be made. Was the novitiate in Africa to be part of the American novitiate, or would it be separate? Fr. Lynn favored an essentially separate structure, with coordination, while the Novice Master, Fr. Trafton believed that there should be a single novitiate for the Order as a whole, with regular interchange of novices. There was much to say for both sides. The cultural, not to mention the geographical, distance between North America and Africa is enormous, and a truly indigenous monasticism would require local control and local understanding. But the unity of the community must also be safeguarded. How could men trained in Africa, out of continuous touch with the rest of the Order, be Holy Cross monks? How would they absorb the tradition? Fr. Lynn prevailed, and Fr. Trafton resigned as Novice Master. He was replaced with Fr. Bede Thomas Mudge, who remained Novice Master for the next eight years.

The first African postulants were received late in 1976, and five men were clothed as novices the following June. All but one were from Ghana. None of them persevered to vows. The novitiate in Liberia had a rocky beginning, not least because the first Novice Master and his assistants could not speak the same languages as the novices and there were many misunderstandings. But as time wore on experience provided what background lacked, and a solid foundation was laid for the growth of the community in Africa.

Holy Cross had begun its life as a self-conscious attempt to build a monasticism which was right for Americans in their own culture. It rejected the idea that monasticism must be imposed on a culture from outside. Fr. Dod and Fr. Huntington intended a monasticism which was fully American. And now, confronting the expansion of the community itself into Africa, the same question presented itself. Was Holy Cross to be a North American religious culture planted in African soil, or were the African monks to fashion a monasticism for their own culture?

The very dualism of this question indicates its American origin. The

Africans themselves who have joined the community in fact see the question very differently. America and Africa are not opposed but complementary. The fullest observance of Holy Cross tradition in liturgy and community life coexists side by side with African life, each enriching the other.

At the 1976 General Convention in Minneapolis the Episcopal Church replaced the unsatisfactory canon on the Religious Life passed in 1913. The new canon defined the content of religious vows, located communities within the structure of Church polity, linked them officially to the Church through a committee of the House of Bishops, and provided for appeal from community decisions through the Presiding Bishop. Many matters were left undefined, particularly the canonical status of unordained Religious. Nevertheless, the Church now had a satisfactory canon, and at its next Chapter Holy Cross voted to seek official recognition as a religious community under canon law—implying officially recognized status as an institution of the Church.

In 1976-77 the Order adopted an entirely new Constitution; the old Constitution had become encrusted with changes. As the community's ethos changed, more and more of the presuppositions of the old documents no longer were valid. Written principally by Fr. Clark Trafton, who also wrote a new Custumal for the Order, the new Constitution embodied the contemporary character of the community's political and governing process, and embedded them more firmly in the Order's official structure. One change so formalized was the decision to change the terms of Superiors. Since 1924 the term at each election had been six years. Now, however, any current or previous Superior who had served a full six-year term could, in the future, be elected only three years at a time.

The community lost ground in numbers in 1977. Four men were life professed, four were dispensed from their vows, and two died. Fr. David Bryan Hoopes and Br. James Borazzas were professed together in April. Hoopes, 33, had been in charge of the community in the Bahamas for a year and a half. Later in the year Br. Orlando Flores (who later added the name Huntington to his religious name), 33, and Br. Jack Harbert, 56, were life professed. Br. Jack's active life in the community was cut short in the fall of 1978 when he had a heart attack and subsequent brain damage that made institutional care necessary.

On March 27, 1977, Fr. Herbert Hawkins, 94, died. In his long life he had been associated with the Order twice: in the 1920s until he was released in 1932 to be married, and then after he returned in 1945. He was the only man life professed twice in the Order. Fr. Hawkins was a difficult man to know well. He was well defended against affection and familiarity. Once as a novice Fr. Mudge was sitting on a stone outside the Middle House at West Park. Fr. Hawkins walked past him on his way to say Mass at the Convent of St. Anne in Kingston. Fr. Mudge, thinking to draw a pleasant comment from Fr. Hawkins, remarked on the lovely weather. Fr. Hawkins whirled about, fixed him with a steely eye, and said, "You sit on stones, you get piles," and stalked off. When the author was a novice, he was assigned for eighteen months to care for Fr. Hawkins in his old age. Every week Fr. Hawkins had to see the doctor in New Paltz, and during the drive he would tell stories from his adventures as the first of the Holy Cross Fathers in Liberia. His favorite concerned the tax the Americo-Liberian government exacted from the tribal people. The government would not accept the iron money sticks used as currency among the tribes, but demanded properly minted European or American coins. Fr. Hawkins regularly made the trek to Pendembu to trade the iron for shillings. When he returned and gave the money to the people, they asked whose head was on the coins. It was that of Queen Victoria. They refused to accept it, making him return, a trip of many days, because they thought the money was no good. His eyes would light up and a wonderful smile would spread across his face as he remembered that line once again: "She done died!" He repeated this story endlessly, always chuckling over the last line. He remembered as a boy seeing the great queen's funeral procession.

On August 23, 1977, Bp. Campbell, 93, died in Santa Barbara. At the time of his death he was the senior bishop of the Episcopal Church by date of consecration, though not by age. After his retirement to Santa Barbara he withdrew from active politics and decision-making in the community, and while the changes swirled about him, the great conservative was serenely uninvolved. Of another of the Brethren who would not, even after his 75th birthday, cease trying to push his point of view, the Bishop said, "That old fool ought to know better at his age!" His ministry in his last years was in some ways the most significant of his whole life. An almost unending stream of people came to see him to seek his wisdom and blessing, and, magisterial as he was, he bestowed it impartially on all. His phenomenal memory was unimpaired, and rare was the churchman who could not find an affectionate conversational connection from his long ecclesiastical experience. He had a way of breaking into conversations which were beginning to verge on the unpleasant. Calling attention to a particularly fine rose in the garden, with an amused twinkle in his eye, he would roar, "Ho, ho, fine day, boys, fine day!"

In the spring of 1978 two men were life professed: Br. (later Fr.) Adam McCoy, 31, and Fr. Carl Sword, 47. Fr. John Walsted and Fr. Peter

Patrick were dispensed from life vows at the Chapter of June, 1978. Fr. Walsted had developed a career as an icon painter. Fr. Patrick, ordained a priest only two years before, had been the Prior in New York City from 1974-77, and then the Prior of Holy Redeemer Priory in Nassau.

At the end of six years as Superior Fr. Lynn could look back on a profound growth in the Order. Numbering thirty-five men when he was elected in 1972, the community had grown to forty-one. Four had died, thirteen had left the community through dispensation but twenty-three had been life professed, more than in any similar period in the Order's history. And while the Order had left its historic work at St. Andrew's, and had terminated work in St. Louis, Connecticut and Texas, it had initiated six new houses and a strong new novitiate in West Africa. A whole new generation of leadership had arisen, and the Order seemed firmly set on its new path.

On June 2, 1978, Fr. Lynn was reelected Superior for three years. Fr. Trafton ran second in the election, garnering significant support. Fr. Lynn immediately made important leadership changes in the community. Fr. Radelmiller was brought from Mount Calvary to be Prior of West Park, his second major move in six months. Fr. Damian Williams, who had been working as a parish priest from the Priory in Toronto since his ordination in January, 1977, was made Prior of Mount Calvary. Fr. Trafton, who had been Prior of West Park, was made Prior of Absalom Jones Priory in Harlem. Fr. Swayne was retained as African Novice Master, and Fr. Mudge as Novice Master in North America and titular head of the novitiate program. Swayne continued as Assistant Superior.

Almost immediately financial problems began to be prominent. For many years the Order had routinely subsidized the budgets of half of the houses of the Order, and the enormous cost of operating the huge novitiate at West Park was regarded as an expense to be borne out of the capital of the Order. Never wealthy, what little capital the Order had was rapidly dwindling. In 1974, for the first time, budget estimates were required from each house. At the same time all houses were instructed to use uniform account numbers. But it was some years before the Order as a whole was uniformly and regularly accounted.

As 1978 and 1979 passed, the financial situation gradually turned into a crisis. Fuel prices skyrocketed, hitting West Park particularly hard. The new monastery, so lovely in its openness to light and nature, was also open to the elements in the wintertime. Shortly after becoming Prior, Fr. Radelmiller was forced to lead the community into a series of drastic economies, which culminated in moving out of the new monastery altogether and back into the original 1904 building, whose construction was much more practical for the climate. The high inflation of the late 1970s hit every house of the Order, and for some time it seemed that even more serious measures would need to be taken. There was talk of selling Mount Calvary, the most valuable property the Order owned, particularly as its 1979 financial picture was bleak. But through hard work and sensible management, that crisis in operating funds was gradually alleviated.

This process brought profound changes to the Order, not simply on a financial level. Perhaps the most important was to put to rest the tradition of dependence on "father figures" to provide whatever was needed. Formerly it was expected that the Superior would provide the money and determine how it was spent. There was little mutual responsibility. Now, however, more and more of the Brethren were becoming directly involved in supporting the community through secular employment in the urban houses and in other ways, and they demanded a more communitarian approach to financial management. For Holy Cross, being a monk no longer meant a childish dependence for the necessities of life.

The second change the financial crisis wrought was to force a re-evaluation of both individual and common vocation. The question began to be asked in earnest, what do you want to do with your life, and how will it benefit the community and others? This forced many of the men to consider their call as monks, beyond the issues of religion narrowly defined, and to look to the question of their relatedness to the larger world. In this movement, a return to Fr. Huntington's vision of active monasticism can be discerned, as well as a response to Fr. Kroll's prophetic cry.

Thirdly, scarcity forced the community to redefine its priorities. The community's inner discussions were permanently enlivened by this process, but it also helped clarify the purpose of the monastic life for many of the Brethren. The need to develop permanent work demonstrated that the monastic life is rooted in particular places and shared with particular people, and those places and people must be adequately maintained. Necessity forced upon the community stability, a new and more focused love of place and Brethren.

One concrete outcome of the financial crisis was the establishment of St. Joseph's Priory in Chicago in the spring of 1979. James Montgomery, the Bishop of Chicago and an Associate of Holy Cross, offered the Order St. Barnabas Church, on West Washington Blvd. The Superior, concerned that his presence at West Park was contributing to the financial hardship there, moved his office to Chicago. Fr. Waywell was appointed Prior and Vicar, and the household included Fr. McHugh and Fr. Wilson, who were to work on development for the Order. Fr. Wilson, who was also the titular

Prior of Bolahun, paid special attention to the needs of the African work. Br. Timothy Jolley and Br. Philip Mantle worked for the Diocese of Chicago.

A second work was established a year later. The Bishop of Albany, Wilbur Hogg, offered the Order the care of St. David's Church, East Greenbush, near Albany. Fr. Gill, Br. Laurence and Br. Orlando were sent there, and for the first year lived in a basement apartment near the Cathedral. A year later they were given care of Trinity Church, Watervliet, as well, and they moved into the rectory there. They were replaced in time by Br. Rafael, Fr. Douglas Brown, Fr. John Kpoto and Fr. Richard Vaggione. The Albany house was never independent, but a work of the monastery at West Park.

At the same time the financial crisis was moving the community in the direction of stability, encouraging work and more focused attention to community, the Order came into contact with the Roman Catholic Camaldolese Benedictines. Fr. Lynn had for some years been a member of the International Anglican-Roman Catholic Commission of Superiors General, and Holy Cross began to be known more widely among Roman Catholic monastic communities. The Camaldolese visited West Park in 1975, mutuality between the two communities was perceived, and a covenant agreement was formulated. The Holy Cross-Camaldolese Covenant was agreed to by the two communities in January, 1977. It committed both communities to work together in the areas of reunion, mutual prayer, communication and exchange.

In 1979, Dom Robert Hale, OSBCam, took up residence at St. Dominic's Priory at the Church Divinity School of the Pacific, which, because of the specifically monastic ethos of the Camaldolese, was renamed Incarnation Priory. The two communities tested the waters of cooperation and eventually decided to form a joint Roman Catholic-Anglican community.

The form of Incarnation Priory is unique in the Christian world. It retains the distinction of Anglican and Roman Catholic, of Holy Cross and Camaldolese. There is no blending of structures and liturgies, but rather the Priory attempts to achieve unity in diversity, the two ecclesial and monastic communities working to inhabit the same space in active peace.

The introduction of the Camaldolese into the life of Holy Cross brought to the fore the question, What sort of monks are Holy Cross? A serious reexamination of the Benedictine tradition in relation to Holy Cross was undertaken. The initial proposal to adopt the Rule of St. Benedict had been offered by Fr. Trafton, and much of the work in the process of considering the Rule was shouldered by Dom Robert and on the Holy Cross side by Frs. Mudge and Wilson. At the annual Chapter of the Order in April, 1980, the community adopted a resolution which asserted that "Chapter, after careful consideration and discussion, believes that our Community is Benedictine in character and nature." It committed the Order to a process of study of the Rule of St. Benedict and contact with other Benedictine communities. The Order was aided in its study by Dom Robert and Dom Colman Grabert of St. Meinrad's Abbey.

Most Anglicans know the Benedictine way primarily through the Abbeys of Nashdom and Three Rivers. Studying the Benedictine world, Holy Cross discovered that it already fit in many ways into the normative pattern of Benedictine communities. The choir office was, and always had been, central to the community's spirituality. Community life had always been primary, particular works ancillary. There was a sensitivity to human growth and development that was perceived by others as characteristically Benedictine. But other aspects of the community did not fit the pattern as readily. The centralized structure of the Order, with a governing Chapter and strong central authority in the person of the Superior, were rather different. Stability had never been practiced by the community; quite the contrary. It had been a matter of some pride to the community that its members (perhaps remembering Fr. Sill) were not allowed to become overattached to particular places and work. The process of election to profession had been taken out of the hands of the members and entrusted to a representative body.

As the time of study proceeded, a consensus was formed. One powerful impetus to this consensus was the realization that Holy Cross is a *monastic* institution. That may not have been the direct intent of Frs. Dod and Huntington, but it is what the community had become. Further, as theory gave way to observation, it was noted that half or more of the community had already in effect chosen stability, through their work and rootedness in the various priories of the Order, and stability was itself necessary to their apostolate. Gone was the day when the Superior could automatically move a member without consultation. Moreover, each priory was seen to be developing characteristic forms of prayer, work and lifestyle, each of them monastic, each of them recognizably related, but each case local, particular. Holy Cross was already Benedictine in many ways.

The Chapter of 1981, therefore, added the Rule of St. Benedict to the Order's formularies, a decision not binding until the next triennial Chapter, in 1984.

On April 28, 1980, Fr. John Baldwin died, 83 years old, life professed for fifty-six years. In his later years Fr. Baldwin concentrated his ministry on itinerant preaching and giving missions. For two generations he traveled up and down the West Coast and throughout Texas and the mountain states and Alaska. He was still actively seeking appointments to the month of his death, even though his Prior could not let him accept them. He had a will of iron and a constitution to match. His erect bearing and precise eating habits endeared him to many, and he had a distinct way of speaking, his jaw thrust forward, trembling until he selected the exact word he wanted to use. From the beginning to the end of his life he was concerned for the precise meanings of words, and delighted in Chapter to spend what seemed like endless hours reformulating words and punctuation. But his greatness lay in his simple faith, expressed with conviction. His sermons always ended with the statement, "What a wonderful God we have." And it was this wonder that he communicated to his listeners.

All but one of the four men life professed during Fr. Lynn's second term took their vows in 1981. Br. Ian Meadowcroft remained in the community only a little more than one year. Br. James Borazzas, who had begun his first year in seminary at the Church Divinity School of the Pacific, left the community in 1981 as well. In February, 1981 Fr. Romuald Brant, 47, and Br. William Brown, 55, were life professed. In March Br. (later Fr.) Paul Lauer, 48, made his life vows. A gifted musician, he was the organist and choirmaster at the Cathedral in Nassau while stationed at Holy Redeemer Priory.

Fr. Lynn's three-year term ended in June, 1981. He stood for reelection, but on the second ballot Fr. Trafton was elected Superior by a single vote. The Chapter also voted to dispense Br. Philip Mantle from his vows. He had decided to remain in Chicago after the house there closed.

Fr. Clark Trafton, 46, had for some years played a key role in the community. As Prior of West Park from 1973-78 he had regularized the finances of the largest house of the Order, pointing the way to a modern financial system for the community as a whole. He had been Novice Master during much of this period, and had guided the formation of the largest group of men to be admitted to the Order up to that time. A key figure in the renewal of the Order from the time of his entrance into the community, he was the principal author of the new Constitution and Custumal. It was Fr. Trafton who had first proposed to the community that it consider adding the Rule of St. Benedict to its formularies. He had been the Prior of Absalom Jones Priory in Harlem for three years, bringing the somewhat chaotic ministry of that house into productive focus. And he had also trained as a psychotherapist at the Westchester Institute and begun practice in New York City. He was a clear alternative to Fr. Lynn.

Fr. Trafton appointed Fr. Allan Smith the Assistant Superior, as well as reappointing him Prior of Tower Hill. He changed the leadership of the community almost entirely, with the exception of Fr. Mudge, who remained Novice Master. Announcing that the Chicago and Nassau houses were to be closed, he appointed as Prior of West Park Fr. David Bryan Hoopes, who had been working in Nassau since 1975. Fr. Adam McCoy, who had been Guestmaster and Subprior of Mount Calvary for two years, was appointed Prior there. Br. William Sibley was made Prior of Toronto, and Fr. Carl Sword Prior of Absalom Jones in New York City. He left Fr. Parker as Co-Prior in Berkeley and Fr. Parsell in Bolahun.

The most pressing problem was to find appropriate leadership for the work in Africa. Chapter in 1981 encouraged the novitiate to move to Ghana, and Fr. Swayne and Fr. Lynn were assigned the task of searching for an appropriate site. That left the novitiate in Bolahun without leadership. Fr. Trafton appointed Br. Jay Launt the African Novice Master and Br. Dean Benedict Robins his assistant. They remained in Africa less than a year.

In July, 1981, Br. Paa Kwesi Josiah, 28, and Fr. Bernard Van Waes, 60, were life professed. Paa Kwesi was the first Ghanaian to be life professed, but he did not remain long in the community. He was assigned to Tower Hill and late in 1982 abandoned the community. In November of the same year Br. Timothy Jolley, 36, made his vows. And in February, 1982, Br. (later Fr.) Robert Hagler, 35, was life professed.

A year of hard work and searching for the appropriate location intervened before the novitiate could move to Ghana. Several sites were offered to the Order for its work there. Bishop John Ackon was especially eager to have the Holy Cross men in his diocese of Cape Coast, partly because he had been trained by the Society of the Sacred Mission at Kelham, England, and wished for a monastic presence in his diocese. He also desired to put his St. Nicholas Seminary under a monastic regime, and make of it a primary seminary for the Church in Ghana. Fr. Swayne was offered the dual post of Provost of the Cathedral of Cape Coast and head of the Church's schools there.

On August 2, 1982, the Brethren left Bolahun and traveled to Monrovia where they chartered a bus. With mishaps of visa and equipment, they entered the Ivory Coast, where another vehicle was hired. At Danane they were detained by a greedy policeman, but finally were extricated at modest cost, and then pushed on to Abidjan. At Abidjan, fed up with the charter crew, the Brethren took Ghana State Transport to Kumasi on Aug. 11, to Accra the next day, and arrived at Cape Coast the next evening, Aug. 12, after paying an exorbitant fare to a driver. Philip Quaque Monastery, named for the first Ghanaian Anglican priest, who is buried in Cape Coast Castle, had begun its life.

The Brethren were given initial lodging by a Cape Coast businessman, Isaac Quansah, who also helped design the plans for the new monastery and seminary to be built some distance from town. Early in 1983 Br. (later Fr.) Vincent Shamo arrived back in Ghana for his Life Profession at his home parish of St. Bartholomew, in Teshie, east of Accra. He was appointed Novice Master. A dean was needed for St. Nicholas Seminary, and Fr. Swayne and Bp. Ackon turned to Fr. Ralph Martin SSM, their old friend from seminary days. By the summer of 1983 the community was well established in Cape Coast, and the beginnings of a fishing venture made the financial situation seem promising for the future.

At the annual Chapter of 1982, Frs. McHugh, Williams and Kpoto were dispensed from their life vows. During his months in Ghana Fr. Lynn had become increasingly uncertain of his vocation to the Order. He returned to the United States in late 1981 and sought counsel, spending part of the winter at St. Joseph's Abbey in St. Benedict, LA. He took the parish of St. Luke in Eleuthera, Bahamas early in 1982, and by the end of 1982 had decided to leave the Order. He was dispensed at a special Chapter in January, 1983. Br. Benedict Robins left the community that winter as well.

Fr. Douglas Brown, 39, and Br. Leonard Abbah, 37, were life professed in the fall of 1983. Two more men were life professed in 1984. Br. Eduardo Bresciani, 32, a native of Chile, was the first Latin American man to be life professed in the Order, but remained in vows only two years. Br. Reginald Martin Crenshaw, 37, was professed in November, 1984. A teacher by training, he had been teaching in parochial schools in New York City while stationed at Absalom Jones Priory since 1982. In January, 1984, Br. Jay Launt left the community.

On March 24, 1984, Fr. Lincoln Taylor, 74, died of a heart attack at Holy Saviour Priory. The final years of his life had been devoted to the monastery in South Carolina, and he had been able to develop the contemplative side of his character there, working on the land. His was a complicated life. Outwardly placid and peaceful, his speech always quiet and calm, he seemed the most placid and reassuring and approachable of men. His leadership risked the existence of the community itself in order to open the door to the winds of reform and change, but for twelve years he guided the community with a strong, if sometimes unseen, hand. To Fr. Taylor, more than any other man since the Founder, Holy Cross owes its character.

His life was celebrated at Trinity Cathedral in Charleston by hundreds of mourners. His ashes are buried beneath the altar at Holy Saviour Priory.

The year Fr. Taylor died was the centennial of the Order, and celebrations were held at every one of the priories. A great service of thanksgiving was held at the Cathedral of St. John the Divine in New York City on June 2, 1984; the Primate of Canada, Ted Scott, preached, and the Presiding Bishop of the Episcopal Church, John Allin, presided.

On the actual anniversary of Fr. Huntington's vow, on November 25, 1984, a service was held in the chapel where he made his monastic profession, then a convent of the Sisters of St. John the Baptist, now a Salvation Army social center. Coincident with the centennial celebration, Fr. Huntington was included by the 1985 General Convention of the Episcopal Church in the Church's Calendar. The first post-Reformation monk to be so honored—the four Memphis Martyrs of the Community of St. Mary were also added to the Calendar—Fr. Huntington is widely regarded as a saint only fifty years after his death.

As part of its centennial observance, the Order embarked on an ambitious capital campaign called the Second Century Fund. This resulted in the acquisition of two new priory buildings, in Toronto and Berkeley, the beginnings of a major expansion of Mount Calvary and the facilities at Tower Hill, and an appreciable increase in the capital available to the Order.

But the most important observance of the centennial was the adoption by the Order of the Rule of St. Benedict to stand beside Fr. Huntington's Rule. The Chapter of June, 1984, made this historic change, and also began the process of adjusting the Order's life to its new Benedictine identity. A new novitiate training structure was adopted, in which men would now be trained in several of the Order's monasteries in order to know which they would like to have their stability. The professed community began the process of moving to stability in particular monasteries, and other functions of the community's life were examined in light of the new commitment.

By becoming Benedictine, Holy Cross came of age. No longer a small, beleaguered byway of the Church, it was, by 1984, the Episcopal Church's largest and most influential community and one of the largest in the Anglican Communion. It had seven well-established, flourishing monasteries, rural and urban, large and small, and more than forty members under vows, American both black and white, Canadian, West Indian, and West African. In its hundred years, twenty-five of its members had remained faithful to death. In joining itself to the great stream of Benedictine tradition, Holy Cross affirmed its own uniqueness and its place in the history of the Church. Against all odds, it had proved that the monastic life is not, as Presiding Bishop Lee had put it, doomed to a "history of shame and suffering." The monastic life of Holy Cross is a gloriously varied, powerful and faithful witness in monastic consecration to the Lord's command: "Take up your cross and come, follow me."

Two pictures may serve to convey the state of Holy Cross at the end of its first century, both in Africa, one old and one new. The Centennial Chapter of 1984 decided that the work in Bolahun was finally accomplished. Clergy of all three nations, Kisi, Bandi and Loma, were now established, and schools and hospitals were undertaken by the local people, often those trained by Holy Cross. And so the Order closed the Liberian monastery and community, looking to the new work and the young men in Ghana. But Fr. Parsell, then 79 years old, believed he still had work to do there. So, like Fr. Allen, in great age he once again made the trip to Lofa County, and there he remains at this writing, building up the churches, caring for the people, and perhaps the most respected missionary of the Church in Liberia. He chose risk, even separation from the day-to-day life of the community in order to pursue the missionary monasticism of the Holy Cross tradition. In so doing, he is at the absolute center of the mystical energies of the community's life.

While Fr. Parsell spends the experience of age in Liberia, a young African prepares to make his life commitment to the monastic life in Holy Cross. And here the mind looks back to that little scene on Stuyvesant Square a hundred years earlier. What greater contrast could there be to Fr. Huntington's Life Profession in that little Gothic chapel on a cold November morning in 1884 than the crowded African Cathedral of Christ Church in Cape Coast, Ghana, on February 23, 1985? Halfway around the world and a century later, Boniface James Ibraimah Adams, son of a Moslem from the north of Ghana, is about to take his vows for life, the 107th man to do so in the Order of the Holy Cross. The hot, dry harmattan is sweeping down off the Sahara. The food is plentiful for the feast, but will everyone have enough tomorrow, or next week? The music, the climate, the languages heard on the street, all are different, utterly different. But one thing is the same. In each place a 30-year-old man, in the vigor of his life, asked what he wants, replies that he wishes to "consecrate myself fully and entirely in body, soul and spirit unto our blessed Lord and Saviour Jesus Christ," and makes the threefold vow, committing himself utterly to God's service.

Who can tell what the energies of holiness can do? This is the power God has unleashed in the world through James Otis Sargent Huntington and the Order of the Holy Cross. A hundred years of faithfulness, prayer, service. A hundred years of very human men, brilliant and slow, mystic and practical, sinner and saint. A hundred years of patiently building the monastic life. So much of that life is hidden in Christ. So much is known to God alone. A hundred years of waiting, waiting for the Word out of Silence. And when the Word speaks, it is of love, of life, and of the future:

"Holiness is the brightness of divine love, and love is never idle; it must accomplish great things. Love must act as light must shine and fire must burn."

Notes

Chapter 1 Backgrounds

[1]Robert William Adamson, *Father Huntington's Formative Years (1854-1892): Monasticism and Social Christianity* (Columbia University diss., 1971), p. 62-3. (See the *Holy Cross Magazine,* 3 (March, 1892), p. 17, for the earliest account of the Order, from which this incident is taken.) Adamson's dissertation is the best account of the Order's early history.

[2]Ibid., p. 5.
[3]Ibid., p. 6.
[4]Ibid., p. 46.
[5]Vida Dutton Scudder, *Father Huntington, The Founder of the Order of the Holy Cross* (New York: E.P. Dutton & Co., 1940), p. 67.
[6]Ibid., p. 66.
[7]Adamson, op. cit., p. 53.
[8]Ibid., p. 55.
[9]Ibid., p. 56.
[10]Ibid., p. 58.
[11]Ibid., p. 59.
[21]Ibid., p. 45.
[13]*The Episcopal Church Annual,* ed. E. Allen Kelley (Wilton, CT: Morehouse-Barlow Co., Inc., 1985), p. 18.
[14]E. Clowes Chorley, *Men and Movements in the Episcopal Church,* The Hale Lectures (New York: Charles Scribner's Sons, 1950), p. 336-41.
[15]Peter F. Anson, *The Call of The Cloister, Religious Communities and Kindred Bodies in the Anglican Communion* (New York: The Macmillan Company, 1953), p. 555.
[16]Ibid., p. 535-36. In 1872 Wadhams became the first Roman Catholic bishop of Ogdensburg, NY, and died in 1891.
[17]Ibid., p. 539, from Fr. Palmer, S.S.J.E., "Brother William Skiles of Valle Crucis," *Cowley* (Autumn, 1944), p. 86.

Chapter 2 The Order's Earliest Days (1880-1884)

[1]Adamson, op. cit., p. 69.
[2]James Otis Sargent Huntington (hereafter JOSH) to Agnes van Kirk, 30 Nov. 1880; OHC Archives.
[3]JOSH to George Huntington (hereafter GH), 11 March 1881; OHC Archives.
[4]Robert Stockton Dod (hereafter RSD) to Rev. Peter Wolcott, 6 March 1881; Adamson, op cit., p. 72. Missing from OHC Archives.

[5]RSD to JOSH, 18 May 1881; OHC Archives.

[6]RSD to JOSH, 18 June 1881; OHC Archives.

[7]Ibid.

[8]JOSH to Agnes van Kirk, 7 July 1881; OHC Archives.

[9]JOSH to GH, 11 Sept. 1881; OHC Archives.

[10]JOSH to Agnes van Kirk, 15 Sept. 1881; OHC Archives.

[11]Ibid.

[12]JOSH to Agnes van Kirk, n.d.; also JOSH to GH, 4 Oct. 1881; both OHC Archives.

[13]JOSH to GH, 31 Oct. 1881; OHC Archives.

[14]JOSH to GH, 8 Oct. 1882; OHC Archives.

[15]All three are mss. in the OHC Archives. As the pages are unnumbered, individual reference to ms. pages is not possible. All quotes from these documents are taken from the mss.

[16]Adamson's distillation from a letter of JOSH to GH, 4 Jan. 1882; OHC Archives: Adamson, op. cit., p. 81.

[17]RSD to Rev. Peter Wolcott; Adamson, op. cit., p. 80. Missing from OHC Archives.

[18]Scudder, op. cit., p. 79-80.

[19]JOSH to GH, 11 Nov. 1881; OHC Archives.

[20]The notes from this retreat (with unnumbered pages) are in the OHC Archives. All quotations from the ms.

[21]All quotes from the ms. notes in the OHC Archives.

[22]RSD, n.d.; OHC Archives. Written from 330 East 13th Street, so dated after spring, 1883 and before he left in March, 1884. Possibly written to Br. Louis, the unsatisfactory brother described by Fr. Allen later in this chapter.

[23]JOSH to GH, 8 Oct. 1882; OHC Archives.

[24]Mrs. F.D. Huntington to GH, 5 Nov. 1882; Adamson, op cit., p. 79-80.

[25]JOSH to GH, 17 Jan. 1883; OHC Archives.

[26]JOSH, 22 Dec. 1882; Scudder, op. cit., p. 80-81.

[27]JOSH to GH, 17 Jan. 1883; OHC Archives.

[28]*Holy Cross Magazine* (hereafter *HCM*) 3 (March, 1892), p. 17.

[29]Sturges Allen, *Early Beginnings of the Order of the Holy Cross,* typescript of ms. in OHC Archives, p. 4-5.

[30]From a ms. copy of an appeal for funds for the Mission, fall 1883 (?), unnumbered pages; OHC Archives.

[31]Ibid.

[32]Edward Henry Schlueter, "Some Remembrances of Father Huntington," typescript, n.d., p. 1-2; OHC Archives.

[33]Allen, op. cit., p. 9.

[34]Schlueter, op. cit., p. 6.

[35]JOSH to F.D. Huntington (hereafter FDH), 5 Sept. 1883; Adamson, op. cit., p. 97-98.

[36]Ibid.

[37]*HCM* 3 (March, 1892), p. 17.

[38]Adamson, op. cit., p. 99.

[39]JOSH to GH, 5 Jan. 1884; OHC Archives.

[40]JOSH to FDH, 18 March 1884; Adamson, op. cit., p. 101.

[41]RSD to JOSH, 5 Nov. 1884; OHC Archives.

[42]JOSH to FDH, 18 March 1884; Adamson, op. cit., p. 101.

[43]Allen, op. cit., p. 8.

Chapter 3 Profession, Social Questions and Slum Work (1884-1892)

[1]Allen, *Early Beginnings,* op. cit., p. 19.

[2]See *The Churchman,* 6 Dec. 1884, p. 623; also Scudder, *Father Huntington,* p. 91-93.

[3]W.R. Huntington to JOSH, 9 Jan. 1885; OHC Archives.

[4]For an overview of this controversy, see Adamson, *Father Huntington's Formative Years,* op. cit., p. 104ff.; Scudder, op. cit., p. 194ff.

[5]Alfred Lee to Henry Codman Potter, 1 Dec. 1884, rpr. in *The Churchman,* 17 Jan. 1885, p. 80-81. See *The Historical Magazine of the Protestant Episcopal Church,* 10 (Dec. 1941), p. 318.

[6]H.C. Potter to A. Lee, 15 Dec. 1884; *The Churchman,* 17 Jan. 1885, p. 80-81.

[7]A. Lee to H.C. Potter, 19 Jan. 1885; *The Churchman,* 31 Jan. 1885, p. 116ff.

[8]H.C. Potter to JOSH, 7 Jan. 1885; OHC Archives.

[9]The Rev'd. E.H. Schlueter, quoted by Scudder, op. cit., p. 114.

[10]R.S. Dod, untitled, on tenements and the need for a new building, ms., p. 19-20; OHC Archives.

[11]H.C. Potter to JOSH, 26 Aug. 1885; OHC Archives.

[12]Sisters of St. John the Baptist, typescript of early memories, p. 93, 96; CSJM Archives.

[13]Adamson, op. cit., p. 118.

[14]JOSH, "The Birth of the Order," *HCM* 45 (Nov. 1934), p. 245.

[15]Ibid.

[16]Allen, op. cit., p. 22.

[17]Ibid., p. 29.

[18]JOSH, "Reminiscences of Henry George," n.d., ms. p. 3-5; OHC Archives.

[19]Ibid., p. 6.

[20]Ibid., p. 6-7.

[21]Ibid., p. 8.

[22]Ibid., p. 9-10.

[23]Louis F. Post and Fred C. Leubuscher, *Henry George's 1886 Campaign, An Account of the George-Hewitt Campaign in the New York Municipal Election of 1886* (New York, 1886; rpr. New York: The Henry George School, 1961), p. 105.

[24]H.C. Potter to JOSH, 10 Oct. 1886; OHC Archives.

[25]George W. Folsom to JOSH, 15 Oct. 1886; OHC Archives.

[26]G.W. Folsom to JOSH, 19 Oct. 1886; OHC Archives.

[27]JOSH to H.C. Potter, 20 Oct. 1886; OHC Archives.

[28]N.Y. *Tribune,* 5 July 1887; clipping in OHC Archives. "Tenement House Morality" was originally published in *Forum* 1 (July, 1887), and rpr. in *The Sterling Weekly* (a Henry George publication), vol. 1, no. 10, 3 Oct. 1896.

[29]N.Y. *World,* 18 July 1887; clipping in OHC Archives.

[30]Allen, op. cit., p. 27.

[31]Reported in the N.Y. *Evening Post,* 26 Oct. 1887; clipping in OHC Archives. Also in a flyer produced by CAIL at the same time; OHC Archives.

[32]Chicago *Daily News,* 26(?) Oct. 1887; clipping in OHC Archives.

[33]N.Y. *Sun,* 27 Oct. 1887; clipping in OHC Archives.

[34]N.Y. *World,* 27 Oct. 1887; clipping in OHC Archives.

[35]Unidentified clipping (2-11 Nov. 1887?); OHC Archives.

[36]Allen, op. cit., p. 31.

[37]Ibid., p. 31-32.

[38]Ibid., p. 28-29.

[39]Henry Rufus Sargent (hereafter HRS) to JOSH, 14 Aug. 1888; OHC Archives.

[40]Allen, op. cit., p. 13.
[41]Milford, DE, *Chronicle,* 23 Nov. 1888; clipping in OHC Archives.
[42]Allen, op. cit., p. 33.
[43]W.D. Howells, *A Hazard of New Fortunes,* 3. iii (1890; New York: New American Library, 1965), p. 200.
[44]Allen, op. cit., p. 36.
[45]Biographical sketch circulated to OHC, summer 1980; OHC Archives.
[46]Unidentified clipping from a Syracuse newspaper, June 1889; OHC Archives.
[47]Allen, op. cit., p. 37.
[48]Unidentified clipping from a NY newspaper, 25 Aug. 1889; OHC Archives.
[49]JOSH, "Miners and Ministers," *The Churchman,* 28 Sept. 1889, p. 9.
[50]Allen, op. cit., p. 37.
[51]RSD to Sturges Allen, 8 Oct. 1889; OHC Archives.
[52]Allen, op. cit., p. 38.
[53]*The Syracusan,* Syracuse Univ., vol. 12, no. 10, 9 May 1890, p. 173. Typescript supplied by Lester G. Wells.
[54]Allen, op. cit., p. 42.
[55]JOSH, "Reminiscences of Henry George," op. cit., p. 14ff.
[56]N.Y. *Herald,* 22 Sept. 1890; clipping in OHC Archives.
[57]Unidentified clipping, Kingston, Ont., n.d. (Jan., 1891?); OHC Archives.
[58]William Paret to JOSH, 5 Jan. 1891; OHC Archives.
[59]S. Allen to W. Paret, 9 Jan. 1891; W. Paret to S. Allen, 10 Jan. 1891; OHC Archives.
[60]Unidentified clipping, 19 Dec. 1891; OHC Archives.
[61]Allen, op. cit., p. 40.
[62]*HCM* 3 (March 1892), p. 18.
[63]N.Y. *Morning Journal,* 1 May 1892; clipping in OHC Archives.

Chapter 4 Westminster (1892-1904)

[1]Allen, *Early Beginnings,* op. cit., p. 61-62.
[2]Ibid., p. 49.
[3]JOSH, "Richard Meux Benson, S.S.J.E.," *HCM* vol. 26, no. 6 (Feb., 1916), p. 162-63.
[4]HRS to William Paret (hereafter WP), 12 April 1893; OHC Archives.
[5]WP to HRS, 13 April 1893; OHC Archives.
[6]WP to Sturges Allen (hereafter SA), 11 May 1893; OHC Archives.
[7]Minutes of Chapter, 13 June 1894.
[8]HRS to Vida Dutton Scudder, 15 Feb. 1939; OHC Archives.
[9]Syracuse *Standard,* 15 March 1894; clipping in OHC Archives.
[10]WP to SA, 2 March 1895; OHC Archives.
[11]Jesse Higgins to WP, 21 March 1895; OHC Archives.
[12]WP to HRS, 17 June 1895; OHC Archives.
[13]H.R. Percival to HRS, 18 June 1895; OHC Archives.
[14]HRS to WP, 1 July 1895; OHC Archives.
[15]WP to HRS, 5 July 1895; OHC Archives.
[16]WP to HRS, 31 Oct. 1895; OHC Archives.
[17]W.F. Brand to Lucretia Van Bibber, 22 Nov. 1895; OHC Archives.
[18]Jesse Higgins to HRS, 13 Jan. 1896; OHC Archives.
[19]Minutes of Chapter, 27 April 1897.
[20]Scudder, *Father Huntington,* op. cit., p. 267.
[21]Allen, op. cit., p. 56.
[22]Ibid.

[23]Ibid., p. 58.

[24]Charles Angell, S.A., and Charles LaFontaine, S.A., *Prophet of Reunion, The Life of Paul of Graymoor* (New York: Seabury, 1975), p. 45.

[25]David Gannon, S.A., *Father Paul of Graymoor* (New York: Macmillan, 1959), p. 76.

[26]Ibid., p. 72.

[27]Angell and LaFontaine, op. cit., p. 45.

[28]Chapter Minutes, 18 Aug. 1898.

[29]Allen, op. cit., p. 60.

[30]Ibid., p. 60-61.

[31]Ibid., p. 61.

[32]S.C. Hughson, O.H.C., "Old Westminster Days," *HCM* 45 (Nov., 1934), p. 250-53.

[33]Henry Vaughn to SA, 10 Dec. 1900; OHC Archives.

[34]JOSH to Lena McGhee, 22 April 1900; OHC Archives.

[35]Charles Grafton to JOSH, 26 July 1901; OHC Archives.

[36]Rule, Prologue II, "Mortification." Quotations from the Rule are taken from the first printed edition, n.d. but printed between 1901 and 1908. It was reprinted with changes in 1931, 1948 and 1975.

[37]Rule, Prologue III, "Of Good Works."

[38]Rule, Prayer V. 2, "Of the Priest as Called to Form Saints for Heaven."

[39]Rule, Mortification V, "Of Recreation."

[40]Rule, Mortification, "Of the Vow of Chastity."

[41]Rule, Prologue II, "Mortification."

[42]Rule, Good Works III, "Of the Officers of the Order."

[43]Rule, Good Works III. 2, "Of the Superior."

[44]Rule, Prologue, "Good Works."

[45]Rule, Prayer I. 1, "The Sacrifice of the Cross Perpetuated in the Sacrament of the Altar."

[46]Rule, Good Works IV, "Of Houses of the Order."

[47]JOSH on a possible move to Philadelphia in 1901; ms. in OHC Archives.

[48]H.C. Potter to JOSH, 10 June 1902; OHC Archives.

[49]F.D. Huntington to JOSH, 6 Oct. 1902; OHC Archives.

Chapter 5 Schools and Crisis (1904-1914)

[1]S.C. Hughson, "Among the Tennessee Mountains," *HCM* vol. 15, no. 10 (June, 1904), p. 161.

[2]Hughson, "Among the Tennessee Mountains. II.", *HCM* vol. 15, no. 12 (Aug., 1904), p. 188.

[3]SA to JOSH, 9 March 1905; OHC Archives.

[4]Ibid.

[5]S. Allen, "Letter from Father Allen," *HCM* vol. 17, no. 3 (Nov., 1905), p. 33.

[6]S.C. Hughson, "Christmas at St. Andrew's," *HCM* vol. 18, no. 6 (Feb., 1907), p. 91.

[7]Ibid., p. 92.

[8]Ibid.

[9]F.H. Sill, "Pater Recalls 1906-1907," *Kent* vol. 2:2 (Winter, 1983), p. 6. Edited from a series in the *Kent News,* Fall 1944.

[10]Ibid., p. 7.

[11]Ibid., p. 9.

[12]A.G. Whittemore, *O.H.C.*, typescript, p. 26; OHC Archives.

[13]Chapter Minutes, 15 Sept. 1906.

[14]Chapter Minutes, 15 Sept. 1908.

[15]Whittemore, op. cit., p. 53-5.

[16]Ibid., p. 58.

[17]E. Clowes Chorley, *Men and Movements,* op. cit., p. 278.

[18]*The Living Church,* vol. 28, p. 221. See George E. DeMille, *The Catholic Movement in the American Episcopal Church* (Philadelphia: The Church Historical Society, 1941), p. 100-05.

[19]JOSH, "The Plan of Campaign," *HCM* vol. 19, no. 8 (April, 1908), p. 122-25. This article was followed by "The Motive Power of the Campaign," *HCM* vol. 19, no. 9 (May, 1908), p. 135-37.

[20]JOSH, "The Real Issue of the Campaign," *HCM* vol. 19, no. 11 (July, 1908), p. 161-64.

[21]HRS to Vida Dutton Scudder, 15 Feb. 1939; OHC Archives.

[22]HRS to SA, 17 Nov. 1908; OHC Archives.

[23]HRS to SA, 3 Nov. 1908; OHC Archives.

[24]Ibid.

[25]HRS to SA, 27 Oct. 1908; in *HCM,* vol. 20, no. 4 (Dec., 1908), p. 56-8.

[26]HRS to SA, 1 Dec. 1908; OHC Archives.

[27]Aelred Carlyle to SA, 3 Dec. 1908; OHC Archives.

[28]HRS to SA, 16 Dec. 1908; OHC Archives.

[29]HRS to SA, 7 Sept. 1909; OHC Archives.

[30]Herbert Kelly to SA, 8 Nov. 1909; OHC Archives.

[31]S.C. Hughson to SA, 8 Nov. 1909; OHC Archives.

[32]Chapter Minutes, 1 Jan. 1910.

[33]JOSH, "Community Life for Men in England and America," *HCM* vol. 23, no. 2 (Oct., 1911), p. 20-21.

[34]JOSH, "Is There a Need for the Active Work of Communities of Men in America?", *HCM* vol. 23, no. 3 (Nov., 1911), p. 33-36; p. 35.

[35]JOSH, "Community Life and Mission Work," *HCM* vol. 23, no. 4 (Dec., 1911), p. 49-52; p. 50.

[36]JOSH, "The Bishops and Communities of Men," *HCM* vol. 23, no. 7 (March, 1912) p. 97-100; p. 100.

[37]JOSH, "Why Attempt to Revive Monasticism?", *HCM* vol. 23, no. 8 (April, 1912) p. 113-17; p. 116.

[38]Scudder, *Father Huntington,* op. cit., p. 270-1.

[39]S. Allen, "In Relation to the Canon on Religious Communities," *HCM* vol. 26, no. 2 (Oct., 1914), p. 43-4.

Chapter 6 The Decision for Mission (1915-1929)

[1]Whittemore, *O.H.C.,* typescript, p. 16-18; OHC Archives.

[2]Hughson, *The Fundamentals of the Religious State,* New York: Longmans, Green & Co. (1915), p. vi.

[3]Whittemore, *O.H.C.,* op. cit., p. 60-61.

[4]Whittemore, *Thanks Be to God,* typescript, p. vi-vii; OHC Archives.

[5]Whittemore, *O.H.C.,* op. cit., p. 63.

[6]*HCM,* Oct., 1918, p. 63.

[7]Fr. Harley Wright Smith, in a conversation with the author, 1983.

[8]"The Consecration at Holy Cross," *HCM* Oct., 1921, p. 286-87.

[9]"Lengthening Cords," *HCM* May, 1921, p. 121-22.

[10]Ibid.

[11]"The Work at Ripon," *HCM,* July, 1921, p. 198-99.

[12]R.E. Campbell, *Within the Green Wall,* West Park, NY: Holy Cross Press (1957), p. 39.

[13]Ibid.

[14]Ibid., p. 40.

[15]Ibid., p. 43.

[16]Ibid., p. 52.

[17]SA to JOSH, 20 Feb. 1922; OHC Archives.

[18]"Father Allen," by Walter H. Overs, in *All for the Love of God, A Holy Cross Omnibus,* ed. Ralph T. Milligan, West Park, NY: Holy Cross Press (1957), p. 238-40.

[19]Campbell, op. cit., p. 64.

[20]H. Maynard Smith, *Frank, Bishop of Zanzibar, Life of Frank Weston, D.D., 1871-1924,* London: SPCK (1926), p. 303.

[21]See *Report of the Anglo-Catholic Congress; General Subject: The Gospel of God; London, July 1923.* London: The Society of SS. Peter & Paul (1923), esp. p. 22-28.

[22]Hughson, "What Is the Episcopal Church?" in *The First Annual Catholic Congress, Essays and Papers, New Haven, Connecticut, November 3-5, 1925.* Central Conference of Associated Catholic Priests (1926), p. 42-43.

[23]Hughson's address is printed in *Report of the Anglo-Catholic Congress: Subject: The Holy Eucharist, London, July, 1927.* London: Society of SS. Peter and Paul (1927), p. 226.

[24]JOSH, "Superior's Letter," typescript, Nov. 1922; OHC Archives.

[25]Joseph Bessom to his father, 6 May 1922; OHC Archives.

[26]Whittemore, *O.H.C.,* op. cit., p. 55-56.

[27]Ibid., p. 62.

[28]Ibid., p. 43.

[29]Ibid., p. 45.

[30]Ibid.

[31]Benedicta Ward, S.L.G., trans., *The Wisdom of the Desert Fathers, Apothegmata Patrum from the Anonymous Series.* Oxford: S.L.G. Press, Fairacres Publications (1975), p. xii.

[32]Whittemore, *O.H.C.,* op. cit., p. 45.

Chapter 7 The Old and The New (1930-1948)

[1]J.O.S. Huntington, "Beginnings of the Religious Life for Men in the American Church," *Historical Magazine of the Protestant Episcopal Church,* vol. 2, no. 1, 1933; p. 39-40.

[2]Joseph Gibson Parsell, OHC, taped interview with Fr. Dana Howard, 9 Jan. 1982; transcription by Georgeann Johnston, p. 9.

[3]Minutes of Chapter beginning 4 Aug. 1931; morning session, 5 Aug. 1931.

[4]J.O.S. Huntington, "A Statement by Father Founder on his Death Bed," 2 p. typescript incorporated in the Minutes of Chapter, after Minutes of Aug. 5, 1935; p. 2.

[5]James Gould Cozzens, "A Democratic School," *The Atlantic Monthly,* March 1920, p. 50-52; rpr. in *Kent,* vol. 2, no. 2, Winter 1983, p. 11-13. Cozzens was in the Class of 1922.

[6]J.G. Cozzens, "Someday You'll Be Sorry," *Saturday Evening Post,* 21 June 1930; rpr. in *Children and Others,* New York: Harcourt, Brace and World, Inc. (var. dates 1930-1964), p. 107-29; p. 108.

[7]Matthew J. Bruccoli, *James Gould Cozzens, A Life Apart,* New York: Harcourt, Brace Jovanovich (1983), p. 106.

[8]Written for *Town and Country,* no. 88 (1 Aug. 1933), p. 38-41, 57; see Bruccoli, p. 106.

[9]J.G. Cozzens, "FHS: A Faith that Did not Fail," *Father Sill's Birthday, March 10, 1956; Kent School's Fiftieth Year,* Kent, Conn.: Kent School (1956), p. 7-10; rpr. in Matthew J. Bruccoli, ed., *Just Representations: A James Gould Cozzens Reader,* New York: Harcourt, Brace Jovanovich (1978), p. 538-42.

[10]J.G. Cozzens, *Men and Brethren,* New York: Harcourt, Brace, (1936). See Bruccoli, op. cit., pp. 128-34.

[11]Graham Greene, *Journey Without Maps,* New York: Doubleday & Co. (1936); quotes from the 2nd ed., Harmondsworth, Engl.: Penguin Books (1971, rpr. 1981), p. 82.

[12]Ibid., p. 85-6.

[13]F. Hastings Smyth to R.E. Campbell, OHC, 11 June 1954. Provided by the Rev'd. T.M. Brown of Toronto, Ont.

[14]Karl Tiedemann, OHC, *An Appreciation of Greatness: The Influence of Fr. Huntington, O.H.C.,* West Park, NY: Holy Cross Press, n.d., p. 32.

[15]Quoted in Scudder, *Father Huntington,* op. cit., p. 366-67.

[16]Whittemore, *O.H.C.,* op. cit. p. 60.

[17]Joseph Parsell, OHC, taped interview with Fr. Dana Howard, 26 Feb 1982, transcribed by Georgeann Johnston, side B, p. 17 (edited).

[18]Bonnell Spencer, OHC, taped interview with Fr. Adam McCoy, OHC, 8 March 1983, transcribed by Georgeann Johnston; p. 3.

[19]Whittemore, *O.H.C.,* op. cit., p. 69.

[20]Robert E. Campbell, OHC, *Within the Green Wall,* op. cit., p. 126-27.

[21]Ibid., p. 127.

[22]J. Parsell, taped interview, 9 Jan. 1982, op. cit., side B, p. 9.

[23]Campbell, op. cit., p. 129.

[24]Bonnell Spencer, OHC, taped interview 8 March 1983, op. cit., p. 6.

[25]A.G. Whittemore to F.H. Sill, 20 Feb. 1941; spread in the Minutes of Council, 14 April 1941.

[26]Spencer, taped interview 8 March 1983, op. cit., p. 8-9.

[27]Whittemore, *O.H.C.,* op. cit., p. 56.

[28]Ibid., p. 48-9.

Chapter 8 Conservatism and Change (1948-1966)

[1]Karl Tiedemann, OHC, "Holy Cross Joke Book," ms., OHC Archives, p. 5ff. This is a short, very rough sketch of an uncompleted work. It occurs halfway through a notebook beginning with Fr. Tiedemann's uncompleted autobiography, "Deo Gratias, Thanks Be to God."

[2]Alan Watts, *In My Own Way, An Autobiography, 1915-1965,* New York: Vintage Books, Random House (1972), p. 222-23.

[3]Joseph Parsell, OHC, taped interview with Fr. Dana Howard, 26 Feb. 1982, transcription by Georgeann Johnston; side B, p. 13.

[4]Watts, op. cit., p. 223. Whittemore's *Thanks Be To God* is being edited piecemeal in *The Whittemore Newsletter,* ed. A.W. Sadler, Sarah Lawrence College; vol. 1, no. 1 is dated March 1, 1982.

[5]James Agee, *The Morning Watch,* Cambridge, MA: Riverside Press (1950), beginning section II, p. 17, and section III, p. 91-2.

[6]Joseph Parsell, OHC, taped interview with Fr. Dana Howard, 9 Jan. 1982, transcribed by Georgeann Johnston; side A, p. 7; edited.

[7]Ibid.

[8]Ibid., side B, p. 11.

[9]R.E. Campbell, OHC, "Biographical Sketch,-Bp. Campbell, OHC," typescript, OHC Archives, p. 3.

[10]Leopold Kroll, OHC, to W.R.D. Turkington, OHC, 17 May 1957; OHC Archives.

[11]R.E. Campbell, OHC, to Sr. Josephine Remley, OSH, 11 June 1957; OHC Archives.

[12]"Statement by the Council of the Order of the Holy Cross," 3 June 1957; OHC Archives.

[13]Lincoln A. Taylor, OHC, taped interview with Fr. Adam McCoy, OHC, 22 Jan. 1983, p. 7; edited.

[14]Sr. Josephine Remley, OSH, "The Order of St. Helena," mimeographed typescript, OSH Archives; p. 10.

[15]Taylor, op. cit., p. 11.

[16]Bonnell Spencer, OHC, to Alan G. Whittemore, OHC, 9 Aug. 1960; OHC Archives.

[17]Taylor, op. cit., p. 17-18; edited.

[18]Ibid., p. 22, 24; edited.

[19]*HCM* 77, no. 3 (March, 1966), p. 24.

[20]Bonnell Spencer, OHC, taped interview with Fr. Adam McCoy, OHC, 8 March 1983, transcribed by Georgeann Johnston; p. 22-3.

[21]Ibid., p. 24.

[22]Ibid., p. 25, edited.

Chapter 9 Reform (1966-1972)

[1]Lincoln Taylor, OHC, taped interview with Fr. Adam McCoy, OHC, 22 Jan. 1983, transcribed by Georgeann Johnston; p. 13-14, edited.

[2]Ibid., p. 18, edited.

[3]Ibid., p. 18-19, edited.

[4]Ibid., p. 19, edited.

[5]Ibid., p. 20, edited.

[6]Sr. Catherine Josephine Remley, OSH, "The Order of St. Helena," mimeographed typescript, OSH Archives; p. 9.

[7]Bonnell Spencer, OHC, *A Four Office Breviary,* West Park, N.Y.: Holy Cross Publications (1968), p. v, "Introduction."

[8]Karl Tiedemann, OHC, "Holy Cross Joke Book," op. cit., p. 8-9.

[9]Taylor, taped interview, op. cit., p. 8-9, edited.

[10]Minutes of Chapter, August 1969.

[11]Bonnell Spencer, OHC, "Paper on the Vows," added to the formularies of the Order in 1970.

[12]Ibid.

[13]Taylor, taped interview, op. cit., p. 12, edited.

[14]Ibid., p. 13, edited.

Chapter 10 Expansion and The Benedictine Decision (1972-1985)

[1]Cyprian William Fields, OHC, "Annual Report of the Superior and the Assistant Superior to Chapter 1972-3," mimeographed typescript, OHC Archives; p. 31.

Bibliography

Many cited sources are found in the Holy Cross Archives. The bulk of the Archives are at the Episcopal Church Archives at the Episcopal Theological Seminary of the Southwest, Austin, Texas. Unless otherwise noted, OHC Archives material is located there.

The *Holy Cross Magazine* is a second major source. It is cited throughout as *HCM*. Individual articles from *HCM* are not cited.

The Minutes of Chapter and Council are kept by the Superior; microfiche copies through 1972.

The various editions of the Rule, Constitution and Custumal are not cited, but can be found in the OHC Archives. Individual letters from the OHC Archives are not cited here. Books published by members of the Order are cited in a separate appendix. Unpublished materials and published articles are cited below.

Unpublished Sources:

Allen, Sturges, O.H.C., "Early Beginnings of the Order of the Holy Cross," typescript, 67 pp. of ms., n.d. [from internal evidence, 1920]; OHC Archives.

Campbell, Robert E., O.H.C., "Biographical Sketch-Bp. Campbell, OHC," typescript, 3 p.; OHC Archives.

_____, "Some Notes About Our Father Founder," typescript, n.d., 10 pp. corrections by author; OHC Archives.

Dod, Robert Stockton, "Constitution of the Order of the Holy Cross," ms. 1881; OHC Archives.

_____, "House Rule of the Order of the Holy Cross," ms., 1881; OHC Archives.

_____, "On Tenements and the Need for a New Building" [untitled], ms., n.d.; OHC Archives.

_____, "Retreat to Novices," ms., Lent, 1882; OHC Archives.

_____, "Rule of the Order of the Holy Cross," ms., 1881; OHC Archives. This document exists copied in several other hands as well.

Huntington, James Otis Sargent, O.H.C., "Reminiscences of Henry George," n.d., ms.; OHC Archives.

_____, "Notes for Retreat Before Clothing as a Novice," ms., 1882; OHC Archives.

_____, "Statement by Father Founder on His Death Bed," 2 p. typescript, incorporated into the Minutes of Chapter, after Aug. 5, 1935.

O'Dell, Eleanor, "Father Huntington, OHC, Minor Instances in Father's Life," typescript, n.d., 9 pp. corrections by author; OHC Archives.

Parsell, Joseph G., O.H.C., taped interview with Dana Howard, 9 January 1982, transcribed by Georgeann Johnston; OHC Archives.

_____, taped interview with Dana Howard, 26 February 1982, transcribed by Georgeann Johnston; OHC Archives.

Remley, Sr. Catherine Josephine, O.S.H., "The Order of St. Helena," mimeographed typescript; OSH Archives.

Sisters of St. John the Baptist, "Early Memories"; typescript, CSJM Archives, Mendham, N.J.

Spencer, Bonnell, O.H.C., taped interview with Adam D. McCoy, O.H.C., 8 March 1983, transcribed by Georgeann Johnston; OHC Archives.

Schlueter, Edward Henry, "Some Reminiscences of Father Huntington," typescript, n.d., 21 pp.; OHC Archives.

Taylor, Lincoln A., O.H.C., taped interview with Adam D. McCoy, O.H.C., 22 January 1983, transcribed by Georgeann Johnston; OHC Archives.

Tiedemann, Karl, O.H.C., "Holy Cross Joke Book," ms., unpaginated; OHC Archives.

_____, "Deo Gratias, Thanks Be To God," ms., unpaginated; OHC Archives.

Whittemore, Alan G., O.H.C., *Long Retreat on O.H.C. Rule,* 1959; OHC Archives.

_____, *O.H.C.,* mimeographed typescript, 1949, iv + 105 pp.; OHC Archives.

_____, "A Talk to the Novices About Our Father Founder," typescript, n.d., 17 pp. corrections by author; OHC Archives.

_____, *Thanks Be To God,* 1954, typescript copy, xxiii + 182 pp.; OHC Archives. Publ. piecemeal by The Whittemore *Newsletter,* A.W. Sadler, ed., Sarah Lawrence College (1982-   ).

Published Sources:

Adamson, Robert William, *Father Huntington's Formative Years (1854-1892): Monasticism and Social Christianity,* (Columbia Univ. Ph.D. diss., 1971).

Agee, James, *The Morning Watch,* (Cambridge, MA: Riverside Press, 1950).

Allchin, A.M., *The Silent Rebellion, Anglican Religious Communities 1845-1900,* (London: SCM Press, 1958).

Angell, Charles, S.A. and LaFontaine, Charles, S.A., *The Life of Paul of Graymoor,* (New York: Seabury, 1975).

Anson, Peter F. *Abbot Extraordinary, A Memoir of Aelred Carlyle. Monk and Missionary, 1874-1955,* (London: Faith Press, 1958).

_____, *The Call of the Cloister, Religious Communities and Kindred Bodies in the Anglican Communion,* (New York: The Macmillan Company, 1953).

Bell, Stephen, *Rebel, Priest and Prophet, A Biography of Dr. Edward McGlynn,* (1937; rpr. New York: Robert Schalkenbach Foundation, 1968).

Benson, Richard Meux, *The Followers of the Lamb, A Series of Meditations Especially Intended for Persons Living Under Religious Vows and for Seasons of Retreat, etc.,* (London: Longmans, Green & Co., 1900).

_____, *Instructions on the Religious Life,* (Oxford: Society of St. John the Evangelist, 1927).

Bruccoli, Matthew J., *James Gould Cozzens, A Life Apart,* (New York: Harcourt, Brace Jovanovich, 1983).

_____, *Just Representations: A James Gould Cozzens Reader* (New York: Harcourt, Brace Jovanovich, 1978).

Cameron, Allan T., *The Religious Communities of the Church of England,* (London: Faith Press, 1918).

Carter, J.F.M., *Life and Work of the Rev. T.T. Carter,* (London: Longmans, Green & Co., 1911).

Carter, Thomas Thelusson, *Harriet Monsell, A Memoir,* (London: J. Masters and Co., 1890).

_____, *Spiritual Instructions, The Religious Life,* (London: J. Masters & Co., 1879).

Chorley, E. Clowes, *Men and Movements in the Episcopal Church,* The Hale Lectures, (New York: Charles Scribner's Sons, 1950).

Clarke, C.P.S., *The Oxford Movement and After,* (London: A.R. Mowbray & Co., 1932).

Cozzens, James Gould, *Children and Others,* (New York: Harcourt Brace and World, Inc., var. dates). Includes all the Dr. Holt stories originally published in *Saturday Evening Post.*

_____, "A Democratic School," *Atlantic Monthly,* March, 1920; rpr. *Kent* 2:2 (Winter, 1983), p. 11-13.

_____, "FHS: A Faith that Did Not Fail," *Father Sill's Birthday, March 10, 1956; Kent School's Fiftieth Year,* (Kent, CT: Kent School, 1956), p. 7-10; rpr. in Bruccoli, *Just Representations,* p. 538-542.

_____, "Kent: A New School," *Town and Country,* no. 88 (1 Aug. 1933), p. 38-41, 57.

DeMille, George E., *The Catholic Movement in the American Episcopal Church,* (Philadelphia: The Church Historical Society, 1941).

Dix, Morgan, *Harriet Starr Cannon, First Mother Superior of the Sisterhood of St. Mary, A Memoir,* (New York: Longmans, Green & Co., 1896).

Gannon, David, S.A., *Father Paul of Graymoor,* (New York: The Macmillan Company, 1959).

The Founders of Clewer, A Short Account of the Rev T.T. Carter and Harriet Monsell to Celebrate the Centenary of the Community of St. John the Baptist in 1952, anon. (London: A.R. Mowbray, 1952.)

George, Henry, *The Land Question and Related Writings,* (New York: Robert Schalkenbach Foundation, 1982).

George, Henry, *Progress and Poverty, An Inquiry into the Cause of Industrial Depressions and of Increase of Want With Increase of Wealth . . . The Remedy,* (1879; rpr. New York: Robert Schalkenbach Foundation, 1979).

George, Henry, Jr., *The Life of Henry George,* (1900; rpr. New York: Robert Schalkenbach Foundation, 1960).

Greene, Graham, *Journey Without Maps,* (New York: Doubleday & Co., 1936; 2nd. ed., Harmondsworth, England: Penguin Books, 1971, rpr. 1981).

Howells, William Dean, *A Hazard of New Fortunes* (1890) (New York: New American Library, 1965).

Hughson, Shirley Carter, O.H.C., "Address" [on the Real Presence], *Report of the Anglo-Catholic Congress, Subject: The Holy Eucharist, London, July 1927,* (London: Society of SS. Peter & Paul, 1927), p. 221-7.

———, "What is the Episcopal Church?", *The First Annual Catholic Congress, Essays and Papers, New Haven, Connecticut, November 3-4, 1925,* (Central Conference of Catholic Priests, 1926), p. 36-48.

Huntington, James O.S., "Beginnings of the Religious Life for Men in the American Church," *Historical Magazine of the Protestant Episcopal Church,* vol. 2 (1933), p. 35-43.

———, "Philanthropy—Its Success and Failure," in *Philanthropy and Social Progress,* (New York: Thomas Crowell & Co., 1893), p. 98-156.

———, "Sin," *Report of the Anglo-Catholic Congress; General Subject: The Gospel of God; London, July 1923* (London: The Society of SS. Peter & Paul, 1923), p. 22-28.

Hutchings, W.H., ed., *Life and Letters of Thomas Thelusson Carter,* (London: Longmans, Green & Co., 1903).

Junge, Werner, *Bolahun: An African Adventure,* trans. Basil Creighton, (New York: G.P. Putnam's Sons, 1952).

Lears, T.J. Jackson, *No Place of Grace, Antimodernism and the Transformation of American Culture 1880-1920,* (New York: Pantheon Books, 1981).

Mary Hilary, Sister, C.S.M. [Hilary Ross], *Ten Decades of Praise: The Story of the Community of St. Mary During Its First Century: 1865 to 1965,* (Racine, WI: DeKoven Foundation, 1965).

May, Henry F., *Protestant Churches and Industrial America,* (New York: Harper & Brothers, Publ., 1949).

Milligan, Ralph T., ed., *All For the Love of God, A Holy Cross Omnibus,* (West Park, NY: Holy Cross Press, 1957).

Muller, James Arthur, "Father Huntington and the Beginnings of Religious Orders for Men in the Episcopal Church; A Review," *Historical Magazine of the Protestant Episcopal Church,* vol. 10 (1941), p. 312-329.

Ollard, S.L., *The Anglo-Catholic Revival, Some Persons and Principles,* (London: A.R. Mowbray, 1925).

Paz, D.G., "Monasticism and Social Reform in Late Nineteenth-Century America: The Case of Father Huntington," *Historical Magazine of the Protestant Episcopal Church,* vol. 48 (1979), p. 45-66.

Post, Louis F. and Leubuscher, Fred C., *Henry George's 1886 Campaign, An Account of the George-Hewitt Campaign in the New York Municipal Election of 1886,* (New York, 1886; rpr. New York: The Henry George School, 1961).

Scudder, Vida Dutton, *Father Huntington, Founder of the Order of the Holy Cross,* (New York: E.P. Dutton & Company, Inc., 1940).

Sill, Frederick, O.H.C., "Our Independent School," (1936), *Kent,* vol., 2:3 (Spring 1983), p. 5-8.

_____, "Pater Recalls 1906-1907," *Kent* 2:2 (Winter 1983), p. 5-10.

Simpson, James B. and Story, Edward M., *Stars in His Crown, A Centennial History of the Community of St. John the Baptist Told in the Context of the History of the Religious Orders in the Episcopal Church,* (Sea Bright, NJ: Ploughshare Press, 1976).

Smith, H. Maynard, *Frank, Bishop of Zanzibar, Life of Frank Weston, D.D., 1871-1924,* (London: SPCK, 1926).

Smith, Martin L., S.S.J.E., ed., *Benson of Cowley,* (Oxford: Oxford University Press, 1980).

Smith, Robert Cheney, S.S.J.E., *The Cowley Fathers in America, The Early Years,* (n.d.).

Thomas, John L., *Alternative America: Henry George, Edward Bellamy, Henry Demarest Lloyd and the Adversary Tradition,* (Cambridge, MA: Harvard University Press, 1983).

Ward, Sr. Benedicta, S.L.G., trans., *The Wisdom of the Desert Fathers, Apothegmata Patrum from the Anonymous Series,* (Oxford: SLG Press, Fairacres Publications, 1975).

Watts, Alan, *In My Own Way, An Autobiography, 1915-1965,* (New York: Vintage Books, Random House, 1972).

Weed, Paul, ed., *Edward Henry Schlueter, A Priest Who In His Day Pleased God* (privately printed, n.d., [1984]).

Woodgate, M.V., *Father Benson, Founder of the Cowley Fathers,* (London: Geoffrey Bles, 1953).

Appendices

I. Published Monographs by Members of the Order of the Holy Cross

BALDWIN, John Sears (1896-1980)
God Came Down, A Plain Statement of the Christian Faith. (West Park, NY: Holy Cross Press, 1958; rev. ed. 1970).
Lessons For Children. [ed.] West Park, NY: Holy Cross Press, 1953).
Why Not Be Natural? (West Park, NY: Holy Cross Press, 1965).

BESSOM, Joseph Harold (1902-1965)
Christian Word Book [with Abbie Loveland Tuller, T.C.G.]. (Washington, CT: T.C.G. Press, 1951).
Gala-fai, Loma Worship and Teaching. (Bolahun, Liberia: Holy Cross Liberian Mission).
The Lord's Life In Loma Lessons. (Bolahun, Liberia: Holy Cross Liberian Mission, 1956).
The Story of God's People. (London: Sheldon Press, 1951; rpr. 1966).

CAMPBELL, Robert Erskine (1884-1977)
Within the Green Wall, The Story of Holy Cross Liberian Mission 1922-1957. (West Park, NY: Holy Cross Press, 1958).

HARRIS, William Edward [Brother Edward] (1896-1970)
Plenty How-Do From Africa. (West Park, NY: Holy Cross Press, 1940).

HARRISON, Jesse McVeigh (1878-1959)
Common Sense About Religion, Being a Synopsis of the Evidence of Reason, Revelation and Experience as to the Truth of the Apostles' Creed. (Franklin Co., TN: St. Andrew's, 1933).

252

Daily Meditations on the Christian Life for Every Day in the Year (2 vols.). (St. Andrew's, TN: St. Andrew's, 1916; 2nd. ed. West Park, NY: Holy Cross Press, 1926).

A Devotional Commentary on the Gospel of St. John. (St. Andrew's, TN: St. Andrew's Book Shop, 1919).

First Century Christianity. (West Park, NY: Holy Cross Press, 1958).

Saint Luke, His Life, Character and Teaching, Being Brief Spiritual Readings for Advent and Lent. (Saint Andrew's, TN: St. Andrew's, 1917).

HUGHSON, Shirley Carter (1867-1949)

An American Cloister. (West Park, NY: Holy Cross Press, 1917; rev. eds. 1931, 1961).

The Approach to God, A Study of the Covenant of Prayer. (West Park, NY: Holy Cross Press, 1932).

Athletes of God, Lives of the Saints for Every Day in the Year. (West Park, NY: Holy Cross Press, 1930, 1957).

Contemplative Prayer. (London & New York: S.P.C.K. & The Macmillan Company, 1935).

Corda in Coelo, Exercises of Affective and Contemplative Prayer. (West Park, NY: Holy Cross Press, 1935).

The Fundamentals of the Religious State. (New York: Longmans, Green and Co., 1915).

The Gloria Psalter. (West Park, NY: Holy Cross Press, 1946).

The Green Wall of Mystery, Venture and Adventure in the Hinterland of West Africa. (West Park, NY: Holy Cross Press, 1928).

The Heart of the Passion, A Study of the Seven Words from the Cross. (West Park, NY: Holy Cross Press, 1925).

The Infant King, The Mysteries of Christmas in Meditation. (West Park, NY: Holy Cross Press, 1920).

The Little Book of Our Lady and a Chaplet of the Blessed Sacrament with Texts for Meditation. (West Park, NY: Holy Cross Press, 4 ed., 1919).

Lord, Hear My Prayer. Ed. Julien Gunn, O.H.C. (West Park, NY: Holy Cross Press, 1953).

Man and the Supernatural. (London: Catholic Literature Association, n.d.).

Our Familiar Devotions. (West Park, NY: Holy Cross Press, 1923).

The Passion of the King: Short Meditations for Lent. (Milwaukee; Young Churchman, 1904).

Pledges of His Love. (West Park, NY: Holy Cross Press, 1921).

Reservation and Adoration: A Historical and Devotional Inquiry. (West Park, NY: Holy Cross Press, 1919).

The Seven Sacraments. (West Park, NY: Holy Cross Press, 1923).

Spiritual Guidance, A Study of The Godward Way. (West Park, NY: Holy Cross Press, 1948).

Spiritual Letters of Father Hughson, O.H.C. (West Park, NY: Holy Cross Press, 1952).

To Tell The Godly Man, Selections from the Writings of Shirley Carter Hughson, O.H.C. Arranged and ed. by William Joseph Barnds. (West Park, NY: Holy Cross Press, 1958).

The Voice of My Prayer, Short Meditations for Sundays and Holy Days. (Milwaukee: The Young Churchman Co., 1907).

The Warfare of the Soul, Practical Studies in the Life of Temptation. (New York: Longmans, Green & Co., 1910).

The Wine of God, A Spiritual Study of Our Lord's First Miracle. (West Park, NY: Holy Cross Press, 1918).

With Christ In God, A Study of Human Destiny. (London and West Park, NY: S.P.C.K., 1947).

HUNTINGTON, James Otis Sargent (1854-1935)

Bargainers and Beggars, A Study of the Parable of the Laborers in the Vineyard. (West Park, NY: Holy Cross Press, 1919).

How to Preach A Mission, Practical Directions for Mission Services. (New York: Edwin S. Gorham, 1916).

The School of the Eternal, Outlines for Use in Retreat or in Daily Mental Prayer (with Karl Tiedemann). (London & West Park, NY: Centenary & Holy Cross Press, 1933).

The Work Of Prayer, (West Park, NY: Holy Cross Press, 1923).

LOOK, Wallace [Br. Gregory] (1921-   )

Later Eyes, with Bill Buck and Jane Hamner. (Bolinas, CA: Malette Dean, Fairfax, CA, 150 copies, 1957).

Lost Eyes (San Francisco: Success Printing, 1961)

PACKARD, Alpheus Appleton (1904-1972)

An Open Door. (Boston: Christopher, 1966).

Twilight: Poems. (Santa Barbara, CA: Schauer Printing Studio, 1959).

PARSELL, Joseph Gibson (1905-   )

Manual of Prayers, Catechisms and Hymns in Bandi. (Bolahun, Liberia: Holy Cross Mission, 1982).

Manual of Prayers, Catechisms and Hymns in Bandi, Kisi, and English.
(London: S.P.C.K., for the Holy Cross Liberian Mission, 1952).

SPENCER, Howard Bonnell (1909-   )
Christ in the Old Testament. (West Park, NY: Holy Cross Press, 1966).
The Church and Christianity. (West Park, NY: Holy Cross Press).
Dietrich Bonhoeffer, Prophet for Our Time. (West Park, NY: Holy
Cross Publ., 1966).
A Four Office Breviary. (West Park, NY: Holy Cross Publ., 1968).
[Collaboration].
A Functional Liturgy. (West Park, NY: Holy Cross Press, 1961). Reprint
from *Anglican Theological Review,* Oct., 1961.
God Who Dares to Be Man, Theology for Prayer and Suffering. (New
York: Seabury Press, 1980).
A Monastic Breviary. (West Park, NY: Holy Cross Publ., 1976).
[Collaboration].
Sacrifice of Thanksgiving. (West Park, NY: Holy Cross Publ., 1965).
They Saw the Lord. (New York: Morehouse-Gorham, 1947; 1961; Wilton,
CT: Morehouse-Barlow Co., 1983).
Thomas Cranmer and the Eucharist. (Private Printing, 1957).
Ye Are the Body, A People's History of the Church. (West Park, NY:
Holy Cross Publ., 1950 [6 printings]; rev. ed. 1965 [6 printings]).
What Has God To Do With Marriage? (West Park, NY: Holy Cross
Publ.)

TERRY, Kenneth Rosier (1922-   )
The Eucharist is an Action. (West Park, NY: Holy Cross Press, 1958).

TIEDEMANN, Karl Ludwig (1890-1968)
An Appreciation of Greatness, The Influence of Fr. Huntington, O.H.C.
(West Park, NY: Holy Cross Press, n.d.).
The Gift of God, A Retreat of Four Days on Self-Givingness. (West
Park, NY: Holy Cross Publ., 1961).
The Glories of Jesus, Thirty Meditations on the Life of Our Lord. (West
Park, NY: Holy Cross Press, 1920).
The Holy Cross, Some Ideals of the Spiritual Life. (London & Milwaukee:
Faith Press & Morehouse, 1935).
The Lord of Love, Thirty Meditations on the Life of Our Lord. (London
& Milwaukee: A.R. Mowbray & Morehouse, 1929).
Priest's Progress. (West Park, NY: Holy Cross Press, 1942).
The School of the Eternal. (see under Huntington.)

WHITTEMORE, Alan Griffith (1890-1960)
Joy in Holiness, A Collection of Letters and Other Writings of Spiritual Direction. Ed. Ralph T. Milligan. (West Park, NY: Holy Cross Publ., 1964).
The Presence of God. (West Park, NY: Holy Cross Press, 1940; 7th printing 1958).

II. Superiors of OHC

1 Nov. 1881-18 March 1884	Fr Robert Stockton Dod
18 March 1884-1 Dec. 1888	Fr James Otis Sargent Huntington
1 Dec. 1886-16 June 1894	Fr Sturges Allen
16 June 1894-5 July 1897	Fr Henry Rufus Sargent
5 July 1897-16 Sept. 1907	Fr James Otis Sargent Huntington
16 Sept. 1907-14 Sept. 1915	Fr Sturges Allen
14 Sept. 1915-6 Aug. 1918	Fr James Otis Sargent Huntington
6 Aug. 1918-11 Aug. 1921	Fr Shirley Carter Hughson
11 Aug. 1921-5 Aug. 1930	Fr James Otis Sargent Huntington
5 Aug. 1930-4 Aug. 1936	Fr Shirley Carter Hughson
4 Aug. 1936-4 Aug. 1948	Fr Alan Griffith Whittemore
4 Aug. 1948-6 Aug. 1954	Bp Robert Erskine Campbell
6 Aug. 1954-22 July 1957	Fr Leopold Kroll
22 July 1957-4 Aug. 1960	Fr William Ryland Downing Turkington (acting 7/22-8/2/57)
4 Aug. 1960-9 June 1972	Fr Lincoln Andrews Taylor
9 June 1971-7 June 1981	Fr Connor Kay Lynn
7 June 1981-	Fr Clark Wright Trafton

Assistant Superiors of OHC

1906-1907	Fr Sturges Allen
1922-1924	Fr Shirley Carter Hughson
1924-1928	Fr Roger Brooke Taney Anderson
1928-1930	Fr Shirley Carter Hughson
1930-1936	Fr John Sears Baldwin
1936	Fr Edwin Clark Whitall
1936-1938	Bp Robert Erskine Campbell
1938-1944	Fr Karl Ludwig Tiedemann
1944-1946	Fr Edwin Clark Whitall

1946-1954	Fr Leopold Kroll
1954-1957	Fr William Ryland Downing Turkington
1957-1958	Fr Sydney James Atkinson
1958-1960	Fr Lincoln Andrews Taylor
1960-1962	Fr Karl Ludwig Tiedemann
1962-1963	Fr Vern Linwood Adams (d. 1/4/63)
1963-1965	Fr Kenneth Rosier Terry
1965-1966	Fr Connor Kay Lynn
1966-1971	Fr William Ryland Downing Turkington
1971-1972	Fr Howard Bonnell Spencer
1972-1974	Br Cyprian William Fields
1974-1981	Fr George Swayne
1981-	Fr Allan Edward Smith

Novice Masters of OHC

1 Nov. 1881-18 March 1884	Fr Dod
18 March 1884-	Fr Huntington

From 1897 the office of Novice Master was elected by Chapter.

1897-1900	Fr Sargent
1900-1903	Fr Sargent
1903-1906	Fr Hughson
17 Sept. 1906	Fr Sargent (immediately resigned)
1906-1907	Fr Mayo
1907-1908	Fr Huntington
1908-1909	Fr Sargent
1909-1912	Fr Officer
1912-1914	Fr Anderson
1914-1915	Fr Hughson

From 1915 the office of Novice Master was appointed by the Superior.

1915-1921	Fr Hughson
1921-1922	Fr Whittemore
1922-1924	Fr Harrison
1924-1925	Fr Hughson
1925-1926	Fr Whittemore
1926-1933	Fr Baldwin
1933-1936	Fr Tiedemann
1936-1941	Fr Whittemore

1941	Fr Kroll
1941-1944	Fr Spencer
1944-1945	Fr Parker
1945	Fr Hughson
1945-1946	Fr Whittemore
1946-1947	Fr Baldwin
1947-1948	Bp Campbell
1948-1949	Fr Whitall
1949-1952	Fr Packard
1952-1954	Fr Kroll
1954-1955	Bp Campbell
1955-1958	Fr Atkinson
1958-1960	Fr Taylor
1960-1963	Fr Terry
1963-1965	Fr Spencer

The position of Postulant Master was created in 1964:

1964-	Fr Packard [Postulant Master]
1965-1968	Fr Lynn
1968-1972	Fr Swayne
1972-1976	Fr Trafton
1976-1983	Fr Mudge (Fr. Swayne Asst. in Africa)
1983-1984	Fr Smith (Br. Vincent Shamo Assistant in Africa)

In 1984 the novitiate was divided:

North America:		*Africa:*	
1984-	Fr McCoy	1984-	Fr Shamo

III. Monasteries of the Order of the Holy Cross

The Houses and Works of the Order of the Holy Cross, 1881-1985

276 East 7th Street, New York, NY
  Oct., 1 1881-May or June, 1882
95 Avenue D, New York, NY
  May or June, 1882-spring 1883
330 East 13th Street, New York, NY
  spring 1883-March, 1885

711 East 12th Street, New York, NY
  March, 1885-Jan. 1, 1886
60 Avenue D, New York, NY
  Jan. 1, 1886-May, 1888
Clergy House of the Holy Cross Mission
Avenue C and 4th Street, New York, NY
  May, 1888-September 21, 1889
417 Pleasant Avenue, New York, NY
  January, 1890-August, 1892
Westminster, Maryland
  August 4, 1892-April, 1904

Holy Cross Monastery
West Park, NY
  April, 1904-
  Until 1967, the Superior or Assistant Superior was the Head of
  House at West Park.

Priors:	Fr. William Turkington	1967-1972
	Fr. John Ryan	1972
	Fr. John Walsted	1972
	Fr. Clark Trafton	1973-1978
	Fr. Nicholas Radelmiller	1978-1981
	Fr. David-Bryan Hoopes	1981-1984
	Br. Timothy Jolley	1984-

St. Michael's Monastery, St. Andrew's School
St. Andrew's, TN
  September, 1905-June, 1972

Priors:	Fr. Sturges Allen	1905-1907
	Fr. Shirley C. Hughson	1907-1914
	Fr. McVeigh Harrison	1915-1918
	Fr. Robert Campbell	1918-1922
	Fr. Edwin Whitall	1922-1923
	Fr. Liston Orum	1923-1924
	Fr. John Baldwin	1925-1926
	Fr. Roger Anderson	1926-1931
	Fr. Francis Parker	1932-1938
	Bp. Robert Campbell	1939-1947
	Fr. Bonnell Spencer	1947-1955
	Fr. Julien Gunn	1955-1965

Fr. Murray Belway	1965-1968
Fr. Lee Stevens	1968-1970
Fr. Sydney Atkinson	1970-1972

Kent School
Kent, CT
  September, 1906-September, 1943
  Headmasters (OHC):

Fr. Frederick Sill	1907-1941
Fr. William Chalmers	1941-1943 (1948)

St. Peter's Church
Ripon, WI
  May, 1921-June, 1925
  Rector: Fr. Karl Tiedemann   1921-1925

St. Athanasius Monastery (1922-1972)
Holy Cross Community in Liberia (1972-1984)
Bolahun, Liberia
  May, 1922-June, 1984

Priors:	Fr. Robert Campbell	1922-1925
	Fr. McVeigh Harrison	1925-1926
	Fr. James Gorham	1926-1932
	Fr. John Baldwin	1932-1937
	Fr. Leopold Kroll	1937-1946
	Fr. Joseph Parsell	1947-1960
	Fr. Sydney Atkinson	1960-1964
	Fr. Allan Smith	1965-1970
	Fr. Connor Lynn	1970-1972
	Br. Rafael Campbell	1973-1977
	Br. Roy Jude Arnold	1977-1978
	Fr. Dominic Wilson	1978-1981
	Fr. Joseph Parsell	1981-1984

St. Mary's Church
Nixon, NV
  1942-1946
  In Charge: Fr. Karl Tiedemann   1942-1946

Mount Calvary Retreat House
Santa Barbara, CA
    October, 1947-

Priors:		
	Fr. Karl Tiedemann	1947-1955
	Fr. Bonnell Spencer	1955-1959
	Fr. John Baldwin	1959-1960
	Fr. Alpheus Packard	1960-1962
	Fr. William Turkington	1962-1966
	Fr. Joseph Parsell	1966-1971
	Br. Kevin Dunn	1971-1972
	Fr. George Swayne	1972-1976
	Fr. Brian McHugh	1976-1977
	Fr. Nicholas Radelmiller	1978
	Fr. Damian Williams	1978-1981
	Fr. Adam McCoy	1981-

Whitby House/James Huntington Priory (1976)
Bishop Mason Retreat Center
Grapevine, TX
    June, 1967-December, 1977

Priors:		
	Fr. Bonnell Spencer	1967-1971
	Fr. John Ryan	1971-1972
	Fr. Thomas Mudge	1972-1974
	Fr. Nicholas Radelmiller	1974-1977

Temporary Project
Savannah, GA
    Easter-September, 1969
    (Fr. Lynn, Fr. Trafton, Br. Rafael, Sr. Josephine OSH, Sr. Columba OSH)

West Indian Projects
I: Guyana
    September, 1969-January 1970
    (Fr. Lynn, Fr. Trafton, Br. Rafael)
II: Jamaica
    January-June, 1970
    (Fr. Mudge, Br. Roy Waywell)
III: Grenada and Trinidad
    June, 1970-Easter, 1971
    (Fr. Trafton, Fr. Mudge, Br. Simon)

Trinity Parish
St. Louis, MO
    June 1971-September, 1972
       In Charge: Br. Cyprian Fields   1971-1972

St. David's Parish
Gales Ferry, CT
    June 1971-June, 1973
       In Charge: Fr. Clark Trafton   1971-1972
               Br. Augustine Brown   1972-1973

Holy Cross Priory
Toronto, Ontario, Canada
    June 1972-
       Priors: Fr. Lincoln Taylor   1973-1975
                 Fr. Brian McHugh   1975-1976
                 Br. Jay Launt   1977-1981
                 Br. William Sibley   1981-

Holy Cross Priory/St. Dominic's Priory/Incarnation Priory
Berkeley, CA
    June, 1972-
       Priors: Br. William Sibley   1972-1976
                 Br. Paul Hayes   1976
                 Fr. Roy Parker   1976-1979
       Co-Priors: Fr. Roy Parker-OHC   1979-1983
                 Dom Robert Hale-OSBCam 1979-
                 Fr. Dominic Wilson-OHC 1983-1984
                 Br. William Brown-OHC 1984-

Holy Cross House/Absalom Jones Priory
New York City
    December 1973-
       Priors: Br. Augustine Brown   1973-1974
                 Br. Peter Patrick   1974-1977
                 Br. Augustine Brown   1977-1978
                 Fr. Clark Trafton   1978-1981
                 Fr. Carl Sword   1981-

Holy Redeemer Priory
Nassau, The Bahamas
   August, 1975-July, 1981
      Priors: Br. Brian Youngward   1975-1976
                    Br. Peter Patrick   1976-1978
                    Fr. David-Bryan Hoopes   1978-1981

Holy Saviour Priory
Tower Hill
Pineville, SC
   September, 1975-
      Priors: Fr. Lincoln Taylor   1975-1979
                    Fr. Allan Smith   1979-1983
                    Fr. Bede Thomas Mudge   1983-

St. Joseph's Priory
St. Barnabas Church
Chicago, IL
   June, 1979-June, 1981
      Prior: Fr. Roy Waywell   1979-1981

House of the Resurrection (dependency of West Park)
Albany and Watervliet, NY
   November, 1979-December, 1983
   Subprior: Br. Orlando Flores   1979-1983

Philip Quaque Monastery
Cape Coast, Ghana
   August, 1982-
      Priors: Fr. Christian Swayne   1982-1986
                    Br. Leonard Abbah   1986-

IV. Life Professed Members of OHC
Biographical Data

This appendix is in two parts. In the first, members of OHC are arranged in order of the date of their Life Profession. Names preceded by a cross (+) died in vows. Those preceded by an asterisk (*) left the community. Those names unmarked are presently under vows in the Order. Names taken in Religion are in brackets.

The second listing is alphabetical and gives biographical information. Stationing is noted by geographical location. Stationing at West Park (or NYC and Westminster previously) is assumed unless otherwise noted.

Life Profession means that one takes the threefold vow of Poverty, Chastity and Obedience for life. This vow can be dispensed, or set aside, by the Chapter at the request of a member, and can be taken again with the permission of Chapter. Members can also be expelled by vote of Chapter, which means that the person is no longer a member of the Order. Expulsion does not affect the Vow, however. A person who has been expelled can be restored to full participation in the Order by a vote of Chapter. After 1977, a person could be dismissed from the Order, his Vow being *ipso facto* dispensed.

The following abbreviations are used (States, Canadian Provinces, and non-theological academic degrees are cited with their normal abbreviations):

Asst	Assistant
B	Bishop
b	born
BD	Bachelor of Divinity
CDSP	Church Divinity School of the Pacific, Berkeley CA
Coll	College
Cur	Curate
D	ordained Deacon
d	died
DCnL	Doctor of Canon Law
DD	Doctor of Divinity
dio	diocese
disp	dispensed from the Life Vow by Chapter
el	elected
Eng	England
ETS	Episcopal Theological School, Cambridge MA
exp	expelled from OHC by Chapter
GTS	General Theological Seminary, New York NY
In-ch	In Charge
Inst	Institute
JSTB	Jesuit School of Theology, Berkeley
LP	Life Professed
LST	License in Sacred Theology
LTh	License in Theology
MDiv	Master of Divinity
Mis	Missionary

P	ordained Priest
PDS	Philadelphia Divinity School
R	Rector
S	Saint
Sch	School
SSJE	Society of St. John the Evangelist
St	State
STB	Bachelor of Sacred Theology
STD	Doctor of Sacred Theology
STM	Master of Sacred Theology
Sup	Superior
U	University
V	Vicar
VTS	Virginia Theological Seminary, Alexandria VA

Members of OHC in order of profession:

1 + James Otis Sargent Huntington
2 + Sturges Allen
3 * Henry Rufus Sargent
4 + Shirley Carter Hughson
5 + Frederick Herbert Sill
6 + William Francis Mayo
7 * Roger Brooke Taney Anderson
8 + Louis Lorey
9 * Harvey Officer
10 + Jesse McVeigh Harrison
11 + Edwin Clark Whitall
12 + Abishai Woodward
13 + Liston Joseph Orum
14 + Robert Erskine Campbell
15 + Karl Ludwig Tiedemann
16 + Alan Griffith Whittemore
17 + James Henry Gorham
18 + Joseph Henry Smyth
19 + Herbert Hawkins
20 + John Sears Baldwin
21 + Charles William Webb
22 + Sidney [Dominic] Taylor
23 + William Edward Harris

24 + Francis William George Parker
25 * Carl Walter Marty
26 * Russell Garvey Flagg
27 * Leopold Kroll
28   Joseph Gibson Parsell
29 * William Scott Chalmers
30   William Ryland Downing Turkington
31 + Frederick [George] Ewald
32   Howard Bonnell Spencer
33 + Joseph Harold Bessom
34 * Herbert Smith Bicknell
35 + Alpheus Appleton Packard
36 + Sydney James Atkinson
37 + Vern Linwood Adams
38 * Julien Gunn, Jr.
39 + Lincoln Andrews Taylor
40   Lee Gerald Elwin Stevens
41 * Kenneth Rosier Terry
42   Raymond Alan Gill
43   George [Michael] Stonebraker
44 * Charles Smythe
45   Allan Edward Smith
46 * Connor Kay Lynn
47 * Robert Murray Belway
48   Thomas Haines Schultz
49 * John Prime Ryan
50 * Robert Edmund Sullivan, Jr.
51   George Eby Hope [Christian] Swayne
52 * Samuel [Kevin] Dunn
53 * Victor Anthony Phillips [Boniface] Challinor
54 * Wallace [Gregory] Look
55   Arthur Eugene [Laurence] Harms
56 * Arthur Robert [Nicholas] Jamieson
57 * John Howard Walsted
58   James Samuel DeMerell
59 * William [Cyprian] Fields
60   Robert [Augustine] Brown
61   Clark Wright [Gregory] Trafton
62 * John Willie [Ambrose] Brice
63   Robert Andrew [Rafael] Campbell-Dixon
64 * Eric James [Martin] Smith

65 * Donald Wayne [Joseph] Wortman
66 * Peter Ernest Ian [Simon] Garraway
67   William Gatewood Sibley
68 * James Brian McHugh
69   Hiram Thomas [Bede] Mudge
70 * Robert Kendrick
71 * Roy Edmund [Dunstan] Waywell
72   Ronald Grant Haynes
73   James Robert [Paul] Hayes
74 * Gerald Frederick Stading
75   Brian Youngward
76   Roy [Jude] Arnold
77 * Stephen Lee [Damian] Williams
78 * Peter John Patrick
79   William Lawrence Nicholas Radelmiller
80 * Jay McIntyre Launt
81   Roy Earl Parker
82   Jack Fowler [Dominic] Wilson
83 * Dean [Benedict] Robins
84 * Philip Mantle
85   Richard [Adrian] Gill
86   Robert Stripling [Stephen-Christopher] Harrell
87 * John Tufa Kpoto
88   David Bryan Hoopes
89 * James Borazzas
90   Orlando Gilbert [Huntington] Flores
91 + Jack Harbert
92   Adam Dunbar McCoy
93   Carl Richard Sword
94 * Ian Archer [Andrew] Meadowcroft
95   Robert Glendon [Romuald] Brant
96   William Johnstone Brown
97   Paul Martin Lauer
98 * Paa Kwesi Josiah
99   Carter [Bernard] Van Waes
100 Robert Nelson [Timothy] Jolley
101 James Robert Hagler
102 Vincent Nee Fio Shamo
103 Douglas Charles Brown
104 Leonard Abbah
105 * Roberto Eduardo Bresciani y Undurraga

106   Reginald [Martin] Crenshaw
107   James Ibraimah [Boniface] Adams
108   Thomas Fogah
109   Richard Paul Vaggione

Biographical Data
Life Professed Members of OHC

104 ABBAH, Leonard, b Ghana 16 Aug 1946. LP 22 Oct 1983. Toronto 1982-84. Ghana 1984-.

107 ADAMS, James Ibraimah (Br Boniface). b Ghana 6 Aug 1955. S Nicholas Seminary, Cape Coast, Ghana 1982-85. D 1985 P 1985. LP 23 Feb 1985. Liberia 1980-82. Ghana 1982-83, 1984-85. Toronto 1984.

37 +ADAMS, Vern Linwood. b Idaho Springs, CO, 30 March 1905. S John's Coll, Greeley CO BA 1934. D & P 1935. In-ch S Michael, Tucumcari, NM, 1935-38. In-ch S John, Farmington, NM, 1938-40. LP 31 Oct 1943. Nixon 1943-46. Santa Barbara 1956-60. d 4 Jan 1963.

2 +ALLEN, Sturges, b Hyde Park, NY, 25 June 1850. U City of New York BS 1869. GTS BD 1880. D 1880 P 1882. LP 1 Dec 1888. Sup 1888-94, 1907-15. Liberia 1921-29. d 26 March 1929.

7 *ANDERSON, Roger Brooke Taney. b Baltimore, MD, 4 Jan 1878. Johns Hopkins BA 1900. GTS BD 1903. D 1903 P 1904. LP 1 March 1907. Chaplain WWI. disp 22 April 1932. R Trinity Church, Waterbury, CT, 1934. d 22 June 1963.

76 ARNOLD, Roy (Br Roy Jude). b Black River, Jamaica 13 Sept 1937. Fordham BA 1985. LP 22 Sept 1974. Santa Barbara 1972-73. Liberia 1974-78. NYC 1978-85. CDSP 1985-.

36 +ATKINSON, Sydney James (Br Sydney to 1953). b Hamilton, Ont., 3 April 1915. U South 1941-44, 1946-47. LP 1 Aug 1943. D & P 1953. Liberia 1948-55, 1958-66. Santa Barbara 1967. Texas 1968-73. d 15 March 1975.

20 +BALDWIN, John Sears. b New Haven, CT, 5 July 1896. Columbia U BA 1916. D 1921 P 1923. LP 21 Dec 1923. Liberia 1932-37. Chaplain WWII. Santa Barbara 1948-54, 1964-74, 1978-80. Texas 1974-77. d 28 April 1980.

47 *BELWAY, Robert Murray. b Toronto, Ont., 6 Jan 1927. U Toronto BA 1951, LTh & STB 1956. D 1955 P 1956. LP 19 March 1963. S Andrew's 1965-69. disp 6 Aug 1969.

33 +BESSOM, Joseph Harold. b Marblehead, MA, 17 Dec 1902. S Stephen's Coll BA. ETS BD 1928. D & P 1928. In-ch S Matthew, Hollowell ME & V S Barnabas, Augusta, ME, 1928-35. R S James, Old Town, ME, 1935-38. LP 25 April 1941. Liberia 1939-56, 1961-64. S Andrew's 1956-57. d 25 Aug 1965.

34 *BICKNELL, Herbert Smith, Jr. (Br Herbert to 1952). b Woonsocket, RI, 29 July 1911. LP 4 Aug 1942. NYU BS 1949. GTS STB 1951. D & P 1952. S Andrew's 1957-68. disp 4 Aug 1969. V S Chad, Tampa, FL, 1968-76. d 11 Feb 1976.

89 *BORRAZAS, James. b Brooklyn, NY, LP 10 April 1977. Berkeley 1980-81. disp 24 Jan 1981.

95 BRANT, Robert Glendon (Fr Romuald). b Deseronto, Ont., 11 Sept 1933. Bishop's U LST 1959. Trinity Coll, Toronto STB 1960. D 1959 P 1960. Cur S George, Trenton, Ont., 1959-61. Cur S Mary the Virgin, Nassau, Bahamas 1961-63. R S Andrew, Exuma, Bahamas 1963-73. R S Mary the Virgin, Nassau, Bahamas 1973-74, R Ch of the Holy Spirit, Nassau, Bahamas 1974-76. LP 24 Feb 1981. Toronto 1979-84. In-ch S Matthias & S John Evangelist, Toronto 1981-83. Santa Barbara 1984-.

105 *BRESCIANI y Undurraga, Roberto Eduardo. b Santiago, Chile 22 Feb 1951. U of Chile 1970-73. LP 1 Jan 1984. Santa Barbara 1982-. disp. 28 Dec 1985.

62 *BRICE, John Willie (Br Ambrose). b Mineola, NY, 31 Aug 1934. MIT BS 1958. LP 28 June 1970. Texas 1970-72. disp 10 Nov 1976.

103 BROWN, Douglas Charles. b Prince George, BC, 26 Nov 1944. Trinity Coll, Toronto BA 1967. U Toronto MA 1968. theology course, Trinity Coll, Toronto 1971. D 1971 P 1972. Cur Christ the King, Toronto 1972-73. Cur S James Cath, Toronto 1973-74. R Parish of Minden, Ont., 1974-77. LP 8 Sept 1983. Albany, NY, 1982-83.

60 BROWN, Robert (Br Augustine to 1980). b Rochester, NY, 2 Oct 1943. U California Santa Barbara BA 1984. LP 25 Oct 1969. Connecticut 1971-72. NYC 1973-78. Liberia 1978-81. D & P 1980. Santa Barbara 1981-84. Cur S George, Brooklyn, NY, 1984-.

96 BROWN, William Johnstone. b Burton-on-Trent, Eng., 13 July 1925. U North Carolina Chapel Hill. Antioch U Santa Barbara 1982-84. LP 26 Feb 1981. Santa Barbara 1980-84, Berkeley 1984-.

14 +CAMPBELL, Robert Erskine. b Florida, NY, 13 Aug 1884. Columbia BA 1906. GTS 1909 STD 1928. U South DD 1928. U Liberia DCnL 1934. D & P 1909. Headmaster S Andrew's 1911-15. LP 21 Dec 1917. S Andrew's 1918-22, 1938-47. Liberia 1922-25, 1955-57. elected VI Bishop of Liberia 30 Nov 1925. Resigned 1936. Sup 1948-54. Santa Barbara 1959-77. d 23 Aug 1977.

63 CAMPBELL-DIXON, Robert Andrew (Br Rafael to 1984). b Corn Island, Nicaragua 5 Oct 1934. Inst Angl de Nicaragua. LP 28 June 1970. Bahamas 1977-81. Liberia 1973-77. D 1979 P 1984. V S Mark's, Bluefields, Nicaragua 1982-86. NYC 1986-.

53 *CHALLINOR, Victor Anthony Phillips (Br. Boniface). b New York, NY, 2 May 1940. public schools. LP 12 March 1966. New York 1973-76. disp 7 June 1976.

29 *CHALMERS, William Scott. b Edinburgh, Scotland 20 Nov 1907. Princeton U BA 1929 MA 1930. GTS BA 1933. D 1933 P 1934. LP 14 Jan 1937. Kent 1940-49. disp 4 Aug 1945. Headmaster, Harvard School, Los Angeles, CA 1949-70. d 9 Dec 1980.

106 CRENSHAW, Reginald (Br Reginald Martin). b Los Angeles, CA, 2 Oct 1947. S Mary's Coll, Moraga CA BA 1969. U San Francisco MA 1979. LP 18 Nov 1984. NYC 1982-.

58 DEMERELL, James Samuel (Br James, then Br Samuel). b Pittsburgh, PA, 6 Nov 1930. U Wisconsin BA 1952. LP 7 Sept 1968. S Andrews 1968-70. NYC 1974-.

52 *DUNN, Samuel (Br Kevin to 1974). b Belfast, No. Ireland 3 Nov 1931. Queens U, Belfast BA 1952. Cambridge MA 1954. Trinity Coll, Toronto MDiv 1974. LP 28 Aug 1965. Liberia 1965-66. Santa Barbara 1969-71, 1974-76. Toronto 1971-74. D 1973 P 1974. disp 7 June 1976. Assoc R S Augustine, Santa Monica, CA 1975-78. R S Timothy, Apple Valley, CA, 1978-1980. R S Mark, Glendale, CA 1980-86. R S Christopher, Wichita, KS 1987-.

31 +EWALD, Frederick (Br George). b Garden, MI, 21 June 1911. LP 4 Aug 1939. Liberia 1961. Santa Barbara 1966-. d 3 Jan 1986.

59 *FIELDS, William (Br Cyprian). b San Antonio, TX, 28 Aug 1924. Southern U BSc 1945. U California Santa Barbara BA 1969. United Theol Coll West Indies LTh 1976. LP 29 Sept 1969. Santa Barbara 1969-71. S Louis 1971-72. disp 4 July 1977. In-ch S Andrew, New York, NY, 1976-77. R All Souls NYC 1978-80. R S Agnes, Orange, NJ, 1980-.

26 *FLAGG, Russell Garvey (Br John to 1935). b Chicago, IL, 4 Aug 1899. De Paul U PhB. GTS BD 1935. D & P 1935. Liberia 1927-28. Kent 1935-40. disp. 4 Aug 1941. Chapl Northwestern U 1940-43. R Trinity, Michigan City, IN, 1943-50. R Good Shepherd, Terrell, TX, 1951-64. R S Matthias, Athens, TX, 1964-67. d 1 Nov 1978.

90 FLORES, Orlando Gilbert (Br Orlando Huntington). b New York, NY, 31 May 1944. LP 3 July 1977. Santa Barbara 1975-80. Albany, NY, 1980-83. NYC 1984-86. Ghana 1986-.

108 FOGAH, Thomas. b Cape Coast, Ghana 14 April 1956. Queens Coll, Cape Coast. LP 9 March 1986. Cape Coast 1986-.

66 *GARRAWAY, Peter Ernest Ian (Br Simon). b Guyana 22 Nov 1927. S Cyril's School and S Stanislaus School, Georgetown, Guyana. LP 12 June 1971. disp 7 June 1976.

42 GILL, Raymond Alan. b Philadelphia, PA, 7 Aug 1915. U Pennsylvania 1935-36. Temple U BS 1941. Nashotah BD 1944. D & P 1944. In-ch S Andrew, West Manayunk, PA, 1944. Mis Liberia 1945-47. V S Bartholomew, Philadelphia 1947-48. LP 30 Oct 1952. Liberia 1953-61, 1968-70. Santa Barbara 1971-72. Berkeley 1974-75. Albany, NY, 1979-82. South Carolina 1982-.

85 GILL, Richard (Br Adrian). b Warsaw, NY, 31 May 1948. LP 28 Aug 1976. St U New York New Paltz BA 1980. NYC 1973-75. Santa Barbara 1975-76. Liberia 1976. NYC 1980-.

17 + GORHAM, James Henry. b Stamford, CT, 6 Aug 1891. Princeton U BA 1913. GTS BD 1916. D 1916 P 1917. LP 12 Feb 1919. Ripon 1923-24. Liberia 1924-32. Kent 1932-37. d 8 Jan 1937.

38 *GUNN, Julien, Jr. b Richmond, VA, 3 Sept 1912. U Richmond BA 1934. VTS MDiv 1940. D 1940 P 1941. R Emmanuel Parish, Cedar Run, VA, 1940-42. R Grace Church, Newport News, VA, 1942-45. LP 6 Jan 1950. S Andrew's 1955-65. R S James, Memphis, TN, 1969-71. Headmaster S Mary's School, Peekskill, NY, 1971-74. disp 27 May 1974. Asst S George, Nashville, TN, 1974-84.

101 HAGLER, James Robert. b 4 Dec 1946. SWTS. Trinity Coll, Toronto. LP 6 Feb 1982. D 1982 P 1983. Toronto 1980-.

91 + HARBERT, Jack. b Seymour, IA, 22 May 1921. LP 6 Aug 1977. declared incapable 20 April 1980. Santa Barbara 1976-78, 1980-. Toronto 1978. d 6 May 1987.

55 HARMS, Arthur Eugene (Br Laurence). b Rock Island, IL, 11 Aug 1929. LP 1 Sept 1966. Santa Barbara 1964-66, 1974, 1982. Liberia 1966-73, 1982-84. Bahamas 1975-77. Albany, NY, 1979-82. Ghana 1984-.

86 HARRELL, Robert Stripling (Br Stephen-Christopher). b Wolfe City, TX, 21 Jan 1943. LP 4 Sept 1976. Santa Barbara 1973. Texas 1974-77. Bahamas 1977. South Carolina 1978.

23 + HARRIS, William Edward (Br Edward to 1945). b Blackheath, Eng., 28 Feb 1896. LP 14 Sept 1928. D 1944 P 1945. Nashotah BD 1947. Liberia 1936-38, 1945-46. S Andrew's 1947-48. d 29 Nov 1970.

10 + HARRISON, Jesse McVeigh. b Hannibal, MO, 8 Feb 1878. U South MA. Washington U LL.B. GTS BD 1906. D 1906 P 1907. LP 1 March 1910. S Andrew's 1915-18. Liberia 1925-26. d 27 Jan 1959.

19 + HAWKINS, Herbert. b London, Eng., 25 June 1883. U Minn CPA 1909. Columbia U BA. Kansas Dio Sch of Theology 1919. D 1916 P 1918. LP (1) 14 Sept 1923. Liberia 1922-26. R S Peter, Geneva, NY, 1926-28. disp 22 April 1932. Chapl S Luke's Sch, New Canaan, CT, 1932-8. R S Paul, White River Junction, VT, 1938-45. R S Paul's Windsor, VT, 1942-45. LP (2) 6 Jan 1950. d 27 March 1977.

73 HAYES, James Robert (Br Paul). b Durham, NC, 1 Oct 1907. Hampton Inst. LP 24 Oct 1973. S Andrew's. Santa Barbara 1971-73. Berkeley 1973-.

72 HAYNES, Ronald Grant. b Baltimore MD 14 Jan 1940. LP 6 Aug 1973. Texas 1970-71, 1973-77. Santa Barbara 1971-72. NYC 1977-78.

88 HOOPES, David Bryan. b San Antonio, TX, 25 June 1943. Findlay Coll BA 1966. Andover-Newton BD 1970. D 1975 P 1976. LP 10 April 1977. Bahamas 1973-81. NYC 1985-.

4 + HUGHSON, Shirley Carter. b Sumter, SC, 15 Feb 1867. U South Carolina 1886. Johns Hopkins U 1893. GTS BD 1896. D 1896 P 1897. LP 3 May 1902. Sup 1918-21, 1930-36. S Andrew's 1906-14. d 16 Nov 1949.

1 + HUNTINGTON, James Otis Sargent. b Boston, MA 23 July 1854. Harvard U 1875. S Andrew's Divinity Sch, Syracuse, NY, 1879. D 1878 P 1879. LP 25 Nov 1884. Sup 1884-88, 1897-1907, 1915-18, 1921-30. d 29 June 1935.

56 *JAMIESON, Arthur Robert (Br Nicholas). b Toronto, Ont., 4 Dec 1941. LP 18 March 1967. Santa Barbara 1965-. Texas 1968-72. Toronto 1973-77. disp 4 July 1977.

100 JOLLEY, Robert Nelson (Br Timothy). b Paris, TX, 2 June 1945. Southwestern Coll, Memphis, TN, BA 1967. U North Carolina Chapel Hill, MA, 1976. American Inst in Aix-en-Provence, Certif. LP 28 Nov 1981. Bahamas 1976. Chicago 1979-81.

98 *JOSIAH, Paa Kwesi. b Ghana 5 Dec 1952. LP 10 July 1981. Liberia 1976-80. South Carolina 1980-81. disp 29 Jan 1983.

70 *KENDRICK, Robert. b New Haven, CT, 26 April 1945. Transylvania Coll, Philadelphia, PA, BA 1967. LP 20 May 1972. disp 2 June 1975.

87 *KPOTO, John Tufa. b Bolahun, Liberia 21 Dec 1935. San Francisco St U. CDSP MDiv 1978. LP 8 Sept 1976. D 1978 P 1980. Berkeley 1974-78. Santa Barbara 1978-82. Albany, NY, 1982. disp 29 Aug 1982.

27 *KROLL, Leopold. b Centralia, WI, 23 Feb 1902. S Stephen's Coll BA 1924. GTS BD 1927. D 1927 P 1928. LP 24 Dec 1930. Liberia 1931-46. Sup 1954-7. exp 22 July 1957. dismissed 7 June 1976.

97 LAUER, Paul Martin. b York, PA, 18 Jan 1933. Millersville St Coll, PA, BSEd 1955. Peabody Conservatory of Music 1960. Royal Sch of Church Music 1980. CDSP MDiv 1984. LP 25 March 1981. D 1984 P 1985. Bahamas 1978-81. Berkeley 1981-.

80 *LAUNT, Jay McIntyre. b Orange, CA, 18 Aug 1947. LP 25 April 1975. Toronto 1976-81. Liberia 1981-82. Santa Barbara 1982-83. disp 31 May 1984.

54 *LOOK, Wallace (Br Gregory). b Eureka, CA, 12 March 1921. Humboldt St U BA 1942. U CA Berkeley. BLibrary Science 1948. U Chicago MA 1951. LP 12 March 1966. S Andrew's 1965-. disp 4 Aug 1969.

8 +LOREY, Louis. b Boston, MA, 28 May 1860. private education. D & P 1905. Member Order of the Brothers of Nazareth 1888-1903. LP 2 Oct 1907. S Andrew's 1914-1929. d 11 July 1929.

46 *LYNN, Connor Kay. b Taft, CA, 22 July 1931. Stanford U BA 1952. CDSP BD 1956, DD 1973. D & P 1956. Mis Liberia 1956-57. LP 17 Jan 1963. Liberia 1963-65. Sup 1972-81. Ghana 1981-82. disp 29 Jan 1983. R S Anne, Stockton, CA, 1982-85. Turks and Caicos Is 1985-.

84 *MANTLE, Philip. b Jamaica. LP 14 Aug 1976. NYC 1974-80. Chicago 1980-81. disp 10 June 1981.

25 *MARTY, Carl Walter. b Stillwater, MN, 20 Oct 1884. Western Theol Seminary 1922-23. D 1926 P 1928. LP 29 April 1930. exp 16 April 1936 effective 1 May 1936. deposed from priesthood 20 Dec 1938. RC priest Dio of Scranton.

6 +MAYO, William Francis. b Peoria Co., IL, 11 March 1861. Racine Coll BA 1884 MA 1888. GTS BD 1888. D 1888 P 1889. LP 24 Feb 1903. d 25 May 1946.

92 MCCOY, Adam Dunbar. b Chicago, IL, 19 Dec 1946. Michigan St U BA 1969. Cornell U MA 1972 PhD 1973. CDSP MDiv 1979. LP 22 March 1978. D & P 1979. Berkeley 1976-79. Santa Barbara 1979-.

68 *MCHUGH, James Brian. b Montreal, Que., 7 July 1946. York U BA 1967. GTS MDiv 1973. LP 20 May 1972. D 1972 P 1973. Toronto 1973-76. Santa Barbara 1976-77. Chicago 1980-81. disp 5 June 1982. R S Stephen, Cincinnati, OH, 1982-84.

94 *MEADOWCROFT, Ian Archer (Br Ian Andrew). b Toronto, Ont., 11 Sept 1939. Toronto Teachers Coll 1959. Queens U, Kingston, Ont., BA 1968. LP 30 Nov 1979. Toronto 1977-80. Santa Barbara 1980-81. disp 24 Jan 1981.

69 MUDGE, Hiram Thomas (Fr Bede Thomas). b Cincinnati, OH, 15 March 1938. Cornell U BA 1960. Nashotah MDiv 1964. D & P 1964. R S Luke, Whitewater, WI, 1965-67. LP 20 May 1972. Texas 1972-74. South Carolina 1983-.

9 *OFFICER, Harvey. Harvard BA 1895. GTS STB 1899. D & P 1898. S Phillip's, St Paul, MN, 1898-99; S Paul's, S Paul, MN, 1899-1900; Trinity Church, Princeton NJ 1902-06. LP 2 Oct 1907. deposed from priesthood 5 July 1921. exp 11 Aug 1921.

13 +ORUM, Liston Joseph (Br Francis to 1920). b Brian, TX, 5 Sept 1892. Selma Military Inst. LP 14 Sept 1916. D 1918 P 1920. S Andrew's 1922-28. d 20 Nov 1928.

35 +PACKARD, Alpheus Appleton, b Brookline, MA, 14 Sept 1904. S Stephen's Coll BA 1926. GTS BD 1929 STB 1930. D 1929 P 1930. In-ch Epis Ch in Willowdale, Romulus & Kendaia NY 1930-31. Cur S Edward the Martyr NYC 1931. R Holy Cross, Kingston, NY, 1931-35. Cur S John, Northhampton, MA, 1936-37. In-ch S George & S Paul, Utica, NY, 1937-38. LP 4 Aug 1942. Liberia 1944-48. Santa Barbara 1956-62. d 17 Jan 1972.

24 +PARKER, Francis William George. b Boston, Eng., 1 Jan 1889. Racine Coll. Nashotah BD 1920 STM 1928. D 1920 P 1921. V S John, Shawango, WI, 1921-26. LP 1 Nov 1929. S Andrew's 1932-39. d 2 Sept 1958.

81 PARKER, Roy Earl. b Los Angeles, CA, 14 Sept 1933. MIT BS 1955. ETS BD 1964. JSTB Berkeley STM 1980. D 1964 P 1967. SSJE 1964-70. Asst Grace Ch, Medford, MA, 1970. In-ch S Jude, Stony Hill, Jamaica 1971-72. LP 20 March 1976. Berkeley 1976-82.

28 PARSELL, Joseph Gibson. b Altoona, PA, 9 Feb 1905. S Stephen's Coll BA 1926. D 1931 P 1932. LP 6 Jan 1932. Liberia 1930-60, 1971-75, 1980-. Santa Barbara 1966-71. South Carolina 1975-80.

78 *PATRICK, Peter John. b Port-of-Spain, Trinidad 7 May 1944. St Andrew's Coll, San Fernando, Trinidad 1967-70. LP 16 March 1975. D 1975 P 1976. NYC 1972-76. Bahamas 1976-78. disp 2 June 1978. R S Andrew's, Tobago 1978-.

79 RADELMILLER, William Lawrence Nicholas. b Pasco, WA, 18 Oct 1939. U Washington BA 1962. Nashotah BD 1965. D 1965 P 1966. Cur S Dunstan, Seattle, WA, 1965-67. V S Mark, Oconto, WI, 1967-70. LP 5 April 1975. Texas 1973-77. Santa Barbara 1978, 1981-83. Mis Quito, Ecuador 1983-85. South Carolina 1985-.

83 *ROBINS, Dean (Br Benedict). b New Orleans, LA, 8 Sept 1948. U New Orleans BA 1970. LP 5 June 1976. Santa Barbara 1976-78. Liberia 1981-82. Berkeley 1983-84. disp 4 June 1983.

49 *RYAN, John Prime. b Lincoln, NE, 8 Jan 1932. Kenyon BA 1954. GTS BD 1957. Trinity Coll MTh. Anselmianum, Rome STD 1978. D & P 1957. Cur S Luke, Bartlesville & V S Elizabeth, Nowata, OK, 1957-59. LP 24 Feb 1964. Texas 1968-71. disp 11 June 1973. V S Michael & All Angels, Tucson, AZ, 1974-75. Asst S Paul, Tucson, AZ, 1975-77. R S Paul, Winslow, AZ, & R S George, Holbrook, AZ, 1977. Chapl to Clergy, Dio of LA 1977-80. Exec Asst to Bp of WY 1980-82. Emmanuel Ch, Shawnee, OK, 1982-.

3 *SARGENT, Henry Rufus. Harvard U BA 1879. GTS BD 1885. D 1885 P 1886. LP 26 May 1894. Sup 1894-97. exp 1 Jan 1910. Downside Abbey 1914. Founded Portsmouth Priory, Portsmouth, RI, 1919. d 15 Oct 1944.

48 SCHULTZ, Thomas Haines. b Pittsburgh, PA, 7 Oct 1933. U Pittsburgh BA 1956. Nashotah MDiv 1959. The Citadel MEd 1986. D & P 1959. LP 24 Feb 1964. Liberia 1964-66. Texas 1968-72, 1974-75. South Carolina 1975-.

102 SHAMO, Vincent Nee Fio, Jr. b Teshie, Ghana 1 Oct 1954. Nunguwa Presbyterian Commercial Sch. S Nicholas Seminary, Cape Coast, Ghana 1982-85. LP 13 Feb 1983. D 1985 P 1985. Liberia 1978-80. Ghana 1982-.

67 SIBLEY, William Gatewood. b Newport News, VA, 19 Feb 1934. U South 1953-57. LP 11 Sept 1971. Santa Barbara 1972-73, 1976-81. Berkeley 1973-76, Bahamas 1981, Toronto 1981-.

5 + SILL, Frederick Herbert. b New York, NY, 10 March 1874. Columbia U BA 1894, LittD 1924. GTS BD 1898, STD 1928. D 1888 P 1899. LP 3 May 1902. Kent 1906-52. d 17 July 1952.

45 SMITH, Allan Edward. b Providence, RI, 1 Jan 1923. Brown U BA 1951. Nashotah MDiv 1954. D & P 1954. Asst S Stephen, Coconut Grove, FL, 1954-56. LP 4 April 1961. Liberia 1961-71, 1974-77. S Louis 1971-72. South Carolina 1977-82. Santa Barbara 1984-.

64 *SMITH, Eric James (Br Martin). b Vancouver, BC, 30 April 1944. LP 12 Sept 1970. Santa Barbara 1970-74. disp 27 May 1974, effective 1 June 1974.

18 + SMYTH, Joseph Henry. b Salem, NC, 10 March 1890. GTS BD 1916. D 1916 P 1917. Asst S Luke's, Newtown, PA, 1916-17. LP 25 Nov 1919. V Trinity Berlin WI & S John, Omro, WI, 1921-27. Ripon 1922-25. Ripon Coll BA 1925. exp 24 July 1925. S Louis U MD 1929. In-ch Trinity, S Louis, MO, 1927-28. Asst Holy Communion, S Louis, MO, 1929-30. In-ch Holy Spirit, Gallup, NM, 1930-31. Bahamas 1944-53, Liberia 1953-62. restored 18 Oct 1960. Santa Barbara 1963-76, S Andrew's 1965. d 5 Nov 1976.

44 *SMYTHE, Charles (Br Charles). b Montreal, Que., 28 Aug 1934. LP 4 Nov 1960. disp 20 Dec 1963.

32 SPENCER, Howard Bonnell. b New York, NY, 31 Dec 1909. Williams Coll BA 1931. Oxford B.Litt 1933. GTS 1933-36, DD 1976. D 1936 P 1937. LP 6 Feb 1940. Kent 1940-42. S Andrew's 1947-55. Santa Barbara 1955-59. Texas 1967-71. Ghana 1983-.

74 *STADING, Gerald Frederick. b Richardton, ND, 4 March 1935. Valley City St Coll, ND, BS 1960. LP 25 June 1974. Texas 1971-75. Berkeley 1975-76. disp 10 Nov 1976.

40 STEVENS, Lee Gerald Elwin (Fr Anthony Gerald). b Durham, ME, 19 July 1912. Bates Coll BA 1933. Powers School of the Theatre 1935-37. Harvard U 1938. GTS STB 1943. D & P 1943. In-ch S Mary & S Jude, NE Harbor, ME, 1943. R Christ Church, Eastport, ME, 1943-47. Chapl USN 1945-46. LP 25 Nov 1951. Santa Barbara 1951-52. S Andrew's 1952-65, 1968-70. Liberia 1966-68, 1971-76, 1982-84. South Carolina 1976-82, 1984-.

43 STONEBRAKER, George (Br Michael). b Washington, D.C., 16 Dec 1929. LP 3 May 1956. St. Andrew's 1953-55. Santa Barbara 1959-62.

50 *SULLIVAN, Robert Edmund, Jr. b Philadelphia, PA, 3 May 1925. Princeton U BA 1949. PDS BD 1952. D & P 1952. V S James, Paulsboro & S Peter, Woodbury Hgts, NJ, 1952-8. LP 29 Sept 1964. Liberia 1964-70. disp 15 June 1970. R S John, Chews Landing, NJ, 1972-.

51 SWAYNE, George Eby Hope (Fr Christian George). b Tweed, Ont., 10 Aug 1933. U Toronto BA. Trinity Coll LTh. D 1958 P 1959. LP 19 March 1965. S Andrew's 1965-66. Santa Barbara 1972-76. Liberia 1976-81. Ghana 1981-.

93 SWORD, Carl Richard. b Bath, PA, 6 March 1931. Penn St U BS 1958. ETS MDiv 1962. Arizona St U MCouns 1972. D & P 1962. Certif. Westchester Inst 1984. In-ch S George, Waynesburg, PA, 1962-63. In-ch S Thomas, Cannonsburg, PA, 1962-64. Asst Trinity, Washington, PA, 1963-64. Staff S Francis Boys' Home, Bavaria, KS, 1964-70. Staff S Francis Boys' Home, Albany, NY, 1970-73. LP 7 April 1978. NYC 1979-.

39 +TAYLOR, Lincoln Andrews. b Buffalo, NY, 2 Dec 1909. Hobart Coll BA 1933. GTS BD 1936, STD. D 1936 P 1937. V Eutawville, SC, 1936-46. LP 24 June 1951. Liberia 1951-58. Sup 1960-72. Toronto 1973-75. South Carolina 75-84. d 24 March 1984.

22 +TAYLOR, Sidney (Br Dominic). b New York, NY, 23 June 1884. NY public schools. LP 4 Aug 1926. S Andrew's 1926-60. d 22 June 1960.

41 *TERRY, Kenneth Rosier. b Richmond, CA, 24 Jan 1922. U California BA 1943, Nashotah BD 1946. D & P 1946. LP 1 June 1952. Santa Barbara 1965-70. disp 14 June 1971. Asst S Luke, Salisbury, NC, 1971-77. V S Mark, Creighton, NE, 1980-.

15 +TIEDEMANN, Karl Ludwig. b O'Fallon, IL, 29 July 1890. Washington U BA 1912. Columbia U MA 1915. GTS BD 1915. D 1915 P 1916. LP 21 Dec 1917. Ripon 1922-25. exp 2 Nov 1925. Keble Coll Oxford 1926-8. restored to OHC 30 July 1930. Nixon, NV 1942-46. Santa Barbara 1947-60, 1964-68. d 21 Aug 1968.

61 TRAFTON, Clark Wright (Fr Clark Gregory). b Marathon, IA, 28 March 1935. Iowa St U BS 1955 MS 1957. CDSP BD 1960, DD 1984. D & P 1960. Certif Westchester Inst 1981. V S Paul, Creston, IA, 1960-65. V Holy Trinity, Atlantic, IA, 1960-63. V Trinity, Winterset, IA, 1963-65. LP 28 June 1970. Santa Barbara 1968-69. Savannah, GA, 1969. Guyana 1969-70. Grenada 1970-71. Connecticut 1971-72. NYC 1978-. Sup 1981-.

30 TURKINGTON, William Ryland Downing. b Philadelphia, PA, 27 Sept 1904. U Virginia BA 1928. VTS BD 1931. GTS MDiv 1932. D 1931 P 1932. Cur S Luke's Chapel NYC 1932-33. LP 30 March 1937. S Andrew's 1938-41, 1943-53. Kent 1941-43. Sup 1957-60. Liberia 1961-62. Santa Barbara 1966-70. Toronto 1975-.

109 VAGGIONE, Richard Paul. b San Jose, CA, 19 Jan 1945. U Santa Clara BA 1966. U Cath Louvain lic. theol. bibl. 1969. GTS STB & STM 1970. Oxford D.Phil. 1976. D 1970 P 1971. LP 29 Sept 1986. Albany 1983-84. Santa Barbara 1984. Toronto 1984-.

99 VAN WAES, Carter (Fr Bernard). b Flint, MI, 26 Jan 1921. Boston U BA 1953. U Texas MA 1970. CDSP BD 1956. D 1956 P 1957. V S Peter, Seward, AK, 1956-57. All Saints, Anchorage, AK, 1957-58. Cur S Mary the Virgin, San Francisco, CA, 1958-59. R S John Baptist, Capitola, CA, 1959-60. Cur S John, Odessa, TX, 1960-63. Teacher, El Paso, TX, 1963-77. LP 10 July 1981. Santa Barbara 1979-82.

57 *WALSTED, John Howard. b Cambridge, MA 5 Feb 1932. U Oregon BS. CDSP MDiv 1959. D & P 1959. S Paul, Salem, OR, 1959-61. LP 6 April 1968. Santa Barbara 1974-78. disp 2 June 1978. R Christ Church, Staten Island, NY, 1983-.

71 *WAYWELL, Roy Edmund (Br Dunstan to 1973). b Warrington, Eng., 21 April 1944. Kelham Theol Coll & GTS. LP 29 July 1972. D & P 1973. Santa Barbara 1974-75. Chicago 1980-81. disp 4 June 1983. V S Thomas, Cleveland, Eng., 1982-84. R Good Shepherd, Momence, IL, 1985-.

21 + WEBB, Charles William (Br Charles to 1929). b Anderson, SC, 26 May 1895. U South 1916. Nashotah 1929. D 1925 P 1929. LP 4 Aug 1925. d 6 May 1944.

11 + WHITALL, Edwin Clark. b Woodbury, NJ, 13 Oct 1878. Nashotah BD 1905. D & P 1905. LP 3 May 1913. Liberia 1929-32, 1939-43. S Andrew's 1922-25, 1952-55. d 11 March 1969.

16 + WHITTEMORE, Alan Griffith. b Boston, MA, 20 June 1890. Williams Coll BA 1912, DD 1937. GTS BD 1915. D 1915 P 1916. LP 12 Feb 1919. Liberia 1926-36, 1949-51. Sup 1936-48. Enclosed 1951-60. d 24 Sept 1960.

77 *WILLIAMS, Stephen Lee (Br Damian to 1977). b Memphis, TN, 27 Nov 1945. Memphis St U BS 1971. Trinity Coll, Toronto MDiv 1976. D 1975 P 1976. LP 27 Oct 1974. In-ch S George, Toronto 1977-78. Santa Barbara 1978-81. disp 5 June 1982. Asst Ascension, Lafayette, LA, 1983-.

82 WILSON, Jack Fowler (Fr Dominic from 1977). b Fairfield, AL, 13 Aug 1945. U Alabama BA 1971. CDSP MDiv 1977. LP 8 April 1976. D & P 1977. Texas 1973. Berkeley 1974-77, 1982-84. Liberia 1977-80. Chicago 1980-81.

12 + WOODWARD, Abishai (Br Abishai). b Cambridge, MA, 12 Jan 1876. Harvard U. Bellvue Hospital nurse's training. LP 15 Aug 1913. declared disobedient 16 March 1919. exp 7 April 1919. disp 14 Aug 1923. restored 5 Aug 1924. d 27 Jan 1936.

65 *WORTMAN, Donald Wayne (Br Joseph). b St Boniface, Manitoba 6 March 1944. U Winnipeg 1961. U Dallas BA 1970. LP 3 Oct 1970. Texas 1968-73. Santa Barbara 1973-77. disp 4 July 1977.

75 YOUNGWARD, Brian. b Montreal, Que., 16 May 1944. LP 14 Sept 1974. Bahamas 1974-76. Santa Barbara 1975-78. Liberia 1978-80. Toronto 1984-.

Index

Abbah, Leonard, OHC, 233
Absalom Jones Priory, 217, 231-233
Academy of Music, New York NY, 53
Ackon, Bp. John, 232, 233
Adams, James Ibraimah [Boniface], OHC, 235
Adams, Vern Linwood, OHC, 176, 193
Adams, William, 12
Aelred, Abbot Carlyle, 108
Agee, James, 184
Alexandrian Fathers, 90
All Saints Convalescent Home, New York NY, 48, 66
All Saints Sisters, 11, 70, 92
Allen, Sturges, OHC, 32, 34, 37-39, 43, 46-50, 54, 56-58, 60-62, 64-67, 69, 70, 72-78, 80-82, 84, 85, 88, 94-96, 99, 100, 106, 108-110, 116, 134, 141, 142, 149-152, 162, 163, 185, 194, 235
Allin, Presiding Bp. John M., 222, 234
Anthony, St., 8
Anderson, Roger Brooke Taney, OHC, 100-, 102, 134, 146, 158
Anti-Poverty Society, The, 53, 58
Arnold, Roy [Jude], OHC, 217
Ascension Church, Chicago IL, 47
Associate, Priests, 56
Atkinson, Sydney James, OHC, 175, 186, 190, 192, 203, 212, 220
Atkinson, Thomas, 13
Atlantic Monthly, The, 59
Atonement, Society of the, 82, 83, 104, 108, 115
Atonement, Franciscan Society of the (Episcopal) 83, 109
Ayres, Anne, 11

Baldwin, Charles Sears, 147
Baldwin, John Sears, OHC, 147, 156, 157, 162, 166, 168, 169, 174, 178, 188, 192, 216, 230
Bassett, Colin, 82
Batterson, Herman Griswold, 10
Belway, Robert Murray, OHC, 193, 196, 203, 211, 212
Benedict, Samuel, 40
Benedictine Nuns, West Malling, 107
Benson, Richard Meux, SSJE, 17, 57, 73, 74, 88, 131
Bessom, Joseph Harold, OHC, 146, 171, 192, 194
Bicknell, Herbert Smith, OHC, 175, 212
Bliss, W.D.P., 55
Borazzas, James, OHC, 225, 231
Borsch, Frederick Houk, 216
Boynton, Bp. Charles, 195
Brant, Robert Glendon [Romuald], OHC, 231
Breck, James Lloyd, 12
Brent, Bp. Charles Henry, 146
Bresciani y Undurraga, Roberto Eduardo, OHC, 233
Brice, John Willie [Ambrose], OHC, 210, 211, 223
Brothers of Nazareth, Order of the, 47, 48, 60, 66, 82, 101, 149, 156
Brown, Douglas Charles, OHC, 229, 233
Brown, Robert [Augustine], OHC, 209, 217
Brown, William Johnstone, OHC, 231
Bruccoli, Matthew, 159
Burnett, C.P.A., 21
Burton, Spence, SSJE, 165